Samuel D. Chapman

History of Tama County, Iowa

Its cities, towns and villages, with early reminiscences, personal incidents and

anecdotes and a complete business directory of the county

Samuel D. Chapman

History of Tama County, Iowa
Its cities, towns and villages, with early reminiscences, personal incidents and anecdotes and a complete business directory of the county

ISBN/EAN: 9783337401177

Printed in Europe, USA, Canada, Australia, Japan

Cover: Foto ©ninafisch / pixelio.de

More available books at **www.hansebooks.com**

HISTORY

OF

TAMA COUNTY,

IOWA.

ITS CITIES, TOWNS AND VILLAGES

WITH

EARLY REMINISCENCES. PERSONAL INCIDENTS AND ANECDOTES,

AND A COMPLETE

BUSINESS DIRECTORY OF THE COUNTY.

BY SAMUEL D. CHAPMAN.

——:——

PRINTED AT THE
TOLEDO TIMES OFFICE.
1879.

PREFACE.

It is now nearly two years since I conceived the idea of publishing a History of Tama County. After I submitted my plan to a number of old settlers who approved of the same and encouraged the enterprise, work on the proposed publication was at once begun. In order to test the enterprise a practical canvass of Tama City, and Toledo, was made and in three or four days time over two hundred subscribers were secured, and I was thus encouraged to continue the work and solicit subscriptions from those living in other towns and in the country.

Of the magnitude of the work I then had no conception. I was of the opinion there were yet living, many of the old pioneers from whom information could be obtained without difficulty; but in this I was greatly mistaken. Few indeed, are the number, as many are dead, while others have left the County. Since the projection of this work, quite a number more have been called to their final resting place, from some of whom we expected to obtain much valuable information. "Man proposes and God disposes." The interviews were never had, and now their lips are hushed in death, and no more will their stories of pioneer life be listened to with interest and pleasure by those gathering around their hospitable firesides.

The author has labored under many adverse circumstances in

PREFACE.

the prosecution of the work. Without a dollar in his pocket or to his credit, without material assistance of any kind from any source, he began the compilation of a work that has required nearly two full years to complete.

As previously remarked, the difficulty in securing information was far greater than anticipated; especially has this been the case with regard to dates. In order to learn the dates of the settlements, several weeks were spent in visiting and interviewing old settlers, besides writing many letters to those who had formerly lived in the County and were supposed to be cognizant of the facts in the case. The conclusions arrived at are satisfactory to my mind, and will be to the mind of any who will take the same trouble to obtain the knowledge. The same care taken to learn the exact time in which the settlements were made, has been taken to verify every fact given. That errors may creep in, however guarded one may be, cannot be doubted; but I believe they will be few indeed.

Although in the compilation of the work much time has been spent, and therefore it has been quite tedious, yet it has not been unmixed with pleasure. Many days and nights have I spent in listening to the stories of the old pioneers; ever hearing something new; now laughing and then crying, as the ludicrous or the pathetic was narrated; and then in the study of the character of our fathers and those of the present generation, time with me has slipped quickly by.

And now, at the close of my labor, I cannot lay down my pen without returning thanks to the many kind friends who have assisted me in obtaining information, and have encouraged me from time to time with words of cheer.

My work is now done, and it is presented to you with the hope that it may please; that its errors you will kindly overlook, and that you will be well repaid in its pursual.

Yours with respect,

SAMUEL D. CHAPMAN.

TAMA CITY, IOWA, SEPTEMBER 1st, 1879.

CONTENTS.

CHAPTER I.

CHAPTER II.

CHAPTER III.

CHAPTER IV.

CHAPTER V.

CHAPTER VI.

CHAPTER VII.

CHAPTER VIII.

CHAPTER IX.

CHAPTER X.

CHAPTER XVIII.

CHAPTER XIX.

CHAPTER XX.

CHAPTER XXI.

CHAPTER XXII.

CHAPTER XXIII.

CHAPTER XXIV.

CHAPTER XXV.

CHAPTER XXVI.

CHAPTER XXVII.

CHAPTER XXVIII.

HISTORY OF TAMA COUNTY.

CHAPTER I.

FIRST SETTLEMENT—ORGANIZATION.

The first settlement of Tama County of which we have record was in the spring of 1849. Previous to this time the county was in a state of unbroken wilderness, the home of the red-men, who roamed at will over its broad prairies, engaged in occupations peculiar to their race. No one, save the old settler, or one who had visited the far West can fully realize the beauty of the country at that time. Tradition has it that Tama County was named after Tama,* the wife of Poweshiek, one of the Chiefs of the Sac and Fox tribes, who resided here when the hardy pioneer sought a future home and brought with him the civilizations of the East, and if by this it was meant to bestow the name of "beauty" upon Tama County the effort has not been lost. Nowhere within the limits of the State could it be surpassed for beautiful scenery, groves, prairies, meandering streams and carpets of flowers and verdure.

Dividing the County north and south, we had upon the north a broad prairie extending as far as the eye could reach, the tall grass gently undulating like the waves of the sea. Upon the south the

*TAMA, beautiful, lovely.

giant oak, the stately elm and the useful hickory, seemingly piercing the very heavens, stood as faithful sentinels over their entire surroundings.   No fallen timber or undergrowth of any kind obstructed the passage; the annual prairie fire making a clean path for all.

A prairie on fire!   Have you ever witnessed one?   The sight is magnificent indeed.   A correspondent to the "Philadelphia Enquirer" on a visit to this State, while traveling up the Mississippi, described in glowing terms the scenery on that "Father of Waters", and thus graphicly sketched a prairie on fire:

"Whilst enjoying the sublimity of the scene, night threw her mantle o'er the earth, and the sentinel stars set their watch in the skies, when suddenly the scene was lighted by a blaze of light illuminating every object around.   It was the prairie on fire. Language cannot convey, words cannot express to you the faintest idea of the grandeur and splendor of that mighty conflagration.   Me thought that the pale queen of night disclaiming to take her accustomed place in the heavens, had dispatched ten thousand messengers to light their torches at the alter of the setting sun, and that now they were speeding on the wings of the wind to their appointed stations.   As I gazed on that mighty conflagration my thoughts recurred to you immured in the walls of a city, and I exclaimed in the fullness of my heart:"

> "O fly to the prairie in wonder and gaze,
> As o'er the grass sweeps the magnificent blaze;
> The world cannot boast so romantic a sight,
> A continent flaming, mid oceans of light."

How changed the scene now.   The timber in many places has been cleared away, and bountiful farms appear in its stead.   The broad prairies have been shorn of their native beauty, and the hand of man has endeavored to excel in their decoration.   The iron horse now courses over the prairie and through the timber where once only the trail of the red man was known.   Villages, towns and cities appear where only the wigwam was once seen. All this change has taken place in twenty-nine years.   What will the next twenty-nine years bring?   Who can tell?

Tama is the fifth County west from the Mississippi, the fifth north from the south line and the fifth south from the north line of the State, occupying a central position; containing an area of 720 square miles: 470,000 acres of land. With its soil, its timber and beautiful scenery, it possesses many attractions of which her citizens may justly feel proud; and has many reminiscences of the past to which she can refer with feelings of great pleasure. History affords no worthier example of greatness than the lives of adventurous pioneers, who, for the sake of independence, weathered the storms of adversity and buffeted the cold winds of a perilous life, in order to provide comfort and homes for their families.

To the pioneers of Tama County belongs a share of this praise for they worked nobly and fought manfully until civilization reached them through time and immigration, and the natural resources of the County.

As before remarked, the county is about equally divided between timber and prairie, the northern tiers of townships being mainly prairie, while the southern is largely timber. When we reach the descriptions of townships, we shall notice this matter more at length. The County is bounded on the north by Black-hawk and Grundy Counties, on the east by Benton, on the south by Poweshiek and on the west by Marshall.

To Isaac Asher belongs the honor of the first settlement, about one-half mile west of the present site of Indian town, in the west part of the County. Mr. A. settled first in Marshall County, on May the 18th, 1847, but the beauty of Indian township, Tama County, attracted his attention, and in the spring of 1849, he permanently settled in Tama County with his wife and eight children, and was the first white settler in the County. He broke the first sod and planted the first crop of corn.*

When the family of Ashers approached their present home they were met by the Indians, who lived near, and who were painted and dressed for war, and demanded that the family return and not attempt to go on; but after a long council of both parties, they were permitted to settle peacefully.

*Mr. Asher has gone to his long home, but his wife still survives and is the oldest white female resident of the County, being the first white woman here.

The next white families that settled in Tama County, were those of Anthony, Robert and William Wilkinson, who came from Coshocton County, Ohio, and permanently located in what is now Salt Creek township, on the 12th day of October, 1849. They were accompanied by their mother and three sisters. Anthony and William had been soldiers in the Mexican war and had just received their land warrants, and in due time located the same. Their brother Robert purchased land near them in the same township. The Ashers and Wilkinsons were the only settlers in 1849.

In June, 1850, Alexander Fowler and Isaac Smith, with their families and Tobias Van Dorn, a single man, settled in York township and commenced improvements on their lands.

R. A. Redman came into the County October 30th, 1850, and settled near the present site of Tama City. At the same time W. L. Brannan, S. J. Murphy, J. H. and W. T. Hollen, and J. Unbarger came in remaining a short time, returning to Marengo during the winter months.

In the summer of 1851, Eli Daily, Anthony Bricker, John Daily and families settled west of the Iowa River in Indian Village township, while David D. Appelgate and his brother Levi, settled north of them in what is now Carlton township.

In the fall of the same year Christopher and D. F. Bruner and families settled on Deer Creek in what is now Howard township. Peter Overmire settled in Toledo township and built the first cabin in that township. About this time Norman J. Osborn and family settled in northern Tama on Wolf Creek, in Perry township, near the present site of Traer, while Daniel A. Dean and his two sons, Ira and Julius, single men, settled in what is now known as Buckingham township; Samuel Giger and family settled in Howard township; Geo. Carter and William Blodgett settled near the present site of Tama City; Wm. Taylor and Newell Blodgett settled near Indiantown, while in the spring of the same year Eli Chase settled near what is now Tama City.

In this year, 1852, other settlers came into the county and cast their lots among those already, upon Tama County soil. In the month of June, John Connell and his brother Joseph, W. D. Hitchner and Jonas P. Wood settled in what is now Perry township; John Connell making his first original entry of land on the 3d day of July. 1852, at Dubuque, Iowa. In the spring of this year James Laughlin and family settled in Carlton township, north and east from Indiantown; James A. Willey settled in Salt Creek township; John C. Vermilya, James H. and T. W. Hollen his brother, and Miron Blodgett also came in the spring of this year and settled in south-western Tama, in what is now Tama township; John Ross, Tallman Chase, William Schamerhorn, Solomon Hufford and families settled near the present site of Toledo. The next spring. B. W. Wilson, T. Skiles and one or two others with their families settled in Richland township south of the Iowa River, and Wm. Cruthers and family in the fall of this year settled north of the river in the same township, while Ed. McKee and Riley Van Dorn and families settled still further north of them, in what is now York township, near Salt Creek, a tributary of the Iowa River.

Isaac Butler, Washington Abbot, J. H. Voorhies and Wm. Martin settled near Indiantown during this year, in Indian Village township, thus increasing the population of the county and giving new neighbors to those who came first.

Every new face was welcomed with hearty good will and the kindest assistance rendered. The best lands were pointed out, while they gathered from far and near to assist in raising the log cabin, which was to shelter them and to mark the place of the new home.

The year 1853 witnessed the coming of a still larger number of pioneers and their families. Early in the spring A. B. Hancock and family settled in what is now Otter Creek township, and later came Abram Tompkins an old soldier of the Blackhawk war and located his land, also John Bishop and family who settled in the same township. These were the first settlers in that township. On June 16th, Joseph Powell, Nathan Fisher, and Levi Haworth and families settled in what is now known as Carroll township, on one of the branches of Salt Creek. In the same spring John

Reedy, G. W. Free, Franklin Davis, William Hillmon, James L. Walkup, Henry C. Foster, and Robert Foster, and families settled near the present town of Toledo, while Ira Taylor and his brother Giles, settled in Perry township. Ira Taylor entered his land this year, on a part of which the present town of Traer is located. In September of this year Thomas A. Graham and his brother James and Z. T. Shugart and families settled in York township, while in the winter George Williams, Levi Marsh, and families settled near the present town of West Irving; James Cronk, Allen Dingee, Geo. Voorhies, and families settled near Indiantown; David Miller, Benjamin Hammitt, Jacob Reedy, and families settled in what is now Howard township near Deer Creek, and commenced their improvements.

In the year 1854, the emigration increased steadily. Joshua Burley, Thomas Everett, Wm. Stoddard and families settled in what is Columbia township, south of Tama City, and south of the Iowa River. They were followed shortly afterward by a great many others, all the various settlements receiving reinforcements.

A state road had been laid out by the legislature running from Marengo to Fort Dodge, through the south side of the County, on July 9th 1853, and during the year 1854, a mail route was established from Marengo to Marietta in Marshall County, and J. D. Smith, now a resident of Richland township was mail carrier. In January of the year 1854 a post-office was established and Anthony Wilkinson made post-master, his commission bearing date February 27th, 1854. About the same time a post office was established north of the Iowa River near the present site of Tama City, with James H. Hollen post-master, his commission bearing date December 23d, 1854; said state Road mail route and post offices being the first in Tama County, gave material assistance to the settlers on the south side of the County, and north of the river, while it also helped those residing in the central part of the county.

Tama County was surveyed by A. L. Brown and his assistants in the years 1843-4-5 and 6. The first original entry of land was made by Noah Dean on section 15, Salt Creek township, May 10th 1848. The next entry was made by Horace N. Atkinson, on section 30 Tama township on May 18th 1848, and now partly occupied by the Sac and Fox Indians.

At this time in her history, Tama County was attached to Benton County for Election, Judicial and Revenue purposes. On the 10th day of March, 1853, the voters of Tama County presented a petition to the County Judge of Benton County, asking for a separate organization, which was duly granted and an order issued for holding an election on the first Monday of May, 1853. Due notice was given and the election was held and returns made to Benton County, showing the following result:

Tallman Chase, County Judge; David D. Appelgate, Clerk of District Court; Norman L. Osborn, Sheriff; John Huston, Prosecuting Attorney; Wesley A. Daniel, County Surveyor; David F. Bruner and Anthony Wilkinson received the votes for School Fund Commissioners, but the office was not filled, they failing to qualify. At the first session of the County Court, held on the first Monday of July, 1853, at John Huston's house, in Indian Village township, David F. Bruner was appointed to the office of Treasurer and Recorder until the August election of that year, and qualified by giving bonds as required by law. On the 7th day of July, 1853, Noah Myers was appointed School Fund Commissioner, until the ensuing election, to fill the vacancy and was duly qualified. This being only a temporary organization and election, only a part of the officers qualified until the regular election, which was held on the first Monday of August, 1853, at which election the following officers were elected:

J. C. Vermilya, County Judge; John Ross, Treasurer and Rrcorder; Franklin Davis, Coroner; W. A. Daniel, Surveyor. Norman L. Osborn, who was elected Sheriff in May, 1853, did not qualify within the time fixed by law, and was appointed to the office July 7th, 1853, by the County Judge. At this election there were 72 votes cast and the Board of Canvassers were John Huston, Robert Wilkinson and Wm. Boohr. At this election the voters had three voting precincts. Those residing in Howard township, met at the house of Rezin A. Redman, and that township was at this election organized legally, and comprised what is now included in the present townships of Columbia, Toledo, Howard, Carroll, Otter creek, Richland, Salt Creek, York and Oneida. The electors of Indian Village township met at the house of Eli W. Daily and organized that township, which comprised what is now the townships of Highland, Indian Village, Carlton, Spring Creek and Lincoln. The electors of Buckingham township met at the house of Norman L. Osborn, and organized that township, which comprised what is now Crystal, Grant, Buckingham, Geneseo, Clark and Perry townships. At an election held at the house of Wm. Murty, on the 1st Monday of April, 1854, Carlton township was organized and contained all that part of Indian Village township as stated, north of the Iowa River, and on the same day Richland township was organized, and contained all that part of Salt Creek township lying south of the Iowa River.

The next election was held on the 3rd day of April, 1854, when a canvass of votes showed that Noah Myers was elected School Fund Commissioner, and Anthony Wilkinson, Drainage Commissioner. The Board of Canvassers at this election were John C. Vermilya, Benjaman Hammitt and Z. T. Shugart. The next election was held on the 7th day of August, 1854, and a canvass of the votes showed the following officers elected: John Connell, Representative, (the first in the County;) David D. Appelgate, Clerk of the District Court; Alford Phillips, Prosecuting Attorney.

A special election was held on the 2nd day of October, 1854, on the question of distraining hogs and sheep from running at large. There were 90 votes cast in favor of the proposition and 49 against it. Total one hundred and fifty nine votes. At the general election held on the 1st Monday in April, 1855, the following vote was had on the "Prohibitory Liquor Law." For prohibtion, 163 votes; against prohibition 126 votes; thus showing the feel-

---

* A small log cabin located about one-half mile east of the present site of Tama City, on section 26. This house was used as a tavern, clerk's office and court house, until the erection of a court house at the county seat.

a term of court to be holden at the house of John C. Vermilya,* and on Friday the 15 day of September, 1854, at 11 o'clock A. M., court was duly opened. The Hon. Wm. Smith, sole presiding judge. There were present, in attendance on the court, David D. Appelgate, Clerk; Alford Phillips, Prosecut'ng Attorney of said county, and Miron Blodgett. Sheriff. There were three civil cases on the docket. First, Rezin A. Redman vs. Noah Myers, School Fund Commissioner, and Robert Carter, for writ of mandamus and injunction: Second, Jacob W. Appelgate vs. Mary A. Appelgate, petition for divorce: Third, Andrew D. Stephens vs. Noah Myers, School Fund Commissioner. All of these cases were continued. David D. Appelgate was Clerk and Miron Blodgett Sheriff.

In the fall of 1853, Hon. James P. Carlton, District Judge of the fourth judicial district appointed Joseph M. Furgeson, of Marshall county and R. B. Ogden, of Poweshiek county, commissioners to locate a seat of justice for Tama county. They met at the house of John C. Vermilya on October 20th, of that year and proceeded to examine a location for a site. They first examined a quarter section near Bruner's mill, in Howard township, which was thought to be too far north. They finally examined and located the town on the present site, it being on the south-west one fourth of south-east one fourth and west one-half of south-east one-fourth of south east one-fourth and south one-half of north-west one-fourth of south-east one-fourth of section fifteen. After the county seat was located the christening it with a name was necessary. It was however agreed that, that honor should be confered upon the oldest person present, and it accordingly fell upon Mr. Adam Zehrung, who in love with Toledo, Ohio, near which he once resided, named it "Toledo "

The next step taken was for the erection of a Court House. The contract was let to T. A. Graham for the sum of thirteen hundred dollars. In due time the house was completed and was used for this purpose until the erection of a new one in 1866.

* A small log cabin located about one-half mile east of the present site of Tama City, on section 26. This house was used as a tavern, clerk's office and court house, until the erection of a court house at the county seat.

This building still stands on the east side of the public square and
is occupied by Jons & Tode as a meat market.   The Court House
was finished according to contract, and District Court convened
therein for its second term on the twenty second day of May, 1855,
Hon. Wm. Smith presiding Judge.   The first criminal case was
at this term, it being the State of Iowa vs. Thomas Evert, on a
charge of larceny.   Alford Phillip, appearing as Prosecuting Attorney.   The case was discharged on motion and bond exhonora-
ted.   This case was brought on appeal from James H. Hollen,
Justice of the Peace to the District Court.   At this term of court
Timothy Brown, Esq., now of Marshalltown, was admitted to
practice.   At the May term following, in 1856, T. W. Jackson, N.
C. Wieting, and E. B. Bolens were admitted to practice at the District Court, at which also appeared as practitioners, I. L. Allen
and Noah Levering who had previously become residents of
Toledo.   C. J. L. Foster and J. W. McKinley practicing attorneys, had at this time removed from the county.   Mr W. H.
Stivers, who is still a resident of Toledo and an able practitioner,
came to the town in the month of August of this year.

The first grand and petit jurors were empaneled at the
second term of the District Court, and were as follows:
C. B. Slade, H. Van Vliet, Giles Taylor, Joseph Jack, W. H.
H. Hill, John Freemer, Henry Stokes, G. P. Yocum, James H.
Hollen, William Blodgett, J. W. Appelgate, H. R. Rich, T. A.
Graham, P. McRoberts, and Jonas P. Wood.

The petit jury were G. Smith, J. D. Gettis, T. Marshall,
N. Bates, E. W. Daily, J. H. Vanhorn, J. H. Voorhies,
L. Olney, John D. Spohr, J. A. Willey, M. Mitchell and N, Fisher.
J. L. Carter was sworn as bailiff.   The first naturalized citizen
was Gotlieb Waggoner, who received his final papers from Judge
Wm. Smith on May 20th, 1856.   The first will probated was the
will of James Hatfield, deceased on the 27th day of November,
1854, in the county court by judge J. C. Vermilya.   The first
letters of administration were issued to Nathaniel E. Horton,
October 23rd, 1854, and Amos Hatfield was the first guardian appointed by the county court, on November 27th, 1854.

The first jury trial was the case of Eli Inman vs. William J. Booher, on note and book account. The jury consisted of George Smith, J. D. Gettis, Thomas Marshall, Nathan Fisher, Norton Bates, E. W. Daily J. H. Van Horn, J. H. Voorhies, L. Olney, J. D. Spohr, J. A. Willey and M. Mitchell. Said jury being duly sworn, after hearing the argument of counsel and charge of the court, retired in the custody of A. S. Curtis, sworn as bailiff. The jury rendered its verdict, finding for the defendant a judgment, and assessed the amount of his recovery at five dollars.

CHAPTER II

1857-61.

From 1857 to 1861 there was no event in the history of Tama County calculated to arouse any particular excitement among her citizens, save the incident of the murder of William Stopp.

The settlers of that day pursued the even tenor of their way, endeavoring to make for themselves and families a home in this unbroken wilderness. Their little troubles were settled by a fair fight and a friendly drink afterwards, and no hard feelings were entertained.

A short time previous to the time of which we write, a German by the name of Olleslangher and a man named Butler, who had more than an ordinary education and attainments and a professional lawyer, came to this County and settled on the farm now owned by J. W. Fleming, in Grant township. If reports are correct, they were of an overbearing and quarrelsome nature.

William Stopp, a young man of but fourteen summers, from Cincinnati, Ohio, accompanied them to this County. The three occupied a small cabin on section 23. Both of these men drank, and caroused and at times cruelly abused the boy. One severe cold night, nearly in the dead of winter, they stripped the boy and gave him a shameful beating then thrust him under the floor of their cabin into a small cellar, where he died before morning from the effects of the cruelty received from the in-

furiated men, and exposure to the severe cold. It was but a
short time before the news spread over the entire neighborhood
and a crowd of excited people at once proceeded to the scene of
murder. In due time both Olleslaugher and Butler were arrested
and placed under bonds. On the 23d day of May, 1857, the
grand jury found a true bill of indictment against these men and
the same day they were brought before the court. A change of
venue was asked and granted to Johnson County. The case was
tried at Iowa City, but they finally escaped their just punishment
through some lack of evidence and informality of the law.
Shortly after they left the County, leaving the whole matter a
mistery at that time, as to the true facts in the case, and their
object in dealing so foully with the boy. But some time subsequent to their trial it was ascertained by the attorney for these
men that the boy Stopp, who at the time of the murder was
about fourteen years of age, was to fall heir to a valuable property in Ohio, when he became of age, and that Butler had succeeded in securing the legal guardianship over him, and without much
doubt removed with the boy to Iowa to accomplish what was accomplished, using Olleslaugher for the purpose, as the gravest
charges, the last severe beating and exposure was done directly
by him but with the approval of Butler.

During the winter of 1856 and 7 the settlers experienced some
long hardships. But all managed to live and had good cause to
be thankful that it was not worse. The young men and women
of this day have little knowledge of what a pioneer life consisted.
Away out upon an almost boundless prairie, alone to experience
the rough and rugged frontier life, deprived of the pleasure of
close communication with old friends and perhaps parents, it
was dreary indeed. But how different it is now; however far
the distance they can be communicated with in a few moments.

The recollection of these hard winters and severe snow storms
are vividly impressed upon the mind of more than one old settler,
and especially the rememberance of the horrors of that long winter, 1857, will never be obliterated while their lives will last.
The snow began to fall on the night of the first of December, and

continued falling for a number of days, until it reached an average depth of about two feet, drifting in places as high as eighteen to twenty feet. Great suffering was experienced in consequence. The settlers relied for their daily wants upon the small crop which they were enabled to raise the previous season, and the wild game which was abundant at that time. The great depth of the snow was a barrier to all travel, and it may well be imagined the suffering was great.

The snow remained on the ground for about three months and during this time some of those who were exposed to the cold froze to death; others narrowly escaped with their lives. A Mr. Crampton and wife, who had been visiting at Mr. Greenlee's, in Perry township, on returning home one Sunday afternoon, a distance of probably half-mile, were over taken by a severe snow storm, lost their way and perished in the cold. The next day, being still stormy the neighbors found her in the forenoon about three miles from home and found him late in the afternoon about seven miles from home, with her shawl wrapped about him. There were convincing evidences that he had carried her for a half mile or more after she was unable to walk. He probably took her shawl to save his own life, after he found she was dead. In the same storm of December 21st, William Randolph, now a resident of Richland township, then living in Carroll township, left his home for the timber to procure a load of wood. On his return he had proceeded but a short distance when caught in a snow storm and it was with great difficulty that he arrived safely at home. We have heard him remark that several times while out that night he thought he would be compelled to give up, lie down and die. The snow in many places had drifted so much that his team could not get through, and he was compelled to effect a passage by raking it away with his hands.

We have little doubt that many weary ones during that long winter, sighed for the comforts of the "Old home", but notwithstanding its dreariness and the suffering of the people, very few became disheartened. We find them in the spring as determined as ever to procure for themselves a home in this truly beautiful country.

In 1860 a Board of Supervisors were elected under an act of the eighth General Assembly, consisting of a member from each civil township in the county. On the 7th day of January, 1851, the Board held their first meeting, at the Court House in Toledo. On motion made by A. C. Marston, Jonathan Peterson, of Carroll township, was elected Chairman *pro tem*, after which P. L. Sherman, of Geneseo township, was elected permanent Chairman. Rules were adopted for the government of the Board, and business at once proceeded with the following named persons responding respectively:

Anthony Bricker, Indian Village township; Wesley Daniel, Buckingham; Turner Forker, Richland; William Gallagher, Jr., Howard; B. A. Hall, Toledo, now of Tama; Robinson Johnson, Highland; Lucius Kibbee, Carroll; A. C. Marston, Spring Creek; G. G. Mason, Oneida; Mefford Mitchell, Otter Creek; Jonathan Peterson, Carlton; S. C. Rogers, Crystal; P. L. Sherman, Geneseo; J. W. Southwick, Perry; T. S. Talmage, Clark; the member from York township being absent.

At this meeting of the Board no business of importance was transacted, and it would be unprofitable as well as unnecessary to present in detail the numerous orders, reports, resolutions, etc. Among so many men, their proceedings partake a good deal of the nature of a legislative body. There are always some cool business heads, as well as a good many "glib-tongues". Some of them are practical, industrious workers, others are of the "loud-mouthed" order and always ready to make a speech of volatile import, more to be heard than for real practical usefulness to their constituency and the tax payer. This is in nowise derogatory to their character as men, they can't help it. It has always been and always will be so. In the Congress of the United States, in State legislatures, a few do the work, while others do the talking. This is neither romance nor elaboration, but solid history sustained by facts as old as any civilized government.

Eight years had come and gone since the independence of Tama

County was recognized. In these years the wild prairies, first the home of the red man, had been reduced to farm tillage, and evidences of wealth, intelligence, comfort and refinement were to be seen in every direction. Indian trails had given way to State and County roads. Villages, churches and school houses had sprang up on the "old camp grounds" of the Sac and Fox and their kindred tribes, natives of the beautiful valley of the Iowa River and its tributaries. Claims upon which the hearty pioneers had settled long before the County Surveyors had disturbed the grasses and flowers that grew in great profusion with Jacob's staff and chain, as they re-surveyed townships and section lines, and established section corners, had been proved up, and with a guaranty from Uncle Sam, the occupants were monarchs of all they surveyed. In peaceable possession of their land and their homes, the out-laws expelled from the County, their lands rich and productive, the people of Tama County can well afford to be joyous and happy. What if their pioneer days were often full of hardships, toil exposure and want; the worst is over. Those years of trial have brought them comfort and plenty, and the future is bright with hope and full of promise. Since then, 1861, seventeen more years have come and gone, each of them adding to the population, wealth and intelligence of the people, until Tama County has come to rank among the richest and most populous in the great State of Iowa, a proud monument in the memory of the brave and heroic pioneers, who settled here first. The following are lines written by an old settler, which we consider very appropriate.

> Of all the dear hopes among men,
>   These are the sweetest in life;
> A hope for salvation—and then
>   A home— for my child—for my wife.
>
> Coming out from the distant east
>   Out from the ocean's strands,
> Away from old Ohio's beech,
>   Out from the blue-grass land,
>
> Coming down from the sunny slopes
>   Of Virginia's mountains,
> The rocky dales of old Vermont,
>   Massachusetts' fountains,

See—here a man, and there a man
    From glen, and dell and bay,
With oxen, wagon, gun and hounds,
    All westward take their way.

And now beside a grassy mound,
    They're tenting on the green;
The thin blue smoke, where they are camped,
    Above the trees is seen.

The night is gone; the early morn
    Salutes the coming day;
In dreams last night new hopes were born!—
    Again they're on their way!

With faces to the setting sun
    Their loved ones left behind;
Their hope, their aim, their object one,
    Each, in each heart enshrined.

For nature's wish in every heart,
    Though often it may roam.
Is still to have some hallowed spot
    That heart may call "Sweet Home.

Then, what was toil, or, what was strife,
    To sturdy souls like those
Who saw the forest yield new life
    And blossom as the rose.

Who saw the prairies robed in green
    Put on new life again!
League after league their lands were seen,
    In waves of golden grain.

They heard the red man's barbarous yell—
    Triumphant roll along.
But soon the hill-top and the dell
    Broke forth in Christian song.

And where the little cabin stood,
    Half hid by shady bough,
Stands towering up above the scene
    The stately mansion now.

And where the dark blue smoke arose.
    From camp-fire's burning brands,
Queen City of the pioneers
    Toledo, in beauty stands.

And, so in pride we gaze upon.
    Her spires and her domes,
We'll not forget the hands that raised
    Our humb'e childhood homes.

But, as the days grow old and die;
    As summers come and go.
Our hearts return to other scenes,
    Of thirty years ago.

To sugar camp where boiling down
    The garnered sap, again,
We listen to the deep mouthed hound
    Close followed by the men.

Cry long and loud upon the track
    Of some poor wounded deer,
Whose doom is sealed—the rifle crack!
    Ah! hear the hunters cheer,

The chase is done—the trophy won;
    And breakfast waits at dawn;
Tis syrup stored—in thin scraped gourd,
    "Corn bread" and roasted fawn.

No days are there like early days,
    No real joy since then;
Time robs us of our happiness
    As we lose faith in men.

O blessed spots! O by gone years,
    O'er you our old hearts yearn,
And as our eyes grow dim with tears,
    To sadder scenes we turn.

To grassy mounds, long years o'ergrown,
    By thickets and by thorns,
Where, precious dust, our loved' ones own,
    Sleep till the coming morn.

Many of the pioneers.
    Are camping on the shore
Of death's dark deep, whose tide of years
    Will wake them never more!

Though some remain, their locks of grey
    Admonish us that still
They're drifting from us day by day,
    Adown life's sunset hill.

CHAPTER III.

The manner and customs of our fore fathers are always fraught with peculiar interest, and read of with pleasure and profit by all. If we compare the pleasures of the times of our fathers with those of to-day, and the customs of those days with our own, we are apt to regard those of the past in an unfavorable light. But by outward appearance alone, things cannot safely be judged. Many things are inwardly beautiful which outwardly appear the reverse.

We have not yet given a description of the dwelling of our fathers; so here it goes. Imagine a home about sixteen feet square, seven and a half feet high, built up with large round or square logs, and covered with roof boards, held on by huge weights and poles, the cracks in the walls filled with mud, which would occasionally fall out, when the wind would whistle through the door, (for there was but one) made of rough boards, with a wooden latch, the string of which always hung out, a sign of welcome to the weary traveler, and the kind neighbor, and you have the exterior, except that upon one side there was a small window, large enough for a sash containing six, eight by ten lights, sometimes with glass in them, but often covered with greased paper. In the interior, you will find upon one side the huge fire place, large enough to contain a back-log as heavy as any man would care to carry, and holding enough wood to supply an ordinary stove a week, on either side are huge pots and kettles, and over all a mantle, on which stands the tallow-dip to give light to all who are in the house, but which will hardly compare with the gas jets of this day; the "little brown jug," which was not so little either, and in many cases well filled with a liquor which teto-tlers decline; in one corner the large bed, for the old folks, un-der which the trundle-bed for the younger members of the family; in another corner stands the old-fashioned large spinning wheel with a smaller one by its side; in another the pine table on which three times a day the food of the family was placed, and which was rapidly taken therefrom by the individual members thereof; in still another may be seen the cumbersome loom; over the door hangs the ever truthful rifle with powder horn, ready for instant use; while around the room are scattered a few splint bottomed chairs and three legged stools; a rude cupboard, holding the glass and queensware composes the furniture—everything of the sim-plest and rudest manufacture.   And yet these homes, simple and rude as they were, were inhabited by a kind, true hearted people. They were strangers to mock modesty, and the traveler seeking lodging for the night, or desirous of spending a few days in the community, if willing to accept the offerings of honest hearts, al-ways found a welcome.   The people were industrious from dire necessity.   All who were old enough were usefully employed. Children were enured to toil and labor and the lot of the women was hard indeed.   Upon them devolved the preparation of the daily food, oft from a very scanty larder; they were re-quired to weave the linen and woolsey, prepare the flax and wool with their own hands, making almost the entire wardrobe of the family, some really doing it all.   It was a life peculiarly trying and wearing to them, yet they bore it with patience and endur-ance.

The family bible was another article found in almost every home, and the minister of the gospel appearing, the two served to turn the thoughts of the people in the right direction.   To these influences we ascribe in a great measure the prosperity of the

County, and the better moral sentiment that has usually prevailed. Without such influence men would be barbarians. Closely allied to this influence is a desire for knowledge that must be appeased. We therefore find the school teacher following closely in the walk of the minister, and schools were established in every neighborhood where a sufficient number of children could be brought together to warrant the services of an instructor.

The cultivation of flax was an important item with many of the early settlers, while sheep raising was hardly ever neglected. The entire clothing of many families was manufactured from these staple sources into cloth by the prudent and tireless house wife.

The flax was, after pulled by the women, and after the seed had been thrashed out, spread on the grass to rot, and when rotted sufficiently was bound in bundles and dressed; that is, the flax and tow were separated. Scarcely any crop, while growing was more beautiful than the flax. From one-half to two bushels of seed was sown on an acre, and the crop amounted to about two hundred pounds.

Great trouble was experienced for many years in the raising of sheep, on account of the great number of wolves that infested the country, but notwithstanding this, enough wool was secured for home use. One article largely manufactured, was called "linsey-woolsey." It was made of equal parts of cotton and wool, and colored according to the taste of the manufacturer. The exquisite shades and delicate colors shown in the dress goods of to-day were not observed in those times, our mothers being content with good, solid colors.

There were few houses where the large and small spinning wheel and the cumbersome loom were not found, together taking up more room than all the rest of the furniture. Having all these implements, and manufacturing so much of their own clothing, our fathers and mothers were almost independent of the rest of the world. To-day all this is changed. The buzz of the little spinning wheel, the whir of the larger ones, and the monot onous click of the loom are heard no more. They are banished to the attic or given over to destruction.

While our fathers and mothers toiled hard, they were not averse to a little relaxation and had their seasons for fun and enjoyment. If they did not receive the oft repeated visits of the theatrical or minstrel troupes, the wonderful magician, or the man with the "intelligent ants," they yet contrived to do something to break the monotony of their daily life and furnish them with a good hearty laugh.

Among the more general forms of amusements was the "quilting bee," the corn husking, or corn shucking, as generally called in this country. Our young readers will doubtless be interested in a description of these forms of amusements, where labor was made to afford fun and enjoyment to all participating. "Quilting-bee," as its name indicates, was where the industrious qualities of that busy little insect that improves each shining hour was exemplified in manufacturing quilts for the house-hold. In the afternoon the ladies for miles around gather at the appointed place, and while their tongues would not cease to play, their hands were busily employed in making the quilt, and a desire was always manifested to get it out as quick as possible, for then the fun would begin. In the evening the gentlemen came, and the hours would then pass swiftly by in playing some boisterous yet innocent game or in the dance. Corn-husking was where both sexes united in the husking. They usually assembled in a large barn which was prepared for the occasion, and when each gentleman had selected a lady partner the husking began. When a lady found a red ear she was entitled to a kiss from each gentleman present; if a gentleman found one he was allowed to kiss every lady present. This feature of the general programme was particularly enjoyable, and a source of unlimited fun and frolic. After the corn was all husked the floor was cleared, the old violin brought out, tuned up, and the merry dance began, usually lasting until broad day light.

"The little brown jug" spoken of as having a place upon the mantle, was often brought into requisition, it affording a means of enjoyment that nothing else could supply. No caller was permitted to leave the house without an invitation to partake of its contents; not to so invite was a breach of hospitality, not to be thought of for a moment. It was brought out upon many occasions and freely dispensed to old and young alike, with no thought of danger. It was a thing of prime importance in all the assemblages of men at log rollings, corn huskings, house raisings, etc.

It seems a great wonder to us that the entire County was not devoted to drunkenness for in the early settlement of all its parts the same universal custom prevailed. No one then seemed to think there could be danger. Now and then a drunkard was made but he was more pitied for his misfortune than for his want of manhood or self-control; it was not the use but only the abuse of it that seemed wrong. It was thought impossible to work without it, and it was therefore always present and the drunken broils occasioned by its use were soon forgotten.

Hunting was a favorite pastime for the men. Game was killed more however, for amusement than to supply the wants and necessities of their families.

House-raising furnished another occasion for assemblage and enjoyment. Buildings were then made of such massive timber that it required a large force of men to erect them, which was done solely by muscular power, all the appliances of modern inventions for this purpose being entirely ignored if not unknown. On these occasions liquor was always free to all present. These raisings were usually important events in every neighborhood and people from far and near came to witness and enjoy them. Log rolling was another mode of useful recreation. When a man had felled the timber on a considerable space of ground, covered as it was with a large growth, it was impossible for him, without aid, to get the logs together so as to burn them. He therefore made a log rolling and invited all his neighbors, who came and with good will and strong muscles, brought the logs together. The work ended with a good supper and a social good time.

Election days were observed as holidays. The men came to

town, voted, drank whiskey, smoked, swore, whistled and fought, all for a little fun.

Look as we may upon the questionable amusement of the early times, we know that kind hearts, neighborly acts and universal good will for all mankind was a genuine passion and therefore we forbear all criticisms.

CHAPTER IV.

The late and more fashionable customs of society had not yet penetrated these regions. The bonnets and shawls worn by our mothers were not cast aside after the first season's wear, but continued to do service as long as they could be kept whole. Our fathers did not aspire to broadcloth suits or beaver hats, but were contented with home-spun jeans and felt or straw hats.

When the County was organized there were no public roads running through it, the first-being the old State Road which was laid out in July, 1853, from Marengo to Ft. Dodge and running along the south side of the Iowa River through Tama County. In August of the same year the A. D. Stephens and Hardin County State Road was located, also in December of that year a State Road running from A. D. Stephens' place to Indiantown was located north from the Iowa River and proved a great benefit to the County. Early in the year 1854, a Road was located from J. H. Hollen's place near the Iowa River, running in a northwesterly direction to James Laughlin's, in Carlton township. In May, 1854, the Blackhawk and Toledo Road was located by the way of Toledo and Buckingham into Blackhawk County, and a Road from Bruner's Mill in Toledo township, to Salt Creek, was located in July, 1854.

Toledo, at this time, was the most important point in the

County. As the County became settled new roads were laid out. More than four-fifths of the entire expenses of the County, we believe, during the first few years of its existence, were for this purpose. Roads were not then run on section lines as now but were located as thought best for the convenience of the people. The broad prairies were open in every direction, and a road running across them at any angle would hurt nobody, but on the contrary would be convenient for all. If one had intimated at that time that these prairies would soon be dotted over with frame houses, barns, school houses and churches, he would have been thought a fit subject for an insane asylum. This no doubt seems strange to our young people and late settlers in the County, but at that time the conclusion arrived at seemed reasonable. In the first place, the question of fuel had to be taken into consideration. As coal had not been discovered within a reasonable distance, wood had to be procured. In the second place, timber for building purposes was required. Railroads were unknown and lumber could not easily be imported. For these reasons our fathers settled in the timber, or on its border, where they could obtain material for the erection of their houses, and fences for their lands, and fuel for their fires.

The nearest and most convenient route from settlement to settlement was sought, and surveyors were so instructed to locate roads. It may be thought that a great saving could have been made to the County by locating the roads as they are now run, but whether these changes were made wholly for the convenience and saving of time to the people now, is a question we are not prepared to discuss.

The Cedar Rapids and Eldora State Road, by way of Wolf Creek settlements was located in July, 1855, also, a road from Vinton to Newton via. Toledo, in June, 1855. This shows the enterprise and determination of the people to have the County open to travel and free communication. Although her streams were poorly bridged, yet they were passable at times and indicated the routes to market and to settlements.

Next follows the location of Mail Routes to different points.

One Mail Route was established through Northern Tama from Vinton to Albion, in the spring of 1857, which gave them better Mail facilities. Toledo was reached in due time in the year 1854.

In coming to a new country the settler has, through necessity, to depend upon a distant market. This was a great draw back to the pioneer. The first year's provisions had about all to be purchased, as they could not reap any benefits from their crops until the second year. The nearest market for the Tama County settler was, at that time, Cedar Rapids, Muscatine and Iowa City. It would take about one week to make the trip. It was customary for the old settlers to take turns in going to market; when one would go he would bring supplies for the whole neighborhood, and in due time another would return. Thus they would do until they had harvested and marketed their crops, then the future would look brighter and more promising.

Many would resort to means of trade and barter. A. would trade B. flour for its value in meat; B. would trade C. a yoke of oxen for a horse; D. would trade E. a half dozen hogs for a cow. Many were the traits to which the people were led to make both ends meet, and numerous laughable incidents are narrated of the crooks and turns that were made—incidents that are laughable to us now, but were serious matters with the poor frontiersman. Notes were given payable in property, and often it would seem impossible for the debtor to meet his obligations. Some holders would hold their notes without attempting to collect them, with the hope that better times would come and the giver be able to pay the money. Favors and accommodations were tendered by one neighbor to another, all working harmoniously together, sharing the last morsel and making room for one more weary one to rest on their cabin floor, permitting no one to go away without fully sharing their humble but generous hospitality.

Great hardships and sufferings were endured on many trips to market; sometimes they were made in mid winter. Frozen limbs frequently attested their exposure and sometimes death. The anxiety of those who remained in their cabin awaiting the

return of those who were out, sometimes became painful from
suspense and frequently their worst fears were realized. But
such good feelings as were shown to one another never have been
excelled, and the strongest band of sympathy existed. To re-
fuse a favor was unknown, but to render one was the first impulse
of their hearts.

After a few years stores were opened among the settlers and
better facilities were offered to purchasers of home necesities.

Not until the fall of 1862 did the settlers of Tama County
receive the benefits of a home market and realize the advantage
of a Railroad. When the Chicago & Northwestern Railroad
reached Tama City, then Iuka, it opened a transportation to
Eastern markets and established a home market for the produc-
ers of Tama County.

CHAPTER V.

This large and excellent County is twenty-four miles from east to west and thirty miles from north to south making twenty full townships of land, containing therefore, seven hundred and twenty sections, or square miles. The principal stream in Tama County is the Iowa River, a broad flowing, swift, bubbling, dancing stream which enters the County near the north western corner of Indian Village township, and crosses in a south easterly course and enters Benton County a little north of the southwest corner.

The face of the County along the river is abrupt, rough, broken and timbered. In only a few places do the prairie vistas open down to the water's edge, affording glimpses of the broad, undulating plains, which open so wide beyond, that the blue of the sky and the green of the rolling sward, seem to mingle in a far off blending.

Three miles west of Tama City a dam is built across the river which furnishes water for one of the best water powers in the State to which we will again refer in another chapter. There are also good dams across the river at Gray's mill in Indian Village township and at Crenshaw's mill in Richland township. Dams might be constructed at many other points on the river within this County and a supply of water power be put into use, unlimited in extent. Indeed, such a stream as the Iowa River, for water powers, is hard to find, and some day it will enrich all this part of the State with its mills, manufactories, factories, foundries, and machine shops. Other, but smaller streams, run through different parts of the County, the principal of which is Otter Creek, raising near the center of the County, and running in a southerly course contributes to the Iowa. Salt Creek upon the east side of the County, runs in a southerly course and empties into the Iowa. Sugar Creek upon the west side of the County, and Deer Creek rising in Spring Creek township, flowing in a southerly direction emptying into the Iowa, also Richland Creek, rising in the southeastern part of the County running east empties into the Iowa. While the north part of the County is well supplied with Wolf Creek, or Big Creek, as it is sometimes known, which flows directly across the County in an irregular course and passes on into Benton County entering into the Cedar River.

The country is rough, and more or less rolling, in close proximity to all these streams, and is covered with a fair growth of timber. None of it could be called very heavy timber, and some of it is brushy barrens. Still, all these streams with a few isolated groves, furnish a fair supply of wood for fuel and other necessary uses.

As previously remarked the County is about equally divided between prairie and timbered land, the former is composed of a soil consisted of the richest prairie loam. In all parts of the State where the counties are prosperous Tama will rank among the foremost in agricultural resources and in the elements of material wealth. The amount of farm products usually raised and sold is enormous. The real resources of the soil are not yet half developed, but when they shall be more fully, and the vast comparatively untouched water powers of the Iowa River and its tributaries shall be utilized, this County will attain a degree of prosperity which will place it foremost in that richest portion of the Prairie State lying between the Mississippi and the Missouri rivers.

The geology of Tama County is of a highly interesting character and to scholars it will be especially valuable. Although, as yet coal and mineral have not been discovered in paying quantities in the County, yet coal exists, and stone has been found not only along the river banks, but in the bluffs in the northern part of the county. Stone can be found in abundance in Lincoln and Geneseo townships and in Fifteen Mile and Six Mile Groves while in the southwestern part of Indian Village township can be found large quarries of stone, from all appearance inexhaustible. This stone is of peculiar formation, and belongs to the sub-carboniferous limestone of the lower series, divided into three classes, St Louis limestone, Keokuk or Kinderhook limestone, and upper and lower Burlington limestone. The solidity and compactness of the formation renders it susceptible of the highest polish. The beds are some twelve feet in thickness consisting of three layers divided as follows;

1st. Thin bedded sandy limestone, 3 feet; 2nd. Thin bedded oolitic limestone, 4 feet; 3rd. Heavy bedded irregular limestone, gray, with bluish tinge, 6 feet; and below this will be found thin beds of carboniferous limestone from 8 to 10 feet.

The Keokuk or Kinderhook limestone is largely composed of fine grained, yellowish sandstone.

The Burlington limestone formation consists of distinct calcareous divisions which are separated by a series of silicious beds. These beds consist of light grayish or yellowish layers of silicious shale and chert together with nodular masses of flint, the whole mixed with a smaller proportion of calcareous matter. It affords much valuable material for economical purposes, but which is confined, however, entirely to its stone. It is seldom that it affords anything suitable for ashlar, but for the purpose of common masonry it is excellent, as it endures exposure to the atmosphere and frost without appreciable change. Good lime can be made from it, but the greater part of the lime is made from the upper division, because it usually produces whiter lime. The upper division furnishes excellent quarry rock

wherever it is exposed. The rock is also strong and endures exposure well. The color of some portions of this division is so
nearly white and its texture somewhat crystaline, that the purer
pieces resemble marble. Although the area occupied by the
outcrops of this formation in the County, is comparatively small,
yet the fossil remains it presents are of the most remarkable
character and profusion. The only remains of vertebrates which
the formation has afforded, are those of fishes and snails which
are numerous in some localities.

The St. Louis limestone formation, as it exists in Tama County
consists of three tolerably distinct sub-divisions, principally dependent on lithological character. They are magnesian, arena
ceous and calcareous. The first and lowest consists of a series
of yellowish gray, more or less magnesian and usually massive
layers. The second is a yellowish or light gray, friable sandstone. The third or upper division is principally composed of
light gray compact limestone, sometimes uniformally bedded, but
it often has a concretionary and even a brecciated character. It
furnishes excellent material for quicklime even when it is so
concretionary and brecciated that it will not serve a good purpose
for building material, and is usually too soft for any practical
use. It contains a great many fossils and is very attractive.

At Indiantown, in this County, the sub-carboniferous formation appears, commencing at the water's level of the Iowa River.

No. 3.   Soft irregularly bedded, Magnesian limestone, passing up into purer
          and more regularly bedded limestone............................40 feet
N o. 2.   Light gray oolitic limestone, in heavy layers................15 feet
No. 1.   Yellowish, shaly, fine grained sandstone....................20 f et

The surface deposits to which the name of Drift is applied, has
a far wider distribution than any other surface deposit. It meets
our eyes almost everywhere, covering the earth like a mantle and
hiding the stratified rocks from view, except where they have
been exposed by the removal of the drift through the erasive act-
i on of waters. It forms the soil and subsoil of the greater part of
the State, and in it alone many of our wells are dug, and our for_
ests take root. Occasionally it is itself covered by another de-

posit; as for example, the bluff deposit, in which case, the latter forms the soil and subsoil. The drift is composed of clay, sand, gravel and boulders, promiscuously intermixed, without stratification or any other regular arrangement of its material.

The clay drift, which is always present in greater or less proportion, is always impure; always finely distributed throughout the whole deposit, but not unfrequently, irrigular masses of it are seperated from the other materials. Its color is usually yellowish from the peroxyd of iron it contains, and which when it is burned into bricks give them a red color.

The sand of the unaltered drift is seldom seperated from the other materials in any degree of purity, but it is not unfrequently the case that it exists in excess of the others; and in some cases small accumulations or pockets of it are found, having a considerable degree of purity while the gravel is derived largely from rocks that are more or less purely silicious, but occasionally they are found to be of granite composition.

So small a proportion of Tama County is occupied by the coal measures that it can hardly be enumerated among the more important of the coal counties, though coal deposits have been found in Northern Tama, and it is not improbable that other discoveries of it may yet be made in other portions.

At Montour, near Indiantown, bed No. 2 is well exposed and is extensively quarried for lime, as it is also at the last named place. Near LeGrand, in the eastern part of Marshall County, and only a few miles west of Indiantown, No. 3 of the preceding section is well exposed, showing a thickness of about forty feet from the level of the River; No. 1 and 2 do not appear they having passed beneath its surface by a westernly dip, aided by the stream. The exposure here is composed most entirely of light brown or buff colored limestone, more or less magnesian, and in some of the more calcareous layers a slight tendency to oolitic structure is seen. Some of the layers are cherty but a large part of it is quite free from silicious matter.

The stone is largely quarried for various purposes, and the finer layers, which frequently have a beautiful veining of per-

oxyd of iron, are wrought into ornamental and useful objects,
and it is known in the market as Iowa Marble. Several other
exposures of the Kinderhook beds are known in Tama and Marshall Counties, one by II. S. Dickson and one by David Houghton.
Those first mentioned are the principal ones.

In this County the oolitic member is well exposed at several
places where it is quarried and used for the manufacture of lime
of excellent quality. It has been proposed to manufacture this
oolitic stone into table tops, mantles, etc., but although it may
be made to receive a fair polish and its oolitic structure gives it
considerable beauty it is feared that the well known tendency
of all oolitic limestone to become fragmentary, will be found to
render it worthless for such purposes. However, that near
Montour and Indiantown promise to prove valuable for such
uses.

CHAPTER VII.

In 1865-6 the subject of a railroad was extensively agitated in this County. A charter had been granted by the State for the building of the Iowa Central railroad, running from St. Louis to St. Paul via. Toledo. At this time N. C. Wieting, the present editor of the "Toledo Times." was publishing a paper in Toledo called the "Iowa Transcript." This sheet was the only Republican paper in the County, and was edited with considerable ability by its proprietor, Mr. Wieting, a whole souled jovial fellow and a talented man. In the files of his paper, now in possession of the County Auditor, R. G. McIntire, to which we had access, we found numerous articles favoring the proposed route. During the days of railroad excitement it was a constant and earnest advocate of the road and did much in influencing the people in its favor.

As already stated, the people of Tama County, at that time were determined to have a north and south railroad. The age was progressive, and they were determined to keep up with the times. Excepting the east and west road, the prairies were trackless but they should remain so no longer, come what would they were bound to have a north and south railroad. A railroad! what an invention! What a blessing! See yon iron horse; with his nostrils breathing fire, his long and shaggy mane, of thick murky smoke, streaming far behind, while in his might and strength, with his

train in the rear, he comes coursing through you neck of timber;
now over that creek, now across the prairie, now again in timber,
until in half the time it has taken us to write it here he is in Toledo, brought up all standing with his freight of bachelors and
babies, married men and mules, ladies and live stock, dry goods
and dutch. Oh! what a rumpus, what a din. But still what a
thing a railroad is. We imagine we heard the people of the
County saying what is to be done in regard to the proposed road.
The time for stopping to consider the policy of such an enterprise
has passed away; and the benefits to be derived from such means
of communication are held to be too self-evident to need any additional argument advanced in their favor; for who, say we, cannot
see in the advanced price of land, in the advantage of a ready market, in the increased facilties of communication, in the spread of
general intelligence, in the cheapened and quickened mode of
transportation, a sufficient inducement to wish such an undertaking success, and say that its benefits are beyond dispute? We
must awake from our stupor; measures must be taken for the securing of stock and having the County become a stockholder to a
liberal amount; of getting individuals, who need only the solicitation of some active friend of the road, to become deeply interested
in its completion. Then, friends of the road, be up and doing;
farmers of Tama County, our interests are at stake, see that you
neglect them not; merchants and mechanics, your welfare, too, is
bound up in this scheme—with it will come your prosperity,
without it you must lose immensly. Then, again say we, let us
all at work. Let our undertaking zeal and determined efforts
show that we desire what we need and must have—a railroad.

Meetings were held for the purpose of creating more interest in
the proposed railroad at Toledo at stated times, when some big
man would address the citizens of the County upon this important
subject. Committes were appointed to confer with the directors
of the road, etc. and after a time the work began in earnest. Men
interested in the road at once began the canvass in various parts
of the County, making speeches in nearly every school house,
church, and log cabin. The opponents of the road were not idle

in the meantime, and used every means in their power to influence
the people against it, but notwithstanding this considerable amount
of money was raised and the grading began, along the proposed
line. After expending some $30,000 in the enterprise, nearly
completing the grade from Toledo to the northern boundary of
the County, the people of Marshall county thinking they would
like to have a north and south road influenced the head men to
change the route and give them the road. When this scheme
came up work suspended, time passed away, and still no road.
Its friends were almost in despair, and its enemies jubilant. The
soothing phrase, "I told you so," was repeated over and over again
to the friends of the road until it became almost monotonous.
We have only to say, Tama County did not get the proposed
north and south railroad but Marshall County did.

In the winter of 1862 three years before the north and south
railroad was proposed the iron horse first made its appearance in
the County. We refer to the Chicago & North Western Railroad,
then known as the Cedar Rapids & Missouri. Without dis-
paragement to the others, this can be said to be the chief road
passing through the County; its volume of business being larger
and its facilities far greater than its competitors. Tama County
subscribed liberally to aid in its construction, and no better investment has she ever made. There has been returned by the road
in the shape of taxes, far more than the subscription. By its aid
the resources of the County have been developed to an extent that
one can scarcely realize. Towns have sprang up along its line
as if by magic, farms have been opened and factories have been
set in operation, employing hundreds of hands, and the wealth of
the East has been poured into our laps. Who would have thought
that we would almost double our population in ten years. In
less than that length of time the population had not only doubled
but nearly trebled. We will venture to say, to-day we have
four times the population we had then, and is constantly increasing.
This road passes through the southern portion of the County
while upon the north the Pacific Division of the Burlington Cedar
Rapids & Northern Railroad passes through a good portion of

the County, giving northern Tama an outlet east. While Toledo has an outlet by a branch railroad running to Tama City, a distance of two miles and one-half, which was constructed in the year 1871, and known as the Toledo & North-Western, Railroad.

CHAPTER VII.

Oh! a wonderful stream is the river of time,
As it runs through the realm of tears,
With a faultless rhythm, and a musical rhyme;
And a broader sweep, and a surge sublime.
As it blends in the ocean of years.

B. T. TAYLOR.

It is not strange that among the pioneer settlers of any new county a deep seated and sincere friendship should spring up that would grow and strengthen with their years. The incidents peculiar to life in a new country, the trials and hardship, privations and destitutions are well calculated to test, not only the physical powers of endurance, but the moral, kind and generous attributes of manhood and womanhood. They were times that tried men's souls and bring to the surface all that there may be in them of either good or bad. As a rule there is an equality of conditions that recognizes no distinction; all occupy a common level, and, as a natural consequence, a brotherly and sisterly feeling grows up that is lasting as time, for a "fellow feeling makes us wondrous kind."

With such a community, there is a hospitality, a kindness, a benevolence and charity unknown and unpracticed among the older, richer and more densely populated commonwealth. The very nature of their surroundings teaches them to feel each other's woes, and to share each others joys. An injury or a wrong may be ignored, but a kindly, generous, and charitable act is never forgotten. The memory of old associations and kindly deeds is always fresh. Raven locks may blench and whiten; full round cheekes fade and hollow; the fire of intelligence vanish from the organs of vision; the brow become wrinkled with care and age; the erect form bowed with accumulating years, but the true friends of the long ago, will be remembered as long as life and reason endure.

The surroundings of pioneer life are well calculated to test the true inwardness of the human heart. As a rule, the men and women who first occupy a new country, who go in advance to open and prepare the land for a future people, are bold, fearless, self reliant and industrious. In these respects, no matter from what remote section or country they may come, there is a similarity of character. In either education, religion or language, there may be a vast difference, but imbued with a common purpose, the founding and building of houses, these differences are soon lost by associations, and thus they became one people, united by a common interest. No matter what changes may come in after years, the associations are never obliterated from the memory.

Many interesting incidents occured during the days of early settlers of Tama County which if had been properly preserved, would be of benefit to poserity, and it is a matter of regret that the formation of the "Old Settlers Association" has not been continuously maintained in Tama County. The presence of such associations in all the Counties of our common country, with well kept records of the most important events, such as dates of arrivals, births, marriages, deaths, removals, nativity, etc., as all can readily see, would be the direct means of preserving to the literature of the country the history of every community that, to future generations, would be invaluable as a record of reference and a ready method of settling important questions of controversy. Such organizations would possess facts that could not be had from any other source. Aside from their historical importance, they would serve as a means of keeping alive and further cementing old friendships, and renewing among the members associations that were necessarily interrupted by the innovations of increasing population, cultivating social intercourse and creating a charitable band for such of their old members as were victims of misfortune and adversity.

Actuated by the purposes suggested in the preceding paragraph the pioneers of Tama County organized a society in 1872, that was known as the "Old Settler's Society of Tama County, Iowa." The first formal meeting was held in the city of Toledo, at the Court House, October 17th, 1872. Rezin A. Redman was chosen Chairman and Thomas A. Graham, Secretary. At this meeting speeches were made by many of those who felt an interest in such an organization. Such business as seemed necessary was transacted, and the meeting adjourned to meet October 24th. At this meeting the organization was made complete. Constitution and by-laws were adopted, wherein any person who having been a resident of the County fifteen years, could become a member of said Association by signing a record kept for that purpose by the Secretary of the Association. The time fixed for holding their annual meetings was the second Wednesday of each year. The following officers were elected:

Anthony Wilkinson, President; D. D. Appelgate, Secretary; Frank Davis, Treasurer; Thomas S. Free, David F. Bruner, W. H. Stivers and John T. Ames were appointed a committee to compile a history of the early settlements of the County.

The last meeting of the Old Settler's Association was held at Traer, October 9th, 1878, where many of the old settlers of Tama County gathered, and participated in a fine time.

CHAPTER VIII.

SAC AND FOX INDIANS.

These Indians were formerly two distinct nations and resided near the waters of the St. Lawrence. They lived together and were considered one people, though they kept up some customs among themselves calculated to maintain a seperate name and language.

The Fox Indians moved to the West and settled in the vicinity of Green Bay, on lake Michigan, but becoming involved in war with the French and neighboring tribes, were so much reduced in number that they were unable to sustain themselves against their hostile neighbors.

The Sac Indians had been engaged in a war with the Iroquois, or Six Nations, who occupied the country which now compasses the State of New York, and had became so weak that they were forced to leave their old hunting grounds and move to the West. They found the Fox tribe, their old neighbors like themselves, reduced in number by the misfortunes of war, and from a matter of necessity, as well as sympathy, they united their fortunes together and became one people. The date of their emmigration from the St. Lawrence is not definitely known. Father Hennepin speaks of the Fox Indians being at Green Bay in 1760, which was at that time called the Bay of Puants.

Just how long they remained at Green Bay is not known, but we do know that before the white man claimed the beautiful lands along the Iowa River, the Musquakie band of the Sacs and Foxes had their favorite hunting ground here, and acknowledged no higher authority than that of their renowned chief, Poweshiek. All were removed, however, with the rest of the Sacs and Foxes to their new home beyond the Missouri. After remaining in Kansas a while they ceded all their lands, in the year 1859 and 1860 to the government for the lands now occupied as a reservation for the original tribe. Three hundred and seventeen Indians of this tribe, after their removal, returned to Iowa and settled in Tama County and here received the misnomer of "Musquakie." The Government permitted them to remain and by virtue of an act passed, March 2nd, 1867, they were permitted to receive their share of the tribal funds, which is the interest only on the amount due them from the Government for their lands.

In August, 1865, Leander Clark, of Toledo, was appointed to act as their agent, and remained in that position until relieved by F. D. Garrety, U. S. A., under the late regulation transfering the Indian Bureau to the War Department. Mr. Garrety was succeeded by Rev. A. R. Howbert, and in April, 1875, Thomas S. Free became agent for the Musquakie band and still remains in that position.

Since Mr. Free has been agent, active steps have been taken for the advancement of the Indians in education and farming, besides many other ways. In August, 1875, a school house was built, at a cost of $1,200 in which school is kept. Mr. A. B. Somers is employed as their instructor. There is not a regular attendance at school, but the school house is kept open and every opportunity improved to teach them, and remove the prejudice existing by reason of their religious belief against education. Books have been distributed among them and in this irregular manner some of them have learned to read and write. The Instructor resides in the second story of the school building and gives his entire time and attention to the advancement of his subjects in agriculture as well as education, and carefully attends to the sick and infirm. The prejudice against the school is caused by the Chief and head men, who are opposed to it and the young men are governed by their disapproval under their tribal relations. Still many have advanced in learning the English language and the requirements of the law, regarding payments of debts, crimes, trespasses, petty misdemeanors and to accept as true the manner in which the law in such cases is applied to the whites.

In a retrospective view of the tribe, while residents of the County we can recall but one marked scene of violence. This occured upon the morning of June 13th, 1874, resulting in the murder of a Pawnee Indian. We give it as given by the "Tama City Press" of June 19th, 1874.

"On Saturday morning about 11 o'clock our usually quiet city was thrown into some excitement over the intelligence that a fearful tragedy had been enacted at the Indian camps, about three miles west of Tama City. After learning that there was some foundation for the rumor we repaired in company with an Attorney, a Physician and a Contractor, to the scene of the tragedy. As near as we could learn, the facts were about as follows:

On the morning of the 12th inst., four Pawnee Indians came to the camp of the Misquakies, and remained all day and the night of the 12th. On the next morning one of them, while but a few steps from the wick-i-up was approached from behind by one of the Musquakies called "Black Wolf," who drew a revolver and fired three shots. The first entered the back of the head, and passing through the brain lodged under the skull in front; the second one passing into the base of the neck passed upward toward the head, and came to the surface near the right ear, and the other was merely a scalp wound. The last two wounds were not necessarily fatal, but the first one bore unmistakable evidence of the intention of him who held the fatal weapon. At the first shot the Pawnee went down, and the other two must have hit him while in the act of falling. When we reached the camp, the Pawnee had been buried, and here, not fearing a dead Indian, we had no necessity for the professional assistance of either of the gentlemen who accompanied us. Soon after, the Coroner. Deputy Sheriff, Indian Agent and several other parties appeared upon the scene, and the dead Pawnee was resurrected, brought to Tama City, together with his murderer, and on Saturday evening an inquest was held by E. M. Beilby, Coroner."

When it was proven that Black Wolf did the bloody deed, a warrant was issued and delivered to Deputy Sheriff Bartlett who arrested him and lodged him in jail. Black Wolf remained in jail until February 18th, 1875, when he was discharged, the witnesses failing to appear against him.

The Chief is Man-an-wan-e-ka, a son of the noted Chief Poweshiek, in honor of whom one of our Counties, is named. He is about 50 years of age, rather intelligent looking, but a man of few words, and highly esteemed by his people. He is a strict tetotaler, says he never drank any whiskey, and talks temperance to his people. Wa-ka-mo is the second or subordinate Chief and the pride of the tribe. He is about 60 years of age, stands six feet high, and has a large and powerful physical structure. He has a keen eye, a quick intellect, but cannot talk English with ease. The Interpreter, Sow-on, is a good looking middle aged man, and speaks the English language fluently. There are also some others who take seats in the council whenever any business of importance is to be transacted.

The reservation belonging to the tribe is located in Tama township, on the Chicago & Northwestern Railroad, three miles west of Tama City, and intersected by the Iowa River. They have 692 acres of land, which they have purchased with their annuities and it is held in trust for their use and benefit, and upon it they pay taxes. They have, by estimate, about 150 acres of land under plow, 60 acres in tame grass, and the balance is wild grass and wood land. The whole tract is under fence, most of the fencing being of good and substantial make. Their chief crop is corn, but they raise potatoes, beans, onions, tobacco, squashes, and other vegetables in quantities to meet their wants. The tribe numbers 345, one hundred and sixty-four males and one hundred and eighty-one females. There has been seven births and three deaths during last year. Their personal property is estimated at $15,000, consisting largely of ponies which is their ideal of wealth. They receive annually from the Government the sum of $11,174.66, as Annuity under treaty relations.

The strongest local attachment exists among them for their present home, it being the home of their fathers. They cannot forget the past with all its associations and will never consent to remove from their present place. They have from the earliest days been friendly to our settlers. They are a peaceful, honest and contented people, posessed with a good degree of moral character and have a bright out-look for the future.

CHAPTER IX.

This chapter we devote to brief histories of each township in rder as organized—Giving date of organization—First settlers—'ownship officers—Interesting incidents, etc. It will be noticed 1at Tama County was organized at an early date, into three ownships, namely; Indian Village, Howard and Buckingham, nd bounded as in Chapter 1, Page 20. We will notice in particu-1r the townships as they are known at present, treating them un-er their respective names.

INDIAN VILLAGE.

This township derived its name from the large number of 1dians, living in the vicinity of old Indiantown, at its organiza-on.

The first settlement effected in the township was in the year S49 by Isaac Asher. E. W. Daily, N. J., A. J. and M. Blodgett, . Chase, J H. Voorhies, E. Stump, P. Rouse, A. Dingee, J. 1ronk, W. Murty, I. Butler, P. Helm, J. Huston, S. B. Dunton, . Jack and T. D. H. Wilcoxen were among the early settlers, 1ming in at an early day and improving farms in various parts f the township.

The Iowa River passes through this township almost diagonal-', in a southeasterly direction, and along its bank will be found one mill known as the Indiantown Flouring Mill, which was established in 1855 by Fisk, Helm & Gray, now owned and operated by Charles Gray, who bought their interest in 1856. This township has peculiar advantages over the adjacent ones, from the fact that a large body of timber lines the bank of the river in its course through the township, and also from the amount of stone to be found here. The bluffs through this section contain abundance of rock for building and other purposes. The quality of this stone and its extent are spoken of in a previous chapter. It contains three towns. Orford, now Montour, Indiantown, (which is known as Butlerville, the name of the P. Office) about two miles apart, and Le Grand Station, located on section 18. The country is fine; the bluffs in general are of gentle ascent and timber and water plentiful, making it a highly productive township.

The township was organized in 1853 with William Taylor, E. W. Daily and L. Appelgate as Trustees. The first election was held at the house of E. W. Daily on the first Monday in August, 1853. The township contains several stone quarries and lime kilns, from which stone are taken and lime made in abundance.

At an early day an exciting shooting affray took place in "Whiskey Bottom"—so called from the immense quantity of whiskey sold there by one Rouse, and the roughness of the people. The old settlers well remember its character. The shooting took place between a Samuel Reed and one Scamerhorn, and resulted in the killing of Reed. It appears from the facts we can gather regarding it, that between this Reed and Scamerhorn a feeling of jealousy existed in regard to a girl that both were wooing. These two men in company with five or six others, were turkey hunting. After proceeding some distance the party seated themselves on a log, when they separated a little while after this a report of a gun was heard and upon examination it was found that Reed was dead, having been shot completely through. Scamerhorn was indicted, but the crime was not fastened upon him, owing to the fact that sufficient testimony could not be had to convict the prisoner.

The first marriage was S. Davidson and Miss A. Asher. July 18th, 1850, three years before the County was organized.

The first school was taught by C. J. Stevens our present County Clerk, at Indiantown in 1856.

The first death was Mariah Blodgett in 1853.

The first birth was Mary M. Blodgett, March 4th, 1853.

But little was done in the settlement of the township until the completion of the Chicago & North Western Railroad, when, in a short time nearly every quarter was occupied.

The township is well improved and has living within its boundaries some of the most enterprising farmers in the County, among whom we many mention J. L. Magee, N. J. Blodgett, W. C. Salsbury, S. Strain, A. B. Taplin, R. M., A. C. and Charles Tenny.

Below will be found the names of those who have served in the offices of Justices, Trustees, and Clerks, from the organization of the townships to the present.

Justices:—W. B. Mumbrow, H. Welton, J. W. Wyman, B. W. Fellows, C. J. Stevens, G. H. Hall, I. Butler, A. Dingee, P. Helm, J. B. Moffitt, J. M. Preston, L. Appelgate, J. H. Stevens.

Clerks:—A. L. Range, T. P. Smith, T. R. Oldham, C. D. Torrey, A. J. Dingee, H. G. Wallace, B. F. Fellows, E. Taplin, J. H. Voorhies, D. D. Appelgate.

Trustees:—R. E. Tewksberry, S. D. Tyner, J. Paxton, E. Garrison, C. and R. M. Tenny, J. M. Mills, J. Abbott, J. Smith, A. B. Taplin, J. Dunn, T. D. H. Wilcoxen, H. G. Wallace, M. and N. J. Blodgett, B. W. Fellows, P. Helm, R. T. Armstrong, C. Gray, G. Blake, C. J. Stevens, A. C. Tenny, J. Moore, J. Bradley, F. Hollingshead, E. Ruggles, J. S. Townsend, A. Dingee, M. Dunn, W. Taylor, E. W. Dailey, J. Jack, L. Appelgate, A. Bricker, I. Asher.

HOWARD.

This township was organized with boundaries as in the year

1854, but afterwards divided into nine townships (see page 20) leaving it as now known in the third tier of townships from the north line and second from the west line of the County.

The township is principally prairie, though containing considerable timber, some of which is very heavy in the south western portion, and along the streams in the west and eastern part. Christian Bruner has the honor of being the first to settle here; he built himself a cabin on section thirty-three in the spring of 1852, near the present village of Monticello. Samuel and Jacob Giger, E. Moler, R. A. Rundals, J. Reedy, R. Ray, J. Hartman, F. Spade, H. Howdyshell R. Blake, E. Myers, A. Harbaugh, D. Miller, B. Hammitt, G. Zehring, P. and L. Otterman, Wm. Gallagher, M. Hill, S. Speer, S. Bird, J. Strain, C. R. Ward, A. Leonard, W. C. Granger, J. Davis and B. C. Freet can also be numbered with the first settlers, all good and industrious farmers, the most of whom are still living in the same neighborhood in which they first settled.

With regard to products, the township will favorably compare with any other in the County. In stock it ranks number one. In intelligence and business enterprise second to none. Being the home of so many good industrious farmers, this is not to be wondered at.

The township is well watered by Deer Creek and its tributaries, passing through a good portion of it.

There is one village in the township, Monticello, a name given it by C. R. Ward a resident of the place, it being the name of the town, and home of ex-President Thomas Jefferson, and has borne the name to this day. For description the reader is refered to another chapter.

The township contians one flouring Mill, established in 1854, by Christain Bruner, now owned and operated by Bruner & Reedy, located in the southwest part of the township on Deer Creek, also one Cheese Factory, with W. C. Granger as proprietor, which was established in 1878.

The first marriage was a double wedding. Mr. W. T. Hollen to Miss. Sarah Bruner, and Mr. Joseph Davis to Miss. Rebecca

Bruner, September 17th, 1854. B. Hammitt, a Justice of the
Peace, officiating.

The first school was taught on section 29, by Miss. Skinner, in
1854.

The first death was, Benjaman Franklin, son of D. F. and
Catharine Bruner, on September 10th, 1853.

The Methodists were the first religious denomination. A
Methodist Minister named Gamin, preached the first sermon at
Christian Bruner's house in 1853. Since that time there has
been a church building erected. The denomination is in a prosperous condition.

We compile the following list of officers from the Clerk's
books.

Justices: B. Hammitt. C. R. Ward, R. Ray, J. Fay, W. C.
Granger, B. Rhodes, J. Stone, H. Dann, W. Guilford, J. Rider. G. Burke, J. Gray. C. Baxter, H. Snodgrass, E. Carpenter, A. Whitely.

Clerks: D. F. Bruner, R. Ray, J. H. Granger, J. W. Rider,
E. S. Beckley, D. K. Gallagher, C. C. Granger and S. W.
Hawke.

Trustees:—W. C. Morrison, J. Ross, F. Davis, S. Giger, W.
C. Granger, D. N. Hill, C. R. Ward, J. Stone, J. Fay, D. Miller
J. Reedy, F. Homan, H. Parker, M. Ross, J. Fuller, P. Otterman,
R. Ray, G. W. McCollister, A. Harbaugh, J. H. Tindall, G.
Burke, E. D. Rice, H. McAnulty, J. T. McCormack, H. H. With-
ington, G. T. Jones, J. Gray, I. A. Richards, J. H. Giger.

BUCKINGHAM.

This is one of the oldest settled townships in the County,
having been organized in the year 1853. To David Dean, and
his two brothers belong the honor of the first settlement, they
having built their cabin on sections 33 and 34, in the year 1852.
But a short time after these gentlemen settled here A. M. Dun-

kle, Mr. Springmire, Pat Casey, and John Connelly,* came in, all settling in the vicinity of Buckingham. From this date the immigration increased quite rapidly. A large number of the first settlers still reside in the township, and nearly all have fine farms and are prominently identified with the history of the township, and County,

Buckingham township is principally prairie, though having in it considerable timber along the streams and southern part. The land is of good quality, and in it are some of the best farms, the finest residences and most substantial improvements found in the County. As a stock producing township it ranks among the best.

Here is the home of J. T. Ames, Esq., one of the largest farmers and hog raisers in the County. He has carried away from different Fairs in the State many blue ribbons. D. and S. Ewing, O. Gravatt, J. V. B. Green, J. W. Fleming and A. Cummings also devote a great deal of labor and attention to this branch of industry and are now heavy farmers,

The southern part of the township is watered by Twelve Mile Creek and on the east it is watered by Rock Creek and its tributaries,

*From some of the early settlers and the records of Tama County we gather this strange history of Mr. Connolly's life. As shown by the testimony of his son at the preliminary examination. He murdered his wife on the 15th of March, 1859, by striking her a blow on the head, and finding her dead he burried her for a few days under the straw and coarse manure in his stable, and then removed her one evening, by his son's aid and burried her on the farm of Mr. T. F. Clark A few years after the son's wife becoming dissatisfied with Connolly's treatment, disclosed enough of the transaction to lead to his arrest, on a warrant issued by N. Fisher J. P. of Toledo and by whom, after hearing the evidence of the case he was held to appear before the next District Court for indictment and trial. He was placed in the custody of constable H. C. Foster at the close of the trial, who took him home with him that evening, intending to start with him the following morning for the jail at Marion, in Linn County.

When it was nearly dark, and while Connelly and Foster were seated near the open door in th front room of the latter's house, Connelly asked for a drink of water. Foster went back to his kitchen, got the water but when he returned there was no Connelly there to drink it nor has there been to this day.

Foster immediately reported to the town his loss, and the people turned out to assist in the search, but could not find him in the darkness, nor have they ever since in the day light. The residents of that time speak of it as a very singular escape.

The township was organized in April, 1853, and comprised what is now Crystal, Geneseo, Perry, Clark and Grant townships. (see page 20) The first election was held on the first Monday in April, 1853.

In 1855 the town of Buckingham was founded and named after ex-Governor Buckingham of Connecticut. The land on which the town is situated belonged to G. Lyman and the Connell brothers, purchased by them of West Wilson, Esq., who entered it in July, 1853. Dr. H. C. Stanley opened the first store, and afterwards sold to D. Connell. Others came and the little Western Village soon comprised four stores, two blacksmith shops one shoe shop, one wagon shop, one tin shop, two churches, one large school house, post office and several dwellings; but no sooner had the town realized success than it was plucked in the bud by the founding of Traer in 1873, within three-fourths of a mile, which attracted the attention of all business and the town of Buckingham was soon a dilapidated ruin, to be no more.

Mr. Horton, an old settler of the township, and son while crossing Wolf Creek, near the present home of W. K. Snow, then known as Indian Ford, was drowned. It seems that they had been working on the opposite side of the creek from the house, and in the evening when returning found that the stream had swollen to a great depth, and that the only way for them to cross was by swimming. Their team, which consisted of four yoke of oxen, was driven into the water and by some cause, both Horton and son were thrown from the wagon into the water and drowned. The bodies, which had been carried down stream a considerable distance were soon recovered.

The first marriage in the township was Mr. Harrison Hill to Miss Charlotte Helm, the fall of 1864, by John Connell J. P.

The first death was a son of M. Spade, in August, 1853.

In 1855 Leander Clark erected a Saw Mill on Wolf Creek, near W. K. Snow's present residence.

The following is the list of township Justices, Clerks and Trustees since the organization of the township.

Justices: J. Connell, D. Dean, T. K. Shiner, L. Clark, J. C.

Wood, C. Gay, N. Reed, G. Jaqua, W. T. V. Ladd, T. L. Drew, E. M. Cugher, W. W. Blanchard, P. H. Mason.

Clerks: J. P. Wood, J. B. Dean, H. T. Gaston, W. A. Daniels, O. Gravatt, B. Roberts, B. F. Thomas, J. Kingery, J. M. Winn, A. N. Bates, B. L. Keeler.

Trustees: D. Dean, N. J. Osborn, S. Dunkle, I. Taylor, J. L. Wood, T. R. Shiner, H. Smith, C. Gay, H. C. Green, J. T. Ames, J. B. Hankison, E. Murdock, A. Gordon, D. S. and W. T. V. Ladd, R. Connell, J. Kingery, D. C. Underhill, M. S. Belknap, H. A. Owens, A. Antram, A. Wood, H. E. Davis, O. Gravatt, A. Cummings, J. Phillips.

RICHLAND.

The southern portion of this township is prairie land and contains some of the finest farms in the County. The Northern and central part, along the Iowa River and Richland Creek is somewhat broken and is principally timbered land. Its first settlement was in 1852 and the first house built on section 23 by A. P. Rich.

The township is well watered, and is fine farming land. Richland Creek passes through the central portion of the township emptying into the Iowa River on section 13, and on the north it is watered by the Iowa River running through the entire township, furnishing living water at all seasons of the year.

The township was organized in the year 1854. It lies in township 82 north, range 14 west, of the 5th, P. M.

G. B. Dunnells, J. Heath, Thomas Skiles, H. Davenport, Thos. and Jas. Marshall, E. Deeter, I. Walters, J. M. and C. E. Ramsdell, J. D. Smith, H. Day and others were among the first settlers of the township.

The township was named after Richland Creek.

James Hanna taught the first school in the year 1855 in a small log cabin, on section 22, which had formerly been occupied by H. Davenport as a residence.

The first marriage was Elias H. Price, and Miss Sarah Hatfield being united in the "holy bands of wedlock" on the 30th, day of May, 1855, by N. B. Hiatt, a Justice of the Peace.

The first death was Jas. Hatfield, who died in the year 1854.

There are two villages in the township, Helena and Eureka. For sketch of these towns the reader is refered to the history of the towns.

The township has one Flouring mill, situated on the Iowa River at Helena, which was established and run by E. Deeter until the year 1863, when it changed hands to B. F. Crenshaw its present owner.

The Chicago & North-Western Railroad passes through the northern part of the township coming in on section 5 and passing out on section 12.

No better improved farms are to be found than in Richland township, and herein live some of the most wealthy and honored of our citizens. Their hospitality is unbounded, the latch string always hangs out and the weary traveler finds a hearty welcome.

Justices:—T. Marshall, C. Hanna, N. F. Taylor, W. Bale, C. Homan N. B. Hiatt, G. Hollenbeck, L. H. Beadle, D. Forker, A. H. Hisey, T. A. Bourner, J. B. Louthan, H. Sabin, H. Cory, F. H. Ramsdell.

Trustees:—E. Deeter, J. Ramsdell, J. Flathers, U. B. Hiatt, J. B. Louthan, A. Wilkinson, H. L. Barnes, J. W. Hiatt, L. H. Beadle, P. Rich, H. Davenport, E. Hatfield, A. Hatfield, I. W. Graham, G. Reed, C. Barns, J. W. Clem, T. Forker, H. Clay, H. Sabin, S. Gould, G. Hollenbeck, J. Gray, J. F. Cram, L. Coolidge, J. J. Huston, O. McKeen, G. W. Bale, E. A. and C. A. Flint, J. Smith, J. Hiatt.

Clerks:—J. Marshall, C. Homan, J. Hoag, N. F. Taylor, R. M. Clem, S. Lewis, T. A. Hopkins, A. Beadle, S. Jackman, H. Sabin, J. F. Cram.

SALT CREEK.

Salt Creek township is the south eastern township in the

County, and lies in eighty-two north, thirteen west. It contains two towns, Chelsea and West Irving.

This township has a fine growth of timber along the banks of the Iowa River which crosses it in a south eastern direction, entering into Benton County. Along the course of the river the land is rough and broken. With this exception the surface is of a general undulating character. It contains some of the finest tracts of land in the County. Salt Creek, which meanders through the County some forty-seven miles enters the Iowa River in this township near the southeast corner, on section 36. The Chicago & Northwestern Railroad passes through the township.

With the exception of Indian Village, this is the oldest settled township in the County, and was first settled by Robert, Anthony and William Wilkinson, who came in the year 1849. G. McChambers, R. W. Wilson, J. A. Willey and L. Marsh, were also old settlers coming in at an early day and improving farms.

The township was organized in the year 1856, and named after Salt Creek.

The first school was taught by Mr. Howard.

The first birth was a son of Wm. Wilkinson's in the year 1851 and died the same year making the first death.

The first marriage was G. McChambers to Miss. A. Lux.

At West Irving, there is a grist mill which was built in 1871, by Fitz, Barrett & Kenner. At an earlier day there was a saw and grist mill owned and operated by G. S. Williams in the same place.

The following list of township officers we compile:

Justices: H. Loomis, A. Hale, L. McChensey, J. W. Taylor, A. J. Stewart, W. Benson, D. A. Stevens, C. R. Smith, E. E. Vickery, M. Smith, J. Hutchison, W. H. Graham, T. Roach, G. McChambers, H. H. Williams, C. C. Coats, T. Finch, J. Gitz and S. Smith.

Clerks: B. Pearson, H. L. Smith, C. S. Barton, J. Collister, W. P. Forsyth, E. E. Vickery, S. Hopper, J. H. Ross, E. A. Stockon, W. Camp, S. Smith, J. Shaler.

Trustees: A. J. Stewart, L. Johnson, A. Kile, T. G. Arbuthnot, S. Dudley, A. Wilkinson, J. Roberts, H. H. Williams G. Crittenden, C. E. Conell, P. D. Smith, A. Wolf, A. J. We: el, B. Rector, M. Smith, R. Wilkinson, E. Hancox, J. Fitz, S. C. Bailey, P. Spence, S. Prill, T. Park. A. Hall, L. Marsh, H. W. Searls, B. Collins, J. A. Willey, S. Miles.

CARLTON.

Carlton township lies in township 84 north and range 16, west. The land is prairie and timber. The timbered portion affords abundance of fuel for the consumer. The prairie portion is fine and productive.

The first settlements were in 1851-2, and the first cabins were built on section 30, by Anthony Bricker, Levi and D. D. Appelgate, who entered their lands, and opened their farms. In the Southwestern part a settlement was founded in the year 1853, now known as the Dobson Settlement. In their part of the township are some fine farms, the land being of good quality. The Dobsons, J. S. Haynes, J. S. Lewis, D. Gray and Wm. Conant came in at an early day, entered land and opened farms.

The township was named in honor of Judge Carlton, Judge of the 4th Judicial District, of Iowa who is well known by many in the County.

Carlton township was organized in the year 1854, and the first election was held at the house of Wm. Murty, on the first Monday of April of the same year.

Silas McClain has the honor of having taught the first school in a small log cabin erected on land owned by Anthony Bricker.

Rev. J. S. Mason of the Presbyterian denomination, preached the first sermon in the township, at the house of J. Laughlin. In the year 1865 a church was erected, known as the Rock Creek Church and now has 40 members. The church is in good standing with Rev. James Stickle as pastor.

Justices: S. Dobson, A. Bricker. G. Rider, W. Krause, H L. Dobson, T. L. Dunn, C. E. Heath, R. Parker, J. Craig, M. Babcock, R. Bunn, J. X. Chambers, T. M. Mulgett, J. Rose, W. G. Dobson.

Clerks: H. L. Dobson, C. E. Heath, S. Strong, T. L. Dunr, J. Craig, E. O. Bowen.

Trustees: J. Lamm, S. Ricker, G. Laughlin, A. Donaldson, B. Clark, G. Finch, R. Fay, F. Hollingshead, J. Peterson, W. Conant, S. Dobson, J. Filloon, G. B. Rider, T. M. Mudgett, S. Strong, S. Myers, R. Parker, C. Bratt, H. L. Dobson, J. Donaldson, S. Berry, D. Gray, L. Myers, J. Rokes, C. Dobson, L. N. B. C. Burt, A. Mericle.

GENESEO.

Geneseo township lies in 86 north, and 13 west. Is well watered by Wolf Creek, or Big Creek, which takes its rise in the north western part of the County. This flows almost east across the township coming in on section 30 and passing out on section 24; with its several tributaries it affords plenty of water for all purposes, and drains the township sufficiently, while along its banks can be found abundance of timber. Stone can be found in this township near the timber, of which there is sufficient for all necessary purposes. The township consists of a fine farming surface; the soil rich and productive.

J. Hill and J. Riley, were the first to settle in the township, coming in and taking claims in section 24. N. Spencer, G. Bussler, J. Tedford, L. and T. F. Clark are also among the old settlers who improved farms in different parts of the township.

The township has within its limits one town—Mooreville, a name given it by G. E. Moore, who established a Flouring Mill at that point about the year 1870. The first store was opened by Wm. Davidson, who after doing business a number of years removed to the town of Dysart and engaged in business at that point. Mooreville to-day has one store and post office with C. A. Williams & Bro. Proprietors, one flouring mill operated by B. & A. Bruner, and one blacksmith shop, by Bugbee & Barns, who established it in 1878.

S. Slade, taught the first school in the fall of 1856.

The first marriage was A. Goodparter to Miss Mary Hill, April 30th, 1854.

The first death was James Riley who died in the year 1855.

The first birth was Louisa, daughter of J. and C. Riley in 1854.

The township was named by N. Spencer, it being the name of a township in New York where he formerly resided.

The township was organized February 5th, 1856. Application made by Nathaniel Spencer.

The land is of good quality. In the township are many fine farms and farm residences and the most substantial buildings found in the County. As a stock raising township it ranks among the best. In number and quality of hogs and cattle they excell. M. Casey, T. F. Clark, A. McElhinney, J. Riley, L. D. and G. W. Hill, and H. Wager, are among the heaviest farmers.

COLUMBIA.

Columbia township lies in township eighty-two, north, range fifteen, west, and is watered in the north by the Iowa river. Along through the Southern and Central portion, Richland Creek and its various tributaries drain the township. The Southern part of the township is principally prairie land, while the portion lying between Richland Creek and the Iowa River is quite rough and is more or less timbered, though containing some fine farms.

The first settlement effected in this township was in the year 1851. Eli Chase was the first settler, erecting a cabin on section 1. Wm. West, E. and H. Morrison, T. Evert, Wheaton Chase, an old Indian interpreter for the Sacs and Fox Indians, J. Burley, J. Waltz, R. Metz and Wagoner are settlers numbered with the first. The most of these men are yet living, or have decendants living in this township, all, we believe, well-to-do farmers and excellent business men.

The township was organized February 5th, 1856 and the first election was held at the house of J. Burley for the purpose of electing township officers.

The first school taught in the township was in a log cabin on section 16 by Elvira O. Stoddard in the year 1855.

The first death was Martha Chase, daughter of W. and E. A. Chase.

First birth was a son of E. and N. J. Chase, March 1st, 1853.

The first marriage was Mr. John A. Carlton to Miss Sarah A. Stoddard, in the year 1855.

The following is a list of township officers since its organization.

Justices: J. D. Gettis, W. Stoddard. G. W. Morrison, W. T. Hanley, I. Toland, J. Fife, M. Bostwick, J. Roads, J. Yates, J. A. Eshbaugh, J. C. Burley, F. Sanborn, S. Wilkinson, T. M. Malin. Wm. Cory. J. H. Fee, W. Hartsock, C. Spire, L. Stoddard, W. F. Eshbaugh.

Clerks—L. F. Stoddard, C. J. Rhoads, Wm. Cory, W. G. Malin, C. Spire, A. P. Leavitt, D. E. Peck.

Trustees—G. W. Morrison, J. W. Coe, J. D. Gettis, G. H. Stoddard, J. Trowbridge, W. M. Voge, J. Waltz, W. Stoddard, J. Fife, H. L. Biggs, S. J. Cady, J. Croskrey, J. Hoag, J. Cory, J. Ross, I. Toland, H. Cory. N. Randolph, T. M. Malin, S. C. Babb, W. E. Eshbaugh, B. C. Berry, H. Bissell, J. G. Sanborn, J. Stokes, T. Trowbridge, A. Zehrung, W. G. Malin, L. Cary, J. Duffey, L. Sexton.

CRYSTAL.

Crystal, one of the finest agricultural townships of the County, joins Spring Creek upon the east, Perry on the west and is bounded on the north by Grant, on the south by Howard.

Wolf Creek flows directly through it from west to east and with its numerous tributaries renders it well watered. Along Wolf Creek there are several fine groves of natural timber, while numerous large and beautiful plantations of trees add to the scenic effect.

The township was formed in 1857 by an order issued by J. C. Vermilya, then County Judge, to J. S. Bishop directing him to call an election. It was a separation from Buckingham township and the formation of Crystal. The first township election was held at the residence of Nelson Felter on the first Monday in April, A. D. 1857. The township was named by Mrs. C. L. Davis from the Crystalline purity of the air.

Nelson Felter and family were the first settlers in the township. They removed from Cook Co., Ill., in 1854 and settled upon section 15. A rude log house 16 by 18 feet was erected upon the banks of Wolf Creek in which the family resided several years, enjoying health and happiness.

Their rude home was open to all travellers and many a weary searcher found shelter with them.

In the course of a few years a number of families had settled around them, among whom we mention J. S. Bishop, V. Shultz, J. W. McCune, A. Quinn, M. Martin, Robert Wylie, A. D. Hoag, J. S. Townsend, C. L. Davis. These settled in various parts of the township, each erecting a rude cabin or rail pen poorly roofed and without floors as a temporary shelter. The first child born was Lyman Felter.

The first school was taught in the Bishop school house by Miss Nettie M. Cyrenus.

Religious meetings were first held at the house of J. S. Bishop by an itinerant Methodist preacher. In the year 1856, a society was organized called the Salem Presbyterian Church, with Robert Wylie and J. S. Townsend as ruling members. The Society has been in prosperous existence to the present time. The number of members enrolled at its organization were 15, at present the membership numbers 66. The first minister was Rev. W. J. Lyons. A Sunday School was organized about the same time with D. S. Dickey as Superintendent.

The township cemetery was largely laid out upon one of the highest and most beautiful hills in the vicinity. It is well cared for and contains some tasteful monuments. The land was donated by C. L. Davis.

The first burial was a little daughter of J. S. and P. Bishop.

Many amusing incidents and experiences of the early settlers might be given did space permit we give only the following:

Live stock and provisions were exceedingly scarce among the early residents and many schemes were resorted to in order to make the limited supply go round. Gilbert McMillen had a number of nice young hogs but was without corn; one day Jas. Vertrees came to him and proposed that as M. had plenty of hogs and no corn, while he had corn and no hogs, they combine and raise hogs upon the shares, he would take the shoats and fatten them and give M. one half of the pork.

The proposal was accepted and Vertrees accordingly took home two of the shoats. In about a week he killed one of these and according to contract divided it, splitting it from the nose to the end of the tail and sending home one half to M. As the side of pork was not much thicker than a board it suddenly dawned upon M. that there was something thin about the contract as the time of "feeding out" seemed decidedly short.

Crystal postoffice was established in 1868, and at the same time a store was built by James Aitchinson. It is now owned and kept by J. M. Foster.

There is also a blacksmith and wagon shop at the same place owned by J. S. Gethman, and another in the south west corner of the township owned by Frank Frohm who has also a hotel and dancing hall which is quite a resort for the German settlers.

Crystal township is noted for the number of its fine stock. West Wilson has a large herd of thoroughbreds and grades while many others are entering more or less extensively into the business of fine stock raising.

There are many heavy tax payers among the farmers of Crystal. Men who, although they came to the country with limited means, have acquired wealth and a competence by honest hard labor. We have space to mention only J. S. Townsend, Peter and Thos. Whannel, and West Wilson.

We glean the following officers from the Clerk's books.

Justices:—R. Wylie, W. Wilson, J. S. Bishop, W. Guilford, O. J. Rice, R. J. Hall, J. B. Wylie, J. A. Plunk, A. Wheatley, G. McCune, W. McTurk, P. Quinn.

Clerks:—J. S. Townsend, J. S. Bishop, W. Wilson, J. A. Bowdle, R. J. Hall, G. McCune, J. D. Hall, W. Wilson, J. R. Felter, A. Wheatley, N. W. Morton, E. Lynde.

Trustees:—J. W. McCune, R. Wylie, O. Burright, N. Felter, R. R. Chambers, C. L. Davis, J. Vertrees, L. Loupee, G. Mc-Millen, O. J. Rice, P. Quinn, J. Morton, S. Reed, J. S. Townsend, R. J. Hall, R. Crawford, J. B. Hill, G. McCune, J. B. Wylie, J. B. M. Bishop, T. Whannel, W. McTurk, O. P. Jones, J. Black.

TAMA AND TOLEDO.

We speak of these two townships connectively from the fact that they were originally one, and continued so until 1868, when they were divided, the North two-thirds assuming the original name, Toledo, and the South one-third that of Tama, in respect of Tama City.

The original township was organized Feb. 14th, 1856, on application made by T. Brown, and lies 83 north 15 west, and is about equally divided between prairie and timbered land. William Blodgett was the first settler erecting a cabin on section 26, in the year 1851, now in the Tama division, In this same year R. A. Redman, J. C. Vermilya and G. Carter came in and improved farms, also W. L. Brannan, J. Unbarger, S. J. Murphy, J. H. and W. T. Hollen came in remaining but a short time. Brannan, Unbarger and Murphy, returned to Marengo, during the winter, while the Hollens returned to Indiana, and in 1851 came back to Iowa, stopping that winter in Marengo and in the spring of 1852 removed to this County, settling on section 27. Numerous others we might mention as old settlers but will not stop to make note.

The growth of timber in various parts of the township is of a thrifty and heavy growth of different varieties, such as cotton wood white and red oak, elm, hickory, etc, furnishing plenty of stove wood. The harder varieties are manufactured into lumber and other necessities to a considerable extent. The prairie land affords the best of tillable soil and numerous are the bountiful farms.

The Northern portion or Toledo township, is watered by Deer Creek and its tributaries and the Iowa River passes through the Southern part or the Tama division, affording good water facilities. We mention elsewhere the usefulness of these streams in affording power for manufacturing purposes. In this respect the township is far superior to any in the County.

In 1868 the voters of the Southern one-third part of Toledo township, which included Tama City, presented to the Board of Supervisors a petition requesting that the South third of Toledo township be set apart as a new township to be known as Tama township. The reasons urged for this division by the petitioners were that they would be much better accommodated with township officers, and it was also understood that it would to a great extent tend to allay the unpleasant strife between the two towns of Toledo and Tama City, growing out of their rivalry. The petition was accordingly granted and the division made.

Each of the townships, after the division, rapidly increased in population and wealth. The Chicago & Northwestern Railroad passes through what is now Tama township, entering on section 36 and exiting on 19.

The only incident of public interest occuring in the township was in the year 1865; some of our readers will remember the excitement it caused. It goes by the name of "The Great Indian Scare." From a participator we glean the following in regard to it: It appears that some little difficulty had occured between the Indians and a Mr. Roberts, who had settled on the Indian Reservation. Two of the Indians having been to town and indulged in "spirit water"or"fire water" as they call whiskey, were on their way back feeling quite boisterous and noisy. On coming to Croskrey's house, where a daughter of Mr. Roberts was staying, asked for shelter. The Indians talked excitedly, and frightened the girl, who secretly escaped through the back door, ran home and told her folks that the Croskrey family had all been murdered in their beds, and that the Indians were going to make a raid upon the town 'that night. This soon spread throughout the neighborhood and town and in three hours time the whole vicinity was in arms. Under the stern dicipline of Capt. W. H. Stivers pickets were sent out, reconnoitering parties were dispatched and the quiet slumberer was called out to meet a formidable imaginary foe, whose mercy was blood, and glory, scalps. Forces were drilled during the long and weary night and muskets, rifles, swords, daggers, pitch-forks, scythes, and all else of a destructive character were in great demand by the panic-stricken citizens. While the slow and monotonous tramp of the guards and the stern command of the officer as he made his usual rounds, carried still greater fear to the hearts of those who were already quaking. After watching and waiting with loaded muskets and poised swords through the long night, reason began to assert its place, and lo, and behold upon examination the family of the Croskreys were found sleeping soundly, unharmed and unmolested. Near by were seen the stalwart frames of the Indians who were charged with such a bloody crime during the night, stretched at full length upon the floor sleeping off the effect of the over draught of "fire water." It is unnecessary to say that the armed forces returned to their homes sleepy but wiser men, and the Indians, when they came to learn of the trouble and anxiety they had caused to the great white man, naturally enjoyed the joke as much as any one.

The first marriage in the township was Mr. G. Wear to Miss Mary Rush, in 1854.

The first birth was W. T., son of J. H. and E. A. Hollen, on February 5th, 1853, and who died the same year making the first death.

The first school was taught at Toledo, by whom we are unable to learn.

The first religious denomination was the Methodists. Rev. David Peterfish preached the first sermon in the year 1853.

The following is a list of those who have served in the respective offices of Justices, Clerks and Trustees in Toledo township since 1864, the previous records having been destroyed.

Justices:—N. Fisher, D. F. Bruner, I. B. Talmage, E. Harmon, G. S. Bailey, G. Raines, H. Bradshaw, N. C. Weiting, S. M. Berger, J. W. Stewart.

Clerks:—W. E. Rogers, L. Allman, J. T. Cary, J McClaskey W. Rickhoff, J. T. Sweat, G. L. Bailey, J. W. Stewart.

Trustees:—W. Hillmon, T. McClelland, A. Hufford, A. J. Wheaton, W. F. Johnston, D. Stoner, N. Lewis, L. Wells. F. Davis, A. LaDow, D. Arb, W. Guilford, H. Galley, J. Rines, J. Q. Clark, T. J. Sweat, T. A. Graham, W. Wade, J. S. Moore A. I. Churchill, K. Dexter, N. Fisher, J. M. Camery, A. H. Sterrett, J. W. Rogers.

Officers of Tama township:

Justices:—E. Harmon, J. Burge, M. A. Newcomb, J. H. Hollen, W. L. Brannan, G. D. Sherman, Chas. McClung, W. T. Carter.

Clerks:—A. M. Batchelder, E. N. Merchant, A. W. Guernsey B. F. Moreland, A. H. Smith, W. H. Ahlbrecht, Thos. Williamson, E. L. Carmichael.

Trustees:—R. W. Wells, J. Fife, N. G. Wheaton, N. Lewis, R. H. Ryan, B. A. Hall, W. Gallagher, C. B. Bentley, W. P. Parker, L. Merchant, G. Hollenbeck, W. Hartsell, J. McKinney, J. Brice Jr., J. B. Dennis, J. Burge, W. E. Newcomb, T. Brice.

OTTER CREEK.

This is one among the finest townships in the County and lies in 83 north range 14 west. The Iowa River runs easterly, south of, but near the southern boundary of this township. Otter Creek runs through its western side, bearing however gradually south easterly as it approaches the southern part and leaves the town ship near its south east corner. The bottom lands of these two streams are very rich and compose nearly one third of the township. The remainder of the township is nearly equally divided between high rolling prairie and bluff land, the latter having considerable timber and is nearly as well settled up as the other parts of the township. These bluff lands of our County as they are called, are by no means barrens, as some of our eastern readers might suppose, but when brought under cultivation are very productive; generally not quite as good for corn but better for wheat than the rolling prairies or bottom lands. They consist of high rolling lands, sometimes hilly, covered with hazel brush and sometimes intermingled with small trees, and some with large timber. This description of bluff lands is true of all in the County.

The first settlement effected in this township was in the year 1853. A. B. Hancox, was the first settler, erecting his cabin on. section 36. A. Tompkins, Robert Carter, S. Lake, N. Lewis, C. Powell and H. Riddle, were among the early settlers, coming in at an early day and taking up land.

The township was organized February 5th, 1856, and the first election was held at the dwelling house of A. Tompkins, on the first Monday in April of that year.

No better improved farms are found, than those in this township. The people are all of the industrious class, and are constantly adding to their wealth. C. E. Hayes, T. Barlow, D. C. Lamb and A. J. Tyler are among the leading farmers and stock raisers of the township.

In this township we find one church of the Catholic denomination, erected about the year 1875, located in the north eastern part of the township.

The first school taught in the township, was in a log cabin on section 19. Miss Harriet Hatfield, teacher.

The first birth was Sumner Tompkins, son of A. and A. M. Tompkins, who was born March 26th, 1855.

The first death was Mrs. Robert Carter, who died March 20th, 1854.

The first marriage was Mr. Logan McChesney to Miss L. A. Hancox, in the year 185÷ by A. LaDow.

Those serving in the offices of Justices, Clerks and Trustees are as follows.

Justices—H. S. Cloud, D. Rusk, G. Pickett, N. Lewis, J. H. Brooks, A. Lane, J. J. and A. M. Staley, E. M. Stevens, S. M. Harris, M. Mitchell, O. Budlong, H. Jacobs and W. P. Soth.

Trustees—M. Mitchell, A. Tompkins, J. H. Vorhies, J. Staley S. M. Harris, J. Higgins, L. Carmichael, A. Baker, E. A. Burnham, C. M. Reed, J. H. Brooks, A. Spalding, A. Sheldon, A. J. Tyler, A. Johnston, S. Stigers, J. L. Jackson, G. McGee, M. W. Varner, M. Hunt, J. P. Evans, J. M. Hayes, W. Wick, J. Farley, E. P. Smith, W. A. Dowd, A. Kosta, T. J. Hoadley, C. Cross, O. Ferris,

Clerks—R. C. M. Wells, J. J. Staley, J. L. Jackson. D. C. Lamb, J. J. Stevens, A. M. Stailey, M. Mitchell, N. H. Bidwell and W. P. Soth.

PERRY.

The township was organized in the year 1858, and the first election was held April 5th, of the same year for the purpose of electing township officers.

Perry lies in township 84 north, 14 west and is one of the wealthiest townships in the County. The township is nearly all prairie though containing some fine timber along the banks of Wolf Creek and its tributaries.

The first settlement made in this township was in the year 1852. N. L. Osborn came in at this date and erected his log cabin on section 10, now owned by Giles Taylor. Still a little later in this year came N. Nash, V. Carpenter, J. P. Wood, John and James Connell, W. D. Hitchner, L. E. Wood, Robert and Daniel Connell, all settling on the north side of Wolf Creek around the village of Buckingham. These were all the settlers during 1852. A few additions were made in 1853, namely Ira and Giles Taylor and families, Mr. Spade, and Q. Helm. After this, imigration increased rapidly; the year 1854 witnessed the arrival of a number too large to enumerate, all of whom improved farms in the township.

The township is well watered by Wolf Creek passing through

the northern portion, and on the south by Salt Creek and its tributaries, which afford advantages in stock raising. There are many excellent farms and the farmers are nearly all well-to-do men. J. G. Sately, James and Peter Wilson, Wm. Sprole and H. A. Hartshorn are among the heaviest farmers.

The township has contained two towns, Tracr and West Union, we speak of the former in another chapter. The latter, formerly known as Charlottsville and later West Union, was laid out in 1855. Mr. Hester opened a general stock of merchandise, and other enterprises, though on a small scale, were started but soon all were gone. The location was a beautiful one, and it seemed that nothing but success would attain her growth but she soon fell and now nothing remains to tell of her past. This place was located near the north east corner of the present town of Traer.

The first marriage in the township was Mr. Nott to Miss M. Taylor, in 1853, Rev. S. W. Ingham officiating. They afterwards moved to Kansas where Mrs. Nott died in 1876. The second marriage was Rev. S. W. Ingham to Miss Cynthia Taylor a sister of the first bride, in the spring of 1854. Rev. D. Petterfish officiating.

The first birth was in the family of Mr. W. D. Hitchner, a daughter, America, born December 1st, 1852.

The first school in the township was taught by Miss Rachel Wood in the summer of 1854, and the first school house was erected in the old town of Buckingham, in the spring of 1856.

The first post office was at Yankee Grove with S. Klingaman as Postmaster.

The first Sabbath School was organized in 1853, at the house of Mr. Osborn, with Mr. Story as Superintendent.

Below is a list of those who have served in the various township offices:

Justices:—J. W. Southwick, J. Wilson, J. A. Stewart, A. Kile, Q. D. Hartshorn, J. R. and R. McCormack, W. Sprole, A. Pratt, R. G. McIntire, W. Rogers, J. Fowler, W. T. V. Ladd, O. T. Brainard, M. B. Higby, D. Connell.

Clerks:—G. W. Bradley, A. Kile, J. Wilson, W. W. Leekins, G. Frank, D. Park, M. L. Seamans, S. M. Elwood, C. C. Collins, W. H. Bowen.

Trustees:—W., H. C. and J. Stokes, J. W. Southwick, H. A. and Q. D. Hartshorn, J. L. Graham, H. Beatty, L. E. Wood Q. Wilson Sr., W. Sprole, C. Loop, A. McCormack, G. Taylor, P. Wilson, S. Everett, H. F. Gaston, J. T. Everett, M. Heath, A. Law, A. McCosh, G. Townsend, J. T. Evans.

SPRING CREEK.

Spring Creek township lies between Lincoln on the north and Carlton on the south, Crystal on the east, and Marshall County on the west.

Wolf Creek in the north and central part, Deer Creek, in the southern portion of the township, place Spring Creek among the most favored townships in the County in regard to water courses. The soil is rich and very productive the surface being gently rolling and well drained.

Lying somewhat remote from the railway lines, which traverse other sections of the County, Spring Creek township relies only upon State and County roads for its thoroughfares; it contains no large towns, but can boast of some of the finest farms in Central Iowa.

The first settlement in the township was made by L. S. Fredericks and Wm. A. Bywaters, who employed a workman named Chapman to erect a cabin and improve certain lands in the vicinity of a large grove, now known as Union Grove, in the fall of 1853. In April, 1854, they brought their families from Jackson County and entered their new home in the grove, jointly occupying for the time a small cabin 14x15. Thos. Jukes also came with them and soon after came E. L. Kuns and family, Chas. C. Knowles, Oscar Hill, J. G. Hull, Wm. B. and O. King, N. C. Knapp, and others, all of whom set to work improving farms, enjoying the free and unconventional life of the pioneer, with its hardships and privations on the one hand, and its freedom and merry-making, on the other.

The beautiful grove wherein the first settlement was made, and which still stands in its primitive vigor and beauty, obtained the name of "Union Grove" from the unity which prevailed among the first settlers in its vicinity, while the towhship derived its name from the numerous springs which rise in the grove and feed the various water courses in the township. The grove is to-day very beautiful, and standing in relief amidst the prairie farms, would make a pleasant summer resort.

At a term of the County Court of Tama County, held on the 10th day of March, 1858, a petition was presented by W. Bowen signed by himself and others, praying a division of Carlton township, on the township line between township 84 and 85, forming a new township to be known as Spring Creek township, which was granted and it was ordered by L. Clark, County Judge, that the first electon in the new township be held at the house of W. B. King, on the first Monday in April of the same year, for the purpose of choosing township officers.

At present there are two villages in the township—Spring Creek and Badger Hill, with a post office in each thriving village.

Miss Mary Wylie, now Mrs. McClain, taught the first school in the township, in a building erected in the grove on land leased of W. B. King.

For the most part the lives of the earlier settlers of this township were devoid of those stirring and often times deplorable incidents which serve to enliven pioneer life and to give coloring to frontier scenes, for although their lands were then wild and unbroken these settlers found themselves by no means upon the frontier of civilization, settlements having already been formed at no great distance upon each side of them.

During the prevalence of the most severe storm in their early experience, Wm. Merrill, attempting to visit the home of one of his neighbors, lost his way, became bewildered, and remaining in the storm nearly all night narrowly escaped freezing to death.

A little son of John and Nancy Hiley wandered away from home one September day 1868, and was lost in the brush a little south of Union Grove, while his mother was gathering plums in the grove. The alarm was given, people throughout the township turned out en-mass to join in the search, and the child was tracked by keen scented hounds to the banks of a small stream, where the trail was lost, and the search was finally abandoned as fruitless. In the early spring the remains of the lost child were found near the creek, by Mrs. Mary Blakely, who is still a resident of the township.

Among the heaviest tax-payers in Spring Creek township at present may be mentioned Messrs J. G. Hull, S. S. Mann, Wm. Merrill, H. Merrill, R. J. Jackson, S. Berry, A. Allard and Hess brothers.

Riding along the highways of the township over the rich rolling land which constitute the home stead of the larger farmers, ones attention is attracted by the appearance of large and elegant residences, notably those of S. S. Mann, S. Berry, and A. Allard,

A plot of ground in the grove, purchased of Wm. Merrill, has been devoted to cemetery purposes by the citizens; and the grounds are well laid out and kept very neat.

Religious services are held at stated intervals in the various school houses in the township.

Spring Creek post office is located at Union Grove, wherein various branches of business are conducted, as follows.

One store established by Jos. Schichtl, in 1874, who carries a general stock and does a thriving trade.

One blacksmith shop, owned by Martin Schichtl, who purchased it of a Grange Association to whom it had been sold in 1874 by W. B. King, who established it in 1872.

A barb wire establishment, operated by J. Kuns and Vince Schichtl.

The second post-office and village, was settled by a small colony from Wisconsin, the Badger State, who gave the settlement the name it bears, in honor of their native State. Business is conducted according to the following representations:

Hess Bros. proprietors of a dry goods and grocery store, established in 1874. P. G. Hess, post-master. •

H. Galloway, blacksmith, business established in 1874.

Flouring Mill, operated by Myers & Wescott, established in 1871.

J. P. Gage, proprietor wagon and repair shop, established in 1877.

A commodious church edifice was completed in the spring of 1879 by the United Brethern Society.

The following township officers we compile from the records.

Justices—J. Mitchell. W. B. King. S. V. R. Kelley, G. M. Finch, V. S. Bartlett, W. Bowen, C. N. Knapp, S. Day, E. W. Thomas, R. Yeoman, S. S. Mann, L. Horn, W. H. Holstead, G. C. Wescott, R. Reichmann, A. C. Marston, A. Benson, W. C. Bunce, W. O. Pond, J. Schichtl.

Clerks—W. Bowen, A. A. Benson, A. T. Willard, G. C. Wescott W. H. Holstead, W. Shattuck, B. Smith, C. French.

Trustees—J. G. Hull, C. N Knapp, R. Jackson, A. C. Marston, W. L. Smith, V. S. Merritt, E. L. Kuns, O. King, T. Baker, J. G. Hull, G. M. Finch, J. Yettey, W. Merrill, L. Horn, A. Bartholomew, C. W. Hiatt, C. French, A. C. Marston, W. Sharp, A. Bates, G. W. Hess, W. Overmire, H. Merrill, A. Benson, W. Shattuck, H. Holstead, S. W. Berry, W. O. Pond, R. Yeoman, G. Wescott, R. Smith.

YORK.

York township, east of Otter Creek and south of Oneida, lies in 83 north and 13 west. A good share of this township is prairie, with timber along the banks of Salt Creek and tributaries. In the eastern part of this township the land is beautiful and very fertile. The western part bordering on Salt Creek is quite broken, and is mostly inhabited by Bohemians who by hard work have succeeded in opening out some fine farms.

The first settlement effected in this township was in the year-
1851, by W. R. Van Doran, who came in at this date and erected a small cabin on section 22. E. McKern, I. Smith, Alexander
Fowler and families came in shortly after and erected cabins in
other parts of the township. The first land entered in the township was by Z. T. and L. H. Shugart, in the year 1853. These
gentlemen still remain on the land holding the original deeds.

The township was organized April 1st, 1856, and the first
election was held at the house of J. R. Graham, and named by
him it, being the name of a township in which he used to reside in
New York.

The first marriage was Mr. Jacob Bruner to Miss Susan Ashby,
February 17th, 1856, by J. C. Vermilya, County Judge.

The first death was Mrs. C. Edmonds, April 22d, 1859.

The first child born in the township was a son of W. R. Van
Doran, in the year 1854.

The township contains one town, Waltham, located in the
north eastern part on section 3. There are two grist
mills, one at Waltham, established in 1856 and opperated by S.
Lewis, and one about the center of the township on Salt Creek,
known as Bruner's Mill, established in 1873. The township also
has one church.

The first school was taught in 1854 on section 14. The teachers name we were unable to learn.

The products of the township are such as are common throughout the County. In horses, cattle, hogs and other stock it ranks
second to none. Here are the homes of W. White, L. H. Shugart,
J. Peck, S. Overturf, M. H. Pierce, J. Kessel, J. Hervert and J.
Scrable all of whom for a number of years have turned their attention to fine stock. They also have as fine farms as can be
found in the County.

Justices—J. R. Graham, E. Robinson, O. T. Brainard, R. O.
Rogers, J. Sale, J. B. VanAuken, J. Holt, J. Townd, V. Kessel,
G. Foster, H. L. Smith and B. Cady.

Trustees—S. Overturf, G. W. Selvey, J. Edmonds, J. R. Graham, J. J. Garrison, B. Twogood, J. Lighbody, S. Dykeman, S.

F. Eccles, S. Miles, A. Mason, L. B. Dodd, J. Holt. W. Ashley, C. S. Barton. W. Alexander R. and H. Rogers, J. Yount. J. D. Hutchinson, T. Weaver. J. H. Shugart, H. L. Smith, P. L. Wintersteen, F. Beneisch, J. Scrable, E. M. Campton, V. Kessel, J. B. VanAuken, V. Hervert, B. Brown, C. Mason.

Clerks—Z. T. Shugart, J. Allen. G. W. Selvey, H. L. Smith, J. T. Cobb, C. Mason. S. J. Bear, D. W. Wintersteen, A. Rogers, B. A. Peck, M. H. Pierce.

CARROLL.

This township lies in 84 north, 14 west, and is bounded on the north by Perry, on the east by Oneida, on the south by Otter Creek and on the west by Howard, and is about equally divided between timber and prairie land. the southern portion is broken and hilly, while on the north it is principally rolling praiarie. The soil is of a good quality and the farmers are among the best in the County. Within the past ten years great improvements have been made. The old log houses have given place to the stylish modern residence; straw sheds to large frame structures. Everything betokens a change for the better.

This is a good stock section and considerable attention is given to this branch of industry.

Its first settlement was in 1853. Levi Haworth, Nathan Fisher and Joseph Powell coming in at this date and improving farms on sections 21, 22 and 23. in the southern part of the township. Then a little latercame E. Fee, Adam, Andrew and Asa Wise, N. Harmon, L. Kibbee, Wm. Hines, Wm. Randolph, John Collins, John Cox, F. Bates and J. L. Stewart, all improving farms in different parts of the township. In the year 1857, a petition signed by N. Fisher and others was presented to the County Judge, J. C. Vermilya, praying for the organization of a new township to be known as Carroll. The petition was granted and the first election was held at the dwelling house of N. Fisher, for the purpose of choosing township officers.

The first marriage was that of Mr. A. Haworth to Miss E. Fee, in the year of 1856.

The first death was Samuel Bailey, who died in 1855.

The first birth was Eli, son of Levi and P. Haworth, April 25th, 1855.

The first school was taught by Miss M. A. Fisher, in the year 1854.

Rev. D. Petterfish, preached the first sermon at the house of N. Fisher, in the summer of 1853, Mr. Petterfish was of the Methodist denomination. •

The township is watered by Salt Creek and its tributaries, rendering it a well and plentifully watered township.

Justices:—T. McEltree, E. Bailey, W. Randolph, N. Jarvis, N. Harmon, W. A. Fee, S. Doolittle, H. Bailey, H. C. Foster, G. M. Fee, A. Wise, C. B. Quintard, J. Fowler, A. M. Smith, J. C. McNeil.

Clerks:—N. Harmon, W. Randolph, A. Maiden, S. Doolittle, J. H. Crawford, J. and A Wise, L. H. Powell, J. M. Smith, J. Roberts.

Trustees:—E. Fee, L. Haworth, J. Powell, A. Wise, J. Colins, T. McEltree, N. Jarvis, J. H. Fee, W. L. McNeil, A. Childers, R. Morrow, A. M. Smith, H. C. Foster, A. C. Cochran, J. T. Surface, G. B. Lawon, L. Powsell, N. Harmon, J. O'Neil, F. A. Belt, A. Loder, R. Foster.

CLARK.

Clark township was organized October 9th, 1860, and the first election was held at the house of David Torrence, November 6th, of the same year.

The township lies in range 85 north, and 13 west. It is a fine body of land, entirely prairie, and nearly all available for cultivation. The soil is very fertile, and at this time there is scarcely a foot of land, but what is in use.

The first settlement made in this township was in the year 1855. A. Parmenter, C. Unger, W. Leach, D. Torrence, J.

Moss, N. Miller, T. S. Talmage, A. Boylan, and G. W. Bradley were the first settlers. The township made no special growth until about the time of the completion of the railroad. There being so much prairie that it seemed a perfect barrier to the settler. Where was the timber for fuel and fencing to come from? was the propounding question of the prospector. But soon the question was solved; the Pacific Division of the B. C. R. & N. Railroad penetrated the township and fuel and fencing was no longer a question of doubt for all necessities were supplied by the advantages which a railroad afford a new country. Mr. A. Parmenter was the first to settle on the open prairie on section 1, in 1855. Now there is hardly a quarter in the whole township that is not under cultivation and Clark ranks among the best townships of the County.

The first marriage was Mr. N. Perkins to Miss M. Moss, in 1859.

The first school was taught by J. Parmenter, in 1862.

The first birth was a daughter of Mr. Boylan, in 1859.

The first death was a wife of Newton Miller, who was caught in a prairie fire and burned to death while returning home from one of the neighbors, in 1857. The full particulars of her death, we were unable to learn.

Dysart, of which we speak in another chapter, is located in this township.

The following we gather from the records.

Justices:—H. Frank, H. Colderwood, J. W. Crissman, S. F. Everett, S. Hanlin, B. F. Thomas, H. Shaffer, D. Torrence, T. S. Talmage, S. L. Cochran, P. P. Wench, S. R. Hunt, J. A. Parmenter.

Clerks:—G. W. Bradley, D. Torrence, T. S. Talmage, O. M. Haney.

Trustees:—J. Moss, C. Unger, G. W. Wiseman, T. S. Talmage, S. R. Hunt, D. Torrence, G. W. Bradley, N. Miller, P. P. Wench, T. L. Cochran, E. Converse, S. F. Everett, J. Enderton, H. Colderwood, M. D. Bonney, B. F. Thomas, J. Dysart, D. Puckett, S. R. Yeoman, L. L. Wheeler, J. T. Converse, A. Sewall.

ONEIDA.

This township was organized October 9th, 1860, and lies in 84 north and 13 west, with Clark township on the north, Benton County on the east, York township on the south, and Carroll on the west. It contains some very fine prairie land and abundance of timber.

Oneida is watered by four tributaries to Salt Creek. No township in the County is any better supplied with water. It has four streams flowing entirely through the township into Salt Creek which passes on through York and Salt Creek townships and empties into the Iowa River.

The farming portions are rich and productive, and extensive farming is a predominant feature of industry in the township while stock raising is not neglected in the least.

A. Fowler, was the first white settler in the township, coming here and settling on section 20, in the year 1852. Also among the early settlers were W Kruthers, J. M. Hull, J. Harden, W. Fowler, D. C. Twogood and G. O. Mason, all opening farms in various parts of the township.

The first marriage was Mr. H. Hull, to Miss E. J. Kerns, in 1857, J. C. Vermilya, County Judge, officiating.

The first school was taught by Miss Hannah Thompson.

Below will be found a list of township officers from its organization excepting 1867, of which there is no record.

Justices:—G. G. Mason, B. Terpening, F. K. Morgan, J. H. Rushton, M. B. Sapp, C. J. Wiles, A. Anthony, W. Mowry.

Clerks:—D. C. Twogood, J. Thomas, J. K. Bull, W. Mowry, W. W. Wiles.

Trustees:—B. Dickerson, R. Terpening, J. B. F. Hill, J. Hardin, J. M. Hill, A. Heath, F. K. Mowry, W. W. Moss, N. Huff, J. C. Wiles, F. K. Morgan, J. H. Burris, W. D. Dean, W. Fowler, A. Cady, M. Sapp, I. E. Babcock, O. A. Turpening.

LINCOLN.

Lincoln township occupies the extreme north-west corner of the County. It is bounded on the north and west by Grundy County on the south by Spring Creek, on the east by Grant township. It has various small streams, the Little Wolf being the largest, all running in a south-eastern direction, and empties into Wolf Creek, in Spring Creek township, near the Badger Hill Flouring mill. Fifteen Mile Grove lies in Lincoln, about three fourths of a mile south of the north-west corner, and covers an area of some fifty acres with as nice timber as can be found in Iowa.

On the 5th, day of June 1861, a petition was presented to the Board of Supervisors of Tama County, signed by voters of township 86, Range 16, praying for a division of Spring Creek, township and the organization of a new township to be known as Lincoln township; petition granted, and first election ordered to be held on the second Tuesday in October, 1861, at the house of Joseph Prescott, when and where township officers were to be chosen.

Lockhart Wilber was the first white settler within the limits of the present township. After him came J. and G. Prescott, and families, from Black Hawk County, in 1855. Not having either house or permanent shelter of any kind to move into, the settlers were forced to make their wagons and tents suffice for domiciles until a log shanty could be erected. While the labors of house building were progressing, night after night were these pioneers listeners to the howling of ravenous wolves, until sleep came to deaden the unwelcome sounds upon their senses.

Their homes were finally reared beneath umbrageous trees in the still beautiful Fifteen Mile Grove. Greenwood Prescott still remains a citizen of the township. S. V. R. Kelley and family the Henrys and the Lewises are also old settlers.

Lincoln township remained comparatively unsettled until about the year 1870, when a German colony began settling within its borders, and to-day it is thickly populated by a good class of German citizens.

The first school house built was on land in Fifteen Mile Grove donated by G. Prescott, and the first school was taught by a daughter of W. B. King.

Early settlers used to claim that this grove was fifteen miles from no where. It has been the scene of various misdeeds, and upon one occasion the corpse of a man was found in the grove, having marks of violence which indicated foul play.

In the year 1876 Stephen and Henry Wilson erected a store and are now carrying a line of groceries etc. successfully.

A blacksmith shop has been in operation here for a number of years. There is an excellent stone quarry in the grove.

The following is the list of the township officers as shown from the clerks' books.

Justices--S. C. Henry, S. V. R. Kelley, J. and G. Prescott, A. C. Brockway, R. Dick, S. H. Baldwin, A. W. Stover, J. F. G. Cold, A. E. Stewart.

Clerks—J. Prescott, S. V. R. Kelley, A. C. Brockway, J. F. G. Cold, C. H. Baldwin.

Trustees—S. C. Henry, S. V. R. Kelley, G. and J. Prescott, F. C. Kelley, H. J. J. Jentzen, D. M. Wane, J. W. Henry, G. C. Henry, W. C. Thomas, J. Linn, A. Stoner, J. Rodman, K. Cowan, J. Dick, A, Eldridge, R. Way, C. H. Baldwin, D. B. Hammersley, A. C. Brockway, D. H. Lambury, R. Dick, G. M. Baldwin, C. Sick, A. E. Seward, S. Robinson, M. H. Rehder, F. E. Kook, J. Daugliesh.

HIGHLAND.

Highland township is one among the finest in the County for agricultural and pastoral purposes and lies in township 82 north, range 16 west and the extreme southwest corner of the County.

J. B. Merritt has the honor of settling first in the township, who came here in the year 1853, from Livingston County, New York, and entered land on section 16, where he still resides.

The next settlers of this township were Samuel Clark, Jacob and John Korns, David Babb, Arthur and Quincy Mansfield, all of whom settled upon their new prairie farms and soon made comfortable homes for themselves and families, and may now be found on their old homesteads reaping the results of their early frontier labors, except David Babb who died in 1878.

The first birth was that of James Hull, second, Willie Merritt.

First marriage was Mary Babb to H. J. Reed, at the residence of David Babb.

The first death in Highland was that of Willie Merritt.

The first school in the township was taught by Miss Lucy Clark of Grinnell, in the fall of 1861 in Central school house.

The first religious meeting in the township was held in the dwelling house of Jacob Korns by Bishop Long, of Pensylvania.

This township was organized October 9th, 1860, and the first election was held at the house of James Adair, on November 5th 1860, for the purpose of choosing township officers.

The officers since its organization as shown by the clerks books were as follows.

Justices:—S. J. Aldin, A. Mansfield, C. W. Moffitt, A. N. Poyneer, E. Phillips, F. M. Clark, D. Babb, B. Crofutt, J. B. Merritt, W. Stewart, E. L. Fish, C. A. Wilson, H. J. Vosberg.

Clerks:—R. Johnson, E. M. Poyneer F. B. Sanborn, A. H. Cowles, D. E. Wing.

Trustees:—J. Korns, A. Mansfield, D. Babb, J. B. Merritt, L. T. Leach, J. G. Cronk, J. Roberts, C. W. Moffitt, F. M. Clark, E. B. Moffitt, L. Snyder, H. I. Reed, J. Ramsey, R. Johnston, J. H. Smith, H. Winders, O. Vandyke, H. J. Vosburg, V. and E. L. Fish, D. E. Wing, V. Smith.

GRANT.

Grant township was organized in the year 1868, and named in honor of ex-President Grant. The township lies in 86 north range 15 west.

The first record we have of its settlement was in the year 1857, when Conklin, and Cornelius Gay, came and built their cabin on section 25. Soon after Evander Murdock built on section 23.

The township is prairie with timber along the streams which intersect it at different parts. It is well watered by Twelve Mile and Four Mile Creeks and their tributaries, which afford advantages to the township as a stock raising section.

The beautiful little grove known as Five Mile Grove in this township, was the scene of the horrible murder of the boy Stopp, at the hands of one Olislaugher, of which we make mention elsewhere.

We give the following list of township officers.

Justices:—W. Kline, T. Weir, C. Fleming, W. C. Seeley, J. R. Davis, J. Stanley, J. McCreath, A. Mitchell.

Clerks:—J. C. Fleming, W. Evans, R. H. Dodd, W. Mitchell.

Trustees:—W. Kline, J. H. Scott, J. Stanley, A. Mitchell, J. Young, L. P. Dinsdale, E. S. Bennett, J. Leonard, R. Whannel, J. Wilson, J. Nichols, G. Maron.

CHAPTER X.

We propose in this chapter to give a short summary of such matters as will show clearly the business and resources of Tama County. To the thoughtful and intelligent reader these items will be invaluable and we commend them to the capitalist as showing truthfully the situation at present. By a careful observation will be seen; first, the extent of our territory; second, the availiable proportion; third, the variety of its productions; fourth, its value as a stock County; fifth, extent of manufactories; sixth, openings for capitalists.

The reader will notice that we date our calculations in the year 1875, from the fact that then the last census was taken, from which, only, we were able to obtain the facts in regard to land productions etc., though during the progress of this chapter we will give a table, showing the assessment of Tama County of this year, 1879, and which will give a portion at a late date.

EXTENT OF TERRITORY.—Tama County is 24 miles wide and 30 long, having within its boundaries twenty full Congressional townships of thirty-six square miles each, making a total of 720 square miles or 455,182 acres.

IMPROVED LANDS.—These are such as are cultivated, or enclosed in fence and used for meadows or pastures as well as plow lands.

According to the census of 1875 there were 255,182 acres under cultivation.

UNIMPROVED LANDS:—The unimproved land as shown by the census of 1875, is 90,222 acres. The greater portion of this has been brought under cultivation since then and is considered as valuable as any in the County.

WHEAT:—Wheat is most extensively raised in the County. The average yield per acre compares favorably with any County of the State. In her earlier days the wheat crop far exceeded that of now; the quality was of an excellent grade and gave full weight. The acreage of 1875 was 97,013 and the yield, 1,437,907 bushels. Of late years the farmers are turning their attention more to stock raising and as a natural consequence corn is being more largely raised and wheat less.

CORN:—Among the products of Tama County as well as generally in the United States, corn is a profitable cereal being the needed article for stock. There were during the year 1875, 72,251 acres of corn tilled in this County, with a yield of 2,842,859 bushels. This amount was mostly consumed within the County.

OATS:—This needful and essential cereal is undoubtedly one of the farmer's most useful productions. The soil and climate of Tama County is especially adapted to this plant and it grows with thrift and hardiness. The yield is large, the price fair, making it a profitable production for the producer. According to the last census, 1875, there were 13,574 acres sown to oats and a yield of 384,469 bushels reaped therefrom. The crops since 1875 have been good and of excellent quality.

BARLEY:—This cereal is not so extensively cultivated as those previously mentioned, although among the Germans of the County it is raised to a considerable extent. The yield is large and the growth is hardy and thrifty. The price is good although not profitable enough for the farmers to give it a special attention.

RYE:—This article is not cultivated in large quantities owing to the low market price, though the soil and climate of Tama

County is suitable for its growth. Large quan.tities could be raised within the County and marketed, 'did the prices compensate for the labor.

BUCKWHEAT:—Large quantities of buckwheat are raised in this County by some of our farmers, but not sufficient attention is given to its culture to make it a leading production.

POTATOES AND OTHER VEGETABLES:—The productions of the garden are not to be over looked. Among these are the different varieties of vegetables so needful to the cellar, such as the potato, cabbage, turnip, bean, pea, radish and other minor articles all of which are peculiarly adapted to Tama County soil and grow with thrift and hardiness. The potato is cultivated to a remarkable extent throughout the County. The Early Rose, Peachblow, Red and White Nechannock all grow thrivingly and produce large quantities. Many of our farmers are making this a speciality and find it a very profitable business. The demand is constantly large, and prices good, both 'at home and abroad. Another favorable feature of the potato raising in Tama County is that the growth is so hardy and healthful, and the climate so especially adapted to them that they keep with full assurance and safety. The Peachblow especially possess this feature; being equally as good in the spring after keeping all winter as in the fall when first taken from the earth. It is not particularly so with the other varieties although they keep well through winter though do not retain that freshness which they possess in the fall. Cabbage is another vegetable that is raised to a large extent but only for home consumption. The other articles which we have enumerated are grown in every part of the County with profit.

MEADOWS:—The culture of tame grass has become a prominent feature with our farmers. The various tame grasses grow in Tama soil as if by magic. There is but little labor needed in raising it and the remuneration is good. The demand is large, as large quantities are needed to winter the vast number of cattle throughout the County. The last census give 15,123 acres assigned to the cultivation of this article, producing 10,169 tons.

In different parts of the County, wild grass is harvested to quite an extent. In the year 1875, as shown by the last census, 27,-667 tons were harvested. The natural or wild grass is very nutritious and gives that nourishment needed by animals.

TIMBER LAND:—Tama County has within her boundaries some as fine timber as there is in the State. The natural growth covers 18,282 acres, and the planted timber 1,589 acres, making a total of 19,871; all of which is in a growing condition and affords the advantages needed to a prosperous population in the way of fuel and other necessities.

HORSES:—According to the census of the year 1875, the last taken, there were 10,419 horses in the County. The character of the horse has been greatly improved in the past few years. Some have been imported from England, France and other countries at a large expense. Previous to this, all breeding horses were of common stock, and the venture to secure a better breed was a new era in horse raising in the County. Colts by these importations were sold as high as one hundred dollars each, and we have known yearlings to sell from one hundred and fifty to two hundred dollars each. There is an increasing demand for imported horses and the breeding of this better class is becoming a source of revenue to the County. All our best farmers are manifesting an interest in the business and we believe the time will soon come when Tama County will rank first among the principal counties in this and other States where the raising of fine horses has been made a specialty for years, and where a greater revenue is derived than from other stock. The question, will it pay to raise the best class of horses? has been fully and satisfactorily answered in the affirmative. It costs no more to raise a good horse than a poor one, and the remuneration is more than double. Many car loads are shipped from this County each year.

CATTLE:—In cattle culture Tama County is fast taking a leading position. The thousands of acres of excellent pasture land well watered, and the immense quantities of corn and fodder raised afford the farmer such advantages that cattle can be raised and marketed at a good profit. For some years past Hon. James Wilson, his brother Peter, West Wilson, L. P. Dinsdale, L. Carmichael and Andrew Jackson have been devoting their time to the improvement of this class of stock and are among Tama County's heaviest stock dealers. All these gentlemen have herds that are a credit to the County, and are constantly adding to the number, variety and quality of their stock. They have some that cost them hundreds of dollars each, and which are of pure blood and undoubted pedigree. We can say in regard to cattle what we remarked in relation to horses, it costs no more to raise the best class than it does the poorest, and the profit is much greater. According to the last census there were 28,589 head in the County. Many of this number, of course, were milch cows.

MULES AND ASSES: —Notwithstanding these animals will do more with the same amount of care, they do not appear to be a favorite with our farming community, there being only 579 head. The average value, at which they are assessed, is $50 each.

SHEEP:—There has been a heavy decrease in the number of sheep in Tama County during the past few years, caused by the low price of wool in the general markets. During the war, wool growing was a most profitable business and largely engaged in by our farmers, but the price of woollen goods has decreased greatly and the profit realized so small, that other business is now much more remunerative. In 1875 we had in this County only 4,851 head of sheep.

SWINE:—This class of stock has received more attention from our farmers than any other, and has generally been the most profitable. The American nation seems "hoggishly inclined," and the price ruling the markets has been such as to tempt our farmers to invest extensively. None seem to abandon the business of raising swine. The quality of hogs has been greatly improved within the past few years by the introduction of the English Berkshire, Chester White, and Poland China. From these and other varieties crosses have been obtained which have proven even more profitable to fatten than the thorough breds. J. T. Ames, A. J. Willey, and others have done much to in-prove this class of stock and deserve the credit of the whole County.

The large yield of corn, the readiness with which the hog fattens, and the market price affords abundant compensation to the farmer or stock raiser. During the past years there have been thousands of hogs shipped from this County and according to the assessors' books of 1875, there were 32,984 hogs. It must be borne in mind that the assessments are made from the first of January, when there are a less assessable number than any other month of the year. The assessment figures will never, therefore, show the exact number, for many pigs that are not assessed before the next yearly assessment, are shipped to the markets.

ORCHARDS:—As a County grows older, the more extensive her orchards and abundant her fruit crop. Tama County now ranks among the foremost fruit growing Counties of the state,—both in regard to the quantity and quality of the fruit growing. In 1875 we had 32,239 trees bearing in the County. This includes apples, pears, peaches, plums, cherries, etc., of which we realized 9,555 bushels of fruit. There were besides this 153,635 trees not in bearing.

APPLE:—The greater part of the land devoted to the cultivation of fruit is used for raising this variety, the principal kinds grown being Jeannette, Winesap, Rambo, Bellflower, Ben Davis, Jonathan, Red Astrachan, Red Streaks, Red June and Early Harvest. These are now considered standard. At present there are thousands of bushels raised in this County each year, and the amount is constantly increasing, the greater number of trees hardly yet reaching maturity, while additions are made each year. During the fall of 1876 there were shipped form the County hundreds of bushels. The apple crop is generally sure each year, the growth is thrifty and healthful. A good price is generally realized from this fruit, and it is found to be of profitable culture. As the orchards become older, the average will be greater.

PEACHES, PEARS AND PLUMS:—There has been some little difficulty in growing these fruits owing to the severe cold. but as the County becomes older, with close attention given the different fruits they are grown to a considerable extent and with a good profit. Plums are especally grown with thriftness and the quality is comparatively good.

CHERRIES.—The principal varieties of this excellent fruit are the English Morella, Early Richmond, and May Duke, the two former being superior to the latter and raised with less difficulty. The yield is usually large and of a superior quality.

GRAPES.—This fruit is becoming one of the staple products of the County. The yield, generally being very heavy where the proper care and attention is given. The market is good and at prices that make its culture profitable. The varieties mostly cultivated are the Concord, Delaware, Hartford Prolific, Isabella and Clinton. The manufacture of wine from the grape is found quite remunerative and is being entered into quite extensively by fruit growers.

SMALL FRUIT:—The small fruits cultivated in this County are the currant, gooseberry, blackberry, raspberry, and strawberry, all of which yield well and are found quite profitable. The quality of each is good and are grown in abundance. The climate and soil seems to be specially adapted to them. There are some who give their especial attenion to the culture of small fruit and find it a remunerative business.

ASSESSMENT OF TA-

The following table shows the Assessment of the County by Townships the purpose of the tax levy the Board of Supervisors ordered that the as- The table is a very interesting one if carefully studied.

	Number of Acres	Value per Acre	Value of Land	Value of Town Property	Neat Cattle	Value	Horses	Value	Mul s & Asses	Value	Sheep
Geneseo	23,095	8 01	165,963	4,529	1,341	14,108	572	16,850	9	350	40
Cla k	22,497	8 82	185,448	31,305	925	10,226	500	15,125	27	1,040	
Oneida	22,502	9 37	194,480		1,200	12,212	488	14,424	40	1,517	14
York	23,183	8 87	201,349	2,255	1,301	14,214	583	19,543	28	1,040	39
Salt Creek	23,217	8 67	200,446	4,440	1,324	15,095	544	17,740	15	595	29
Buckingham	22,360	9 11	189,018	405	1,505	15,380	498	15,380	13	430	26
Perry	22,158	8 96	18,761	1,2,3	1,673	15,075	489	14,240	23	710	28
Carroll	22,974	8 39	183,803		882	7,948	415	11,790	20	690	
Otter Creek	22,723	8 92	202,221		1,380	11,044	741	18,880	27	750	1
Richland	23,093	8 36	191,729	2,195	1,143	10,458	534	14,852	31	1,170	
Grant	22,733	6 50	144,245		989	10,529	441	1,580	46	1,360	10
Crystal	22,785	7 57	158,841		1,510	16,836	530	13,183	38	1,370	58
Howard	23,157	8 55	188,510	1,310	1,368	13,461	651	19,103	12	380	230
Toledo	14,589	11 26	164,651		816	9,046	293	11,424	9	307	134
Tama	6,251	12 34	77,210	4,310	336	4,755	192	3,570	10	475	101
Columbia	22,718	7 65	172,975		1,282	13,414	467	16,359	15	685	
Lincoln	22,439	9 37	207,304		847	10,248	424	13,152	67	2,634	14
Spring Creek	22,433	8 14	165,798	1,364	962	5,838	610	10,018	56	975	215
Carlton	23,331	7 63	174,217		1,027	9,690	591	14,938	21	760	120
Indian Vill ge	21,152	7 35	16,195	4,906	1,458	13,888	582	15,238	9	267	86
High and	22,456	8 15	181,805		1,223	10,129	495	12,691	13	515	28
Chelsea	584	13 84	8,087	15,918	103	1,268	59	1,920			
Traer	475	32 09	15,243	66,790	111	1,538	191	6,695	2	215	
Toledo City	126	65 57	8,253	115,690	121	1,353	146	3,643	6	60	
Tama City	732	20 06	14,686	164,032	233	2,476	177	4,361	2	55	12
Montour	218	28 33	6,176	32,054	189	1,738	109	2,785			7
Totals	455,294	8 26	3,753,091	455,627	25,240	254,850	11,460	318,895	543	18,360	1,192

and Towns as made by the Assessors thereof. In equalizing it for
sessment be reduced five per cent on Toledo and Lincoln Townships.

Value	Swine	Value	Vehicles	Value	Value of Merchandise	Capital Employd in Manufactures	Moneys and Credits	Taxable House hold Property	Corporation Stocks	Taxable Farming Utensils or Mechanic's Tools	Other Taxable Property	Total Personal Property	Total Value of All Propery
2.5	3.493	4.207	12	225	1.000		6.325			5	2,528	45,686	216,178
	1,552	3.492	42	1,060	12,905	175	6,030	905		100	8,487	59,595	279,818
14	1,721	2,842	6	250			1,500				200	32,959	226,439
30	1,817	3,319	26	860	550		3,275	330		560	290	44,011	247,615
25	2,080	3,355	12	385	850		5,963				908	44,854	249,540
40	2,434	4,625	27	660			6,020				460	42,935	232,358
19	2,701	4,787	13	540			2,870	210				38,583	326,865
	1,642	2,068	15	24							42	22,739	206,022
1	3,337	3,794	30	755			4,075	380			1,295	43,904	249,125
	2,407	3,551	27	740	1,800	590	510			100	1,141	34,913	228,857
7	1,942	2,776										26,252	172,197
46	2,445	3,916	26	600	410		2,785			50	495	39,691	197,582
230	3,084	5,420	40	796			1,756				851	42,000	264,320
184	1,153	2,130	36	900	725		9,507	410			523	35,136	195,487
79	439	740	4	130			3,595				312	13,566	75,086
	2,030	4,022	15	490			495	25			496	36,496	209,451
30	2,715	4,810			375		75			82	105	31,511	228,815
131	3,110	4,848	13	190	2,793	3,600	3,472				87	31,952	190,114
100	2,018	3,324	20	386	525		2,205				772	32,670	205,887
66	2,010	2,756	37	680	464		3,196	340			1,459	38,354	207,955
24	3,008	3,929	12	285			250	50			94	28,067	208,872
	241	335	11	297	5,100	75	1,513				590	11,499	35,104
	61	122	78	1,220	23,155		22,750	880			3,360	59,325	141,368
	172	367	71	2,024	28,162		47,455	1,695	26,575	100	9,684	120,998	214,861
9	138	287	82	2,093	18,459	2,525	15,374	600	8,728	20	4,159	59,116	237,835
7	377	495	35	740	9,075		12,438				1,664	28,942	67,172
1,020	48,377	76,316		16,677	106,318	6,965	162,424	5,795	95,303	1,047	40,372	1,045,342	5,254,078

CHAPTER XI.

TEMPERANCE.

Tama County, like all other organized territory has had its Temperance revivals, its seasons of drunkenness and seasons of sobriety. As stated in the first part of this work, one of the first acts of the settlers was the prohibiting of intoxicating liquors, and at the general election held on the 1st Monday in April, 1855, the following votes were cast on the Prohibitory Liquor Law. For Prohibition, one hundred and sixty-three votes, and against Prohibition, one hundred and twenty-six votes; thus showing the feeling of the settlers on this important question. At this early day a great many drank; not to do so in the eyes of this class of people was to set yourself above your neighbor and become his judge, a state of things which was not to be encouraged. As near as we can learn the first barrel of whiskey was brought to the County by a man named Rouse living on Whiskey Bottom. It was from this circumstance that Whiskey Bottom obtained its name. Notwithstanding, we are told that whiskey in those days was very pure, it made a surprising number of drunkards, and when the Washingtonian movement swept over the country it is not to be wondered that this County was struck by the huge wave and driven along with the current.

Occasionally strangers would appear in the various settlements proclaiming themselves missionaries of this great and powerful movement, secure some school house or log cabin and give the people a temperance lecture. After a while a temperance organization was effected to carry on the temperance work, and known as the Sons of Temperance, an organization which was at that time being extensively introduced all over the country. This was a secret organization, composed of males eighteen years old and upwards. In a short time this organization had its divisions all over the County; a very strong one existed in Toledo, at the time. A good work was accomplished by them, the effect of which will last throughout eternity.

Other organizations have existed at different times and in different places, each endeavoring to accomplish a special work. For a number of years past, in our villages and large towns, the temperance men have either put forward recognized temperance men for the local officers and voted for them as such, or have been content to vote direct upon the question of license or no license, allowing the political parties of the day to nominate such men as they chose, while pledging them to carry out the will of the people as expressed at the ballot box.

Although intemperance exists among us to an ordinary extent, in common with the rest of the country, we know it has greatly decreased within the last twenty years. We do not believe that, according to the population, there are one-fourth as many drunkards in our midst as there were at an early day. This leads us further to declare that we do not believe the efforts put forth by temperance people have been a failure in times past. That organizations have lived and flourished for a while and then gone down, prove nothing. All these organizations are but human instrumentalities, and are brought forth by the necessities of the hour. Their design is to accomplish a certain purpose apparent at the time. It is not to be expected that they will be as enduring as the hills, or like the church, so strong that "the gates of hell shall not prevail against them". If they accomplish a good work for the time being, well enough. If it is found there is a radical defect in their organizations, necessitating change, let it be made, and let us not imagine, because they are defective and have not accomplished all the good their most sanguine supporters anticipated, that nothing has been done.   All over the country can be found sober, honest and good men, who but for the efforts put forth by the means of some temperance organization that has ceased to exist, would now fill a drunkards grave. Then we would bid God speed to every effort of temperance men and women, knowing that as temperance increases our country will become more and more prosperous.

CHAPTER XII.

OLD AND NEW COURT HOUSE AND COUNTY JAIL.

As previously remarked Tama County during the first term of District Court was without a seat of Justice, therefore, the first session was held at the dwelling house of J. C. Vermilya, County Judge, where the proper steps were taken for the erection of a Court House, whereby a contract was let to T. A. Graham for the building of the same, for the sum of $1,300. Lot 2 in block 5, in Toledo, was selected for the site, and in the latter part of the year 1854, the Court House was completed, and the second term of Court was held therein.

The house was a commodious frame building two stories in hight and answered the purpose for which it was built until the people realized the need and necessity of a larger one. The old building was disposed of in the year of 1866.

During the year 1865 the people of Toledo and vicinity, agitated the question of a new Court House. At a meeting held in Toledo, there was a Court House Association, organized and the following trustees were chosen: W. F. Johnston, Wm. H. Harrison, D. D. Appelgate, T. A. Graham, N. C. Weiting, and G. R. Struble, with A. J. Free as Secretary. The question of the erection of a new Court House was settled, and the Association advertised for bids upon the plans and specifications submitted. The bid of P. B. McCullough of Toledo, Iowa, was adopted, and the construction was begun by him, but, failing to fill contract, H. B. Belden, agreed to finish it under the contract. Under Mr. Belden's charge the building was finished at a cost of something over $22,000 of which the County paid about $5,000.

THE BUILDING AND SURROUNDINGS.

The building is a fine structure centrally located in Toledo City on the Public Square, and presents a picturesque spectacle, approached from any direction. The ground on which it is situated is beautifully decorated with trees of different kinds, and inclosed by a tasty and substantial fence, affording the citizens of Toledo a beautiful park suitable for out-door gatherings.

The building is one of neatness and constructed after modern style, two stories high and covers an area of 45 x 72 feet. The material of which the main part is constructed is brick. The basment is stone, giving it a solid and sure foundation, the upper stories are of an excellent quality of brick. The whole building is roofed with corrugated iron.

There are two entrances to the main building one from the north and the other from the south. The structure is surmounted by a fine belfry which rises from the center. From this belfry a sublime view can be obtained of the surroundings for miles around. A large hall passes through the entire building.

The first floor is very systematically arranged into different departments and occupied as offices for the various officers of the County. Each department is furnished with all the necessities that are needed to make them commodious and comfortable. The large fire and burglar proof safe in each office and vault render the keeping of all records and funds secure and safe. In the south end will be found a large stair-way leading up into the second story and Court Room. This room throughout is well seated and furnished which make it comfortable quarters for its occupants. Besides the Court Room there is a large and commodious gallery, a jury room and a hall at the entrance.

Farther up is the belfry reached by a stair-way running from the second story. The building, surroundings and conveniences are referred to with no little degree of pride by the people of

Toledo and Tama County. We pass from this public enterprise to that of the

COUNTY JAIL.

This building is a fine two story brick structure, and stands 30x34 feet on the ground and erected under the supervision of David Stoner, of Toledo.

The upper story is occupied by the jailor and contains six pleasant rooms. The lower story, or the jail, contains a large wrought iron cage, 22x25 with sleeping apartments for the confinement of the prisoners. The outer door, leading from the dwelling to the jail, is also wrought iron, and the inner one is a grated door. The entire building is covered with an iron roof. A neat fence surrounds the lot on which it stands, which adds much to its general appearance. The jail was first occupied in the latter part of 1870, and from that time there has been over three-hundred prisoners confined therein. Sheriff Austin took possession of the dwelling on the eighth day of January, 1874. The building stands on the corner of Broadway and State Streets, opposite the northeast corner of the Court House square.

Below will be given a full list of officers filling the various County offices.

Judges:—Tallman Chase, J. C. Vermilya, Leander Clark, John Allen, T. F. Bradford, T. A. Graham, Maj. T. S. Free.

Clerks of District Court:—D. D. Appelgate, L. B. Blinn, C. J. Stevens.

Sheriffs:—N. L. Osborne, M. Blodgett, W. Garner, H. C. Foster, T. Murry, H. A. Williamson, K. Dexter, R. E. Austin.

School Fund Commissioners:—N. Myers, D. F. Bruner, L. S. Fredrick.

Surveyors:—W. A. Daniels, C. Irish, J. P. Wood, H. Jacobs, C. W. Hiatt, W. H. Holstead.

Treasurers:—D. F. Bruner, J. Ross, T. J. Staly, A. J. Wheaton, J. H. Struble, T. Schaeffer, D. Forker, L. B. Blinn.

Recorders:—D. E. Bruner, T. J. Staly, A. J. Wheaton, J. H. Struble, J. Yeiser, J. R. McClaskey, T. S. Free, J. B. M. Bishop.

Coroners:—F. Davis, C. Olney, T. W. Jackson. I. J. Wilkins, N. Fisher, M. A. Newcomb, G. W. Cowles, E. M. Bielby, J. C. Kendricks.

County Superintendents:—W. Helm, J. Ramsdell, T. L. Downs, J. R. Stewart, T. Hurd, A. H. Sterrett, A. H. Brown.

Representatives: —J. Connell, T. W. Jackson, Jas. Wilson, A. Tompkins, W. G. Malin, G. Jaqua.

Auditors:—T. S. Free, A. J. Bowdle, R. G. McIntire.

Supervisors:—L. Clark, G. Jaqua, A. N. Poyneer, J. Ramsdell, S. W. Hutton, J. W. Lauderdale, T. F. Clark, H. H. Withington, J. Dysart, R. M. Tenny, T. Forker, J. M. Young, J. A. Willey, A. Wilkinson, I. Toland, G. W. Morrison, W. Cory, M. B. Sapp, C. W. Dobson, J. Peterson, W. Conant, A. Donaldson, C. Bratt, P. L. Sherman, J. Wilson, J. J. Keeler, L. Kibbee, P. McRoberts, S. Doolittle, J. Powell, W. Merrill, C. W. Knapp, W. T. Willard, G. M. Morehouse, A. C. Brockway, W. C. Thomas, G. Prescott, S. H. Baldwin, S. C. Rogers, J. S. Townsend, C. C. Guilford, T. S. Talmage, H. B. Clemans, J. W. Fleming, W. F. Johnston, D. D. Appelgate, G. Jaqua, W. T. V. Ladd, R. Johnston, A. M. Poyneer, T. Hufford W. Gallagher, E. S. Becklsy, M. Mitchell, N. Lewis, A. Tompkins. A. M Stayly, A. C. Tenney, A. Bricker, J. B. Dresser, G. W. Selvey, Z. T. Shugart, L. B. Ladd, H. L. Smith.

Tama County is in the eighth Judicial District which comprises Linn, Cedar, Jones, Johnson, Iowa, Tama, and Benton Counties. The following is a list of the Judges and Attorneys serving in the District and Circuit Court.

Hon. William E. Smith, G. J. Cook, W. E. Miller, N. W. Isbell, C. H. Conklin, N. M. Hubbard. J. A. Rothrock, Hon. John Shane, A. Phillips, N. C. Wieting, I. A. Allen, C. R. Scott, W. G. Thompson, Milo P. Smith.

CHAPTER XIII.

Tama County has had comparatively few marked scenes of violence and crime, which is a good thing to record, although in early days there existed in this and adjoining Counties a combination of outlaws, horse thieves, counterfeiters and murderers, that fastened themselves upon the country of the Iowa River valley and Northern Tama, previous to 1860.

About the confines of American civilization there has always hovered, like scouts before the march of an invading army, a swarm of bold, enterprising, adventurous criminals. The broad, untrodden prairies, the trackless forests, the rivers unbroken by the keels of commerce, furnishes admirable refuge for those whose crimes drive them from companionship with the honest and law-abiding. Hovering there, where courts and civil processes could afford but a weak bulwark of protection against their evil and dishonest purposes and practices, the temptation to pray upon the comparatively unprotected sons of toil, rather than to gain a livelihood by the slow process of peaceful industry, has proven two strong to be resisted. Some of these reckless characters sought the outskirts of advancing settlements for the express purposes of theft and robbery; some because they dare not remain within reach of efficient laws; others of limited means but ambitious to secure homes of their own, and with honesty of purpose, exchanged the comforts and protection of law afforded by the old settled and populous districts for life on the frontiers, and not finding all that their fancy painted, were tempted into crime by apparent immunity from punishment. In all new countries the proportion of the dishonest and criminal has been greater than in the older and better regulated communities where courts are permanently established and the avenues of escape from punishment for wrong doing more securely guarded. This was notably and particularly the case in the early settlement of Tama and surrounding Counties.

At the time of which we write, a strong and well organized band of desperadoes held almost undisputed and unobstructed dominion throughout this whole region of country and very few of the honest settlers were fortunate enough to preserve all their property from being swept into the meshes of the net-work these land pirates had spread around them. Good horses and their equipments were the most easily captured and most readily concealed, and consequently the most coveted by the outlaws as well as the most unsafe property that early settlers could own.

Owners of fast or really good horses never presumed to leave them unguarded for a single night unless the stable was doubly locked and barred, and a faithful dog either left within the stable or at the stable door, and oft times the owners would sleep in the stable with their trusty rifles by their side, while many never thought of going to his stable or wood pile after night-fall without his gun.

Among this gang of cut-throats were the Bunker boys, Charles and William. These men were the representative characters of the gang. The operations of the gang extended from one end of the country to the other—from Texas up through the Indian territory, Arkansas, Missouri, and Iowa, to Wisconsin; from the Ohio River, at Pittsburgh, through the State of Ohio, Indiana, Illinois, and Iowa, to the Missouri River, as far as civilization extended. Their hands and depredations were directed against society everywhere, and they prayed upon the substance of honest toilers, merchants, and buisness men, with reckless and da

ing impunity, sparing no one who was not in some way allied
with their plunder stained combination.

In 1860, a gentleman by the name of Small, a resident of Polk
County had three valuable colts stolen from the prairie just east
of the city of DesMoines, which by the way was not much of a
city at that time. And when Mr. S. missed his colts, he procured
the assistance of Constable Seaman, of the same County, and
started on the trail, which they followed to the residence of the
Bunkers, in Hardin County, where they very soon found the
colts. Advancing to the house, the pursuers were met by the
mother of the Bunkers who barred their way, ax in hand. At
length, and without violence, an entrance was effected and one
of the boys arrested. Securing him they kept guard until day-
light when another Bunker came in sight, and after a long chase,
he too, was captured. The colts were haltered and the party
started for DesMoines. While in Tama County they were joined
by a man named Klingaman, and as the story goes they proposed to hang one of their prisoners until he should reveal the names
of his partners in crime. They had succeeded so far as to sus-
pend him in mid air,—without however, intending to continue
the process until he was dead—when the other Bunker sprang
away and started for freedom at a rushing gate. Klingaman and
Seaman started in pursuit, leaving Small to take care of the aerial
Bunker. Small became so much interested in watching the pursuit and flight that he forgot to lower the body and by the time
Klingaman and Seaman returned with the recaptured brother,
the first was as dead as a smelt. As a matter of precaution, and
to prevent his telling tales, the other Bunker was submitted to
the same strangling process, and with the same result. Thus
both bodies were left, suspended on a Tama County tree, in what
is known as "National Grove" in Perry township. They were
found hanging soon after and the perpetrators gone. Klingaman,
so says our informant, was drowned the next spring, near Helena,
in the Mississippi river, having fled to that point to escape justice,
and Seaman and Small were arrested shortly after, but escaped.
The former was never seen or heard of afterwards. Small, after

passing several years in the Rocky Mountains returned to his farm and family in Polk County. In 1877, Small was arrested at DesMoines, by Deputy Sheriff, Wm. E. Applegate, and again escaped from custody but afterward gave bond for his appearance at the February term of Court, 1878. At this term he was tried and found guilty of murder in the first degree. A new trial was asked, and granted by Judge Shane. At the February term of District Court, 1879, the case was dismissed. Small paying all costs of prosecution.

As already stated murder has been rare in this County, yet occasionally we are shocked with the announcement of a terrible murder committed in our midst. It would be folly for us as a historian, to recall these bloody deeds one by one as they were committed, therefore we will only speak of a few.

On the morning of the 8th day of October, 1866, the alarm was given that Abram Felter, a resident and farmer living in Buckingham township had murdered his wife. Friends of the deceased at once gathered and an investigation was made, when it was discovered that she had been killed while in a quarrel, from all appearance with an ax at the hand of her own husband. An inquest was held upon the body by the coroner, and after examining the body and carefully investigating the matter the Jury returned a verdict that the deceased came to her death by violence and unlawful means by the hands of her husband, Abram Felter, who was immediatly arrested and committed to jail.

On the twenty-first day of February following, the Grand Jury of the County found a true bill of indictment against him for murder in the first degree. The case being called he was tried found guilty and sentenced to the penitentiary at hard work for life. To day. from all reports, Felter is serving his time in comparatively good health.

Frank Mulligan shot and killed a man named Garvey in a saloon owned by G. Mence, in Tama City, then known as Iuka, February 15th, 1869, while in a drunken row. The Grand Jury found a true bill of indictment against Mulligan for murder in the second degree, and he was sentenced to one year's hard work in the penitentiary, and the cost of prosecution.

Thomas Robecheck, and Joseph Prusha, Bohemians, were neighbors living in Otter Creek township. A feud had existed between them for some time which resulted in the murder of Prusha. Meeting on the 26th of July, 1875, the day the murder was committed, a quarrel ensued, with the above result. Prusha's body was found by the road side shortly after. Robecheck was arrested and indicted at the September term, 1875, for willful murder. The trial resulted in a verdict of guilty, and Robecheck was sentenced to the penitentary at Anamosa, at hard work for sixteen years and the cost of the suit.

On the 9th day of July, 1877, Martin Meshek shot and killed Constable C. S. Whitely, a highly respected resident of Carroll township, who was trying to arrest Meshek for assault and battery. In this case Meshek was arrested, and at the September term of Court, 1877, the Grand Jury found an indictment against him for murder in the first degree. He was tried, found guilty and sentenced for the term of ten years. After the sentence was pronounced the attorneys for the defendant asked for a new trial which was overruled and the case was carried to the Supreme Court, where a new trial was granted at the June term, 1879. The case will probably be disposed of at the next term of District Court.

The cases of Wm. Taylor for the shooting of Perry Wheaton, September 14th, 1878, and that of W. H. Houd, for the murder of J. L. Smith, Aug. 14th, 1878, were called up and diposed of at the last term of District Court. Taylor being sentenced to penitentiary for ten years, while Houd was sent for two years. The last and most foul is the murder of Michael Straka, a Bohemian, August 29th, 1878, by the hands of some unknown villian for the sum of $250. At this writing the murderer is still at large.

There are other cases of murder and crimes of which we might speak, but we will leave the matter.

CHAPTER XIV.

In 1856 a few citizens of this County interested in Agricultural and Mechanical Arts met in Toledo for the purpose of effecting an organization having for its object improvement in the agricultural interest of the County, and on September 25th, of this year a Fair was held. The display of different products of the County was fair both from field and garden. The stock was a fine show and manifested the interest Tama County farmers took in this creditable pursuit at so early a date. This Fair proved a success in almost every particular, and it was determined that renewed efforts should be made to make the society efficient and permanent, but their zealous efforts failed and the organization, after holding two or three more Fairs ceased to exist.

From time to time Fairs were held at different parts of the County, without a permanent organization until a Fair was established at Tama City in 1866, of which we will speak again.

We cannot well help drawing a comparison between the Fairs then and now. At that time, although they were spoken of as being successful, the entries were few indeed in comparison to what are now made each year. Blooded stock then was scarce. No such fine herds of cattle as are now owned and exhibited each year by L. Carmichael, Andrew Jackson, the Wilsons and others; no such droves of hogs as J. T. Ames and others show; no improved horses like those of M. and J. Wylie's, W. McGowan's Dr. W. Corns' and J. H. Hollen's to carry off the ribbons.

The floral hall at an early day would blush if placed side by side with the buildings now owned by the Societies and filled each year to overflowing.

As already stated, the first agricultural society at Toledo ceased after a few years. No other organization of the kind existed at that place until the year 1873. On July 12th, of this year at one o'clock P. M., A. J. Wheaton, West Wilson, T. A. Graham, L. B. Nelson, A. W. West, W. H. Stivers, N. Huff, J. Reedy, P. Lichty and others, met at the Court House in Toledo, for the purpose of organizing the Agricultural Association of Tama County. West Wilson was called to the chair and W. H. Stivers was chosen Secretary, *pro tem.* Remarks were made by various persons and the feasibility and importance of the proposed organization discussed. Articles of incorporation of said association were duly adopted, agreed upon and placed on record. The next meeting held on the 19th, a tract of land on section 15, belonging to F. Davis was purchased for the fair grounds. P. Lichty, J. S. Townsend and D. F. Bruner were appointed a committee to prepare and fence the ground, while N. Huff, E. Taplin and J. O'Niel were appointed a committee to prepare the trotting track.

The first annual meeting of the association was held on the 1st 2nd and 3rd days of October, 1873. The officers were as follows: President, A. J. Wheaton; Vice-President, West Wilson; Secretary, W. H. Stivers; Treasurer, L. B. Nelson. The fair proved a success in every respect as every one will testify who visited it. Yearly exhibitions were held upon the grounds from the time of organization of the society until 1878 when by some cause the society failed.

TAMA COUNTY AGRICULTURAL SOCIETY.

The people of Tama County interested in agriculture and the improvement of the same, met in Union Hall, Iuka, now Tama City, on August 4th, 1866, for the purpose of discussing the question of organizing a County fair. The meeting was called to order. A large number of delegates from different parts of the County were present and the issues discussed with considerable interest and length. Nothing definite was determined upon until the next meeting, held on the 18th of the same month, when the organization was made complete with Judge Salsbury of Indiantown, President; West Wilson, of Crystal, Vice-President; John Ramsdell, of Richland, Treasurer; and A. M. Batchelder, of Iuka, Secretary. Articles of incorporation were drawn up and adopted. The first fair was held on the 10th and 11th days of the following October, and proved a success. Since that time fairs have been held each year on the grounds, with increased success. The grounds are well adapted for the purpose and are situated within the limits of Tama City, at the time of the organization of the society known as Iuka, and are the finest and most convenient in the County. The officers and Board of Directors for the present year, 1879, are as follows:

President, L. Carmichael; Vice-President, W. G. Malin; Secretary, C. H. Kentner; Treasurer, B. A. Hall; Trustees, B. F. Swanton, A. B. Taplin, J. H. Hollen, Wm. Earnest and Wm. Cory. These men are all tried and true, and will work with a will to make the Society a credit to the County.

TRAER DISTRICT AGRICULTURAL SOCIETY.

This society was organized at Traer, February 28th, 1874, and given the above name. At a meeting of the society, March 14th, 1874, the following officers were elected for that year: President, West Wilson; VicePresident, J. R. Steer; Secretary, G. Johnston; Treasurer, J. T. Wild. The first fair was held September 10th and 11th of the same year. The operations were a grand success, both in attendance and financially. From year to year the society has given a good exhibition at their grounds.

The ensuing officers were men of energy and have done all in their power to make the fair a successful and beneficial exhibition to every farmer in the County.

Every citizen of the County should take an interest in the exhibitions of the different societies in the County and use his utmost endeavors to make the annual meetings successful. Nothing tends more to incite farmers to action than the comparison of their stock or the products of their labor. We attribute in a great measure the advanced steps taken by our people in the improvement of fine stock and the growth of the various products to these exhibitions.

CHAPTER XV.

We now take up the interesting history of Tama County during the late war and note with pride the active part she took for the right during the stirring events of the four long years when the dark clouds threatening the destruction of our Union hovered over her, each and every one hoped, even against hope, that they would pass away and that peace and prosperity would continue to reign, but such was not the case.

On the twelfth day of April, 1861, the enemy, who for weeks had been erecting their batteries upon the shore, after demanding of Major Anderson a surrender, opened fire upon Fort Sumpter. For hours an incessant cannonading was continued; the fort was weakened, provisions were almost gone, and Major Anderson was compelled to haul down the old flag, that flag which had seldom been lowered by a foreign foe, was trailed in the dust by the hands of a local enemy. Oh! how the blood of patriots boiled when they learned of the outrage. No where was greater indignation manifested than in Tama County. Partisan feelings, which before had existed were swept away, and the language of the immortal Douglass, verified, in which he said "but two parties can exist, patriots and traitors."

When the President issued the call for 300,000 men, Tama County responded without delay; seemingly all were ready to go forth in defence of their country. Meetings were held in various parts of the County, participated in by all parties, then known as patriots, and resolutions were adopted setting forth in the strongest terms undying devotion to the Union. About the 12th of August, 1861, a company numbering one-hundred men was organized at Toledo, and the following officers elected: A. Stoddard, Captain; T. B. Martin, First Lieutenant; T. W. Jackson, Second Lieutenant. The names of the company are given elsewhere.

As the company left Toledo, for the place of rendezvous, hundreds of people were present and many were the tears shed and the hearty "God bless you," given over the departure of loved ones. But there was not one of that whole number who would have had any one of the departing boys turn back. Shortly after this company had left W. II. Stivers and L. Clark organized companies and were off to the seat of war. Another company was also organized and sent out under the command of John A. Staly as Captain. A number of Tama County young men also joined a cavalry company raised by Tama, Marshall and Story Counties. W. P. Hepburn, of Marshall County, Captain, Paul A. Queal of Story County, 1st Lieutenant, Wm. II. Stoddard of Tama County, 2nd Lieutenant.

In addition to these there were a large number of enlistments of men for old companies whose ranks had been decimated by disease and bullets during the war. Grey headed men, who had almost reached their three-score years and ten, and boys not yet out of their teens went to the camp and through the most urgent solicitation were accepted. Neither old age nor youth kept them back, and when rejected from either cause or from physical inability, would insist on being received, believing themselves as capable of doing a soldier's duty as many who had already gone. Hundreds of as brave men as ever handled a musket or drew a sword went out from this County, some never to return. In many homes throughout the County we find the vacant chair, and witness the mournful look of those ever watching for one that cometh not. Upon the streets day by day we

meet those wearing armless sleeves or walking in a way that tells
plainly that the sound of the foot-step is not made by flesh and
bone.   Inquire the cause and we shall probably learn that while
charging the enemy at Vicksburg, Shiloh or elsewhere, a cannon
ball deprived them of a limb or arm.   But no word of com-
plaint do we hear; the only regret expressed being that it was
not possible to do more for their country.

While they were away upon the tented field, the patriotic
men and women at home were not idle.   The County officials
at a meeting called August 5th, 1861, passed a resolution allowing the sum of five dollars per month for the relief of soldiers'
families, and an additional sum of two dollars per month for each
child under twelve years of age.   During the entire four years
of war, we think but little actual suffering was experienced by
any at home on account of the absence of their providers who
were away serving their country.

Occasionally word would be received of the gallant conduct
upon the battle field of some company from this County, and
although hearts were made sore by the fact that the blood of
many had been shed, yet all rejoiced that none failed to preform
their duty.

Time passed, and the rebellion was brought to an end and
peace was proclaimed throughout the land.   All over the
country the shouts went up from loyal hearts, and as our "brave
boys in blue" returned the joy increased.   The long struggle
was over, the sacrifice made, the Union saved and Tama
County did her part.   Now those that are left are gathered at
home and occasionally relate to us the scenes of those terrible times, and our hearts almost cease to beat as they describe
the battles in which they were engaged, and tell us how
the strife raged the fiercest, where so many of their brave com-
rades fell, or how one by one in the dreary prisons or in the hos-
pitals, passed away from earth those who but a short time previously were full of health and hope.   But amid all this we have a
saved country, and should we not be thankful to the One Ruler
of all that it was in the power of man to make the sacrifice by
which all this was accomplished?

OUR BOYS IN THE FIELD.

If time and space allowed, gladly would we follow our boys to the tented field and recount the individual acts of bravery of each, but this we cannot do and can only speak in general, giving a short description of such regiments as were composed partly of men from this County.

Our soldiers, we find are as modest as brave, and not disposed to volunteer information for publication, so what we do give is gathered from the records. The first in order will be

COMPANY C—TENTH IOWA.

Company C was organized at Toledo and assigned to the 10th Iowa Infantry, with Colonel N. Perczel, commanding, and was mustered into the service of the United States on the 6th day of September, 1861, under proclamation of the President, bearing date July 23rd, 1861, at Camp Fremont, Iowa City, with Albert Stoddard, Captain. The company was first ordered into rendezvous at St. Louis, Mo., where they were uniformed and equipped for the service. The company participated in skirmishes and battles at Bloomfield, Mo., resulting in the dispersion of the rebel force under the command of Jeff Thompson; Charleston Mo., January 8th, 1862, where four of our boys were wounded, A. Myers, A. H. Kellogg, C. Maholm, and A. Tice. On the 13th and 14th, Sexton, Mo., was captured resulting in the evacuation of Island No. 10, and on the 7th and 8th of February. Tiptonville, Tenn. was taken, capturing between five and six thousand prisoners, and then came the memorable battle of Corinth on the 3rd and 4th of October. In this battle John M. Stebbins, second Sergeant was killed, A. M. Roberts and Wesley Randall wounded; Randall died from the effects of the wound, November 8th, 1862. This battle lasted two days when the enemy gave way. Skirmishing and fighting were indulged in at Farmington, Iuka, Grand Gulf, and Holly Springs. At Missionary Ridge, Wm. E. Applegate, G. W. Guilford, J. Newport and Melvin Rhoads were wounded. The long seige at Champion Hills, and Vicksburg came next, resulting in the retreat of Joe. Johnson from Champion Hills and the capture of Vicksburg, but

not however, without heavy losses. At these battles J. B. Han-
cox, J. Budka, C. J. Herrick, C. W. Peck, P. Ramsey, J. C.
Rouse, and C. Van Horn, were killed. J. W. Gower, V. P.
Gray, J. H. Larmer, J. K. Lux, T. S. Brennon, B. Dunbar,
N. P. Stevenson, W. Appelgate, C. L. Bailey, G. W. Guilford,
A. H. Harmon and C. Moisner wounded. There was fighting
and skirmishing at Mission Ridge, Decatur, Savannah, Columbia,
Fayettville and Cox's Bridge, but without bad result.

On the 28th of September, 1864, the non-veterans were mustered out of the service and in August, 1865, the veteran volunteers were mustered out of the service of the United States at
Little Rock, Arkansas. There were one-hundred men in the
company from this County, and during the war, or from the time
of mustering in until the company was mustered out, the causualities were eight killed, twenty-six wounded, nineteen died.

COMPANY G—FOURTEENTH IOWA.

Company G, 14th Iowa, was organized at Davenport, Iowa
and was mustered into the United States service at Davenport, November 2nd, 1861. The company contained fifty-eight men from
this County, with Wm. H. Stivers. Captain, who resigned January 24th, 1862, and the following day George Pemberton, of Soctt
County, was elected captain in his stead. At the battle of Shiloh, August 6th, 1862, the greater part of the company were taken
prisoners of war, after fighting bravely and maintaining their position from morning until 5 o'clock in the evening. The captured
were as follows: Wm. Gallagher, S. Eccles, P. Wilson, B. F.
Thomas, J. A. Pope, James Fox, B. Brennon, J. Burright, M.
Clark, R. F. Clark, E. Dykeman, J. B. Edwards, R. Ritch, J. R.
Felter, W. L. Goit, M. L. Grubbs, I. Hunnicutt, W. Heath, G.
Hate, J. H. Luke, D. Miller, J. R. Myers, J. E. McCune, J. B.
Overturf, E. Stokes, D. Southwick, J. B. Wiseman, H. H.
Williams and D. S. Young, while E. G. Oldroyd, H. Loomis,
and J. Miles, were wounded. At the battle of Pleasant Hill, La.,
Arpil 9, 1864, after a severe fight the enemy was defeated but
not however without loss. Here 1st Lieutenant J. A. Shanklin, W.S.

Townsend and H. Spangler fell mortally wounded; G. W. Bates J. B. Edwards, W. Heath, and J. H. Wilkins, wounded; E. Kern, J. Morton, and G. Loucks Jr., captured. At the battle of Tupelo and Town Creek on the 14th and 15th of July, 1864, the enemy's lines were broken and their men so terrified that their officers could not rally them to make a stand, although trying it several times. The rebels were defeated with comparatively small loss, Elijah Gallion being the only one wounded in the fight from this County. On the 8th, day of May, 1864, at the battle of Bayou De Glaize, Gideon Hate was wounded slightly in the left leg. The company participated in the battles of Corinth, Fort de Russey and numerous other battles.

The company was mustered out of service Nov. 16th, 1864, at Davenport, Iowa. The casualties were three killed, nine wounded and ten died.

PROMOTIONS.—Wm. H. Gallagher 2nd Lieutenant, November 2nd, 1861, 1st Lieutenant, January 25th, 1862, Captain, January 7th, 1863; S. F. Eccles 1st Sergeant, November, 2nd, 1861, 2nd, Lieutenant, January 25th, 1862; J. A. Shanklin 2nd Corporal, October 9th, 1861, 1st, Sergeant January 29th, 1862; G. A. Walroth 4th Sergeant October 8th, 1861, 1st Sergeant November 2nd 1861; W. Breese 4th Corporal December 14th, 1861, from private; J. A. Pope 6th Corporal, October 10th, 1861, from private; J. Gaston 8th Corporal, October 6th, 1861, from private.

J. H. Stevens Surgeon, commissioned Aug. 19th, 1862.

W. H. Stivers, Captain Nov. 2nd 1861, commissioned Nov. 4th, 1861, resigned Jan. 24th, 1862; W. Gallagher, 1st Lieutenant Jan. 25th, 1862, from 2nd Lieutenant, missing at Shiloh, April 6th, 1862, Captain Jan. 7th, 1863.

COMPANY E—TWENTY-FOURTH IOWA.

This company was raised in Tama and Iowa counties, with Leander Clark as Captain and mustered into the service of the United States by Capt. H. B. Hendershott, U. S. A., at Muscatine, Iowa, September 17th, 1862 under proclamation of the President bearing date July 2nd, 1862, Colonel E. C. Byam,

commander. The company while in the service participated in
some severe battles and skirmishes, such as the battles of Port
Gibson, Cedar Creek, Champion Hills, Mansfield, Winchester,
and Vicksburg. At Port Gibson, 1st sergeant John Rokes was
wounded. At Cedar Creek on the 19th, of October, 1854, James
Rokes, M. Mitchell, and R. T. Shelley were taken prisoners, and
R. Filloon, M. Mink and A. J. Boberts, wounded. Next came
the battle of Champion Hills, which resulted in the defeat of the
enemy, but not with out loss. In this battle G. H. Stoddard and
John Gross were killed while in action and F. Verner, A. J.
Lamm captured, and William Hillmon was wounded, dying
five days after from the effect. At Mansfield, J. Wande and W. L.
Conant were captured, while S. R. Rushton was wounded and
captured.

On September 18th, 1864, company E. took part in the battle
of Opequan or Winchester. At this battle the enemy was entirely routed and driven pell mell from the field. W. Dobson was
captured, J. Pass and E. Bruner wounded. The company participated in closely contested fights and skirmishes at Jackson,
Fisher's Hill, Sabine Cross Roads, Alexandria and other places.
S. S. Dillman, 1st Lieutenant was killed September 19th, 1864.
There were in the company from this County sixty-six men.

PROMOTIONS.—Leander Clark, Captain August 21st, 1862,
Lieutenant Colonel January 1st, 1865. Major James
Rokes, 2nd sergeant August 18th, 1862, 1st Lieutenant by com-
mission, September 20th, 1864, Captain, November 19th, 1864; S. S.
Dillman, 2nd Lieutenant August 21st, 1862, 1st Lieutenant
April 4th, 1863; E. S. Edwards, 1st, Corporal from private, Oct-
ober 3rd, 1862.

The causualities were four killed, seven wounded, and twelve
died.

The company was mustered out of service at Savannah, Ga.,
July 17th, 1865.

COMPANY F—TWENTY-EIGHTH INFANTRY.

Company F. was mustered into the service of the United States by Capt. II. B. Hendershott, U. S. A., at Iowa City, Oct. 10th, 1862, under proclamation of the President of the United States, bearing date July 2nd, 1862, John A. Staly, Captain. The company while in the service participated in the battles of Sabine Cross Roads, Fisher's Hill, Cedar Creek, Champion Hills, Winchester, Opelousas, Port Gibson, Helena, Vicksburg, Jackson, and numerous other battles and skirmishes. At the battles of Sabine Cross Roads or Mansfield La., April 8th, 1864, Adam Jack, and S. Harlacher were killed while Colonel John Connell, John II. Scott, J. Hart and F. Schaffer wounded. At the battle of Fisher's, Hill L. Loupee and J. Behenneck, were wounded. In the battle of Cedar Creek, Oct. 19th, 1864, E. D. Beckley, H. D. Fuller, J. M. Hammitt, J. Young, J. H. Davis, S. W. Myers J. Wood were wounded, and E. W. Bunce and J. Chess were captured. May 16th, 1863, at the battle of Champion Hills Company F. was in the thickest of the fight and the officers and men conducted themselves like veterans. After a few minutes of hard fighting the enemy was driven from the field in confusion. At this battle Samuel W. Hammitt, B. W. Russell, David Shelton, T. Southers, J. A. Knapp and George Williams fell mortally wounded; J. W. Hiatt, Wm. Nixon, S. W. Arbuthnot, C. Godfrey, H. M. Miller, G. A. Moss and J. E. Rockenfield were wounded. While J. Blair, J. Chess, John Wilson and Capt. John A. Staly were taken prisoners. It is said that Capt. Staly and his men disputed the advance of the enemy in a very efficient and highly successful manner. Another severe engagement ensued near Winchester, Va., on the 19th day of September, 1864, where both officers and men stood boldly forth in defense of the old flag, and did their duty nobly. Wounded, J. Crawford, W. Hanna, S. Bruner, J. B. M. Bishop, F. Sheldon, II. A. Read and C. W. Sipes; captured, W. Nixon, W. Grubbs, E. S. Beckley and J. Young. At Opelousas, La., W. Bywaters, W. Grubbs and S. W. Myers were captured while in action, and at the battle of Port Gibson, P. II. Mason, J. Myers, and J. L. Fitzgerald were wounded. At Helena, Ark, B. F. Brennon, F. M. Conner and D. Shelton were captured, and S. G. Clark was wounded. while J. W. Flathers was captured at Jackson.

The 28th Infantry contained 130 men from this County, and the casualties were eight killed, twenty-six wounded and twenty-one died.

PROMOTIONS.—Theodore Schaeffer 1st Lieutenant Aug. 8th, 1862. Captain Jan. 13th, 1864; J. S. Furguson 2nd Sergeant, 1st Sergeant, November 1st. 1862; D. W. Emerson 7th Corporal, November 1st, 1862, from private. W. A. Daniel from assistant Surgeon to Surgeon, December 21st 1864; H. H. Weaver 5th Sergeant August 8th, 1862, 1st Lieutenant January 13th, 1864; J. H. Davis 4th Corporal, August 5th, 1862, appointed 1st Lieutenant; C. P. N. Barker 2nd Lieutenant, March 10th, from private; B. W. Wilson Lieutenant Colonel, April 7th, 1863, from Captain, Company B.

The regiment was mustered out of the service at Savannah Georgia, July 31, 1865.

Tama County was represented in nineteen regiments and fifty companies. There were forty-two men killed in battle, ninety-one wounded and eighty-three died a natural death while in the service.

On the following pages may be found a statement taken from the reports of the Adjutant General of the State and revised by some one familiar with each regiment and company. We have tried to make it correct and reliable having spent many weeks in the work of compilation.

TAMA COUNTY VOLUNTEERS.

ABBREVIATIONS

Asst...............................Assistant.
Adjt...............................Adjutant.
Capt...............................Captain.
Com...............................Commissioned.
Cor...............................Corporal.
Col...............................Colonel.
Cav...............................Cavalry.
Captd...............................Captured.
Dis...............................Discharged.
Hon...............................Honorable.

Lt...............................Lieutenant.
m. o...............................Mustered out.
m. in...............................Mustered in.
Maj...............................Major.
Pri...............................Private.
Pro...............................Promoted.
Res...............................Resigned.
Ser...............................Sergeant.
Trans...............................Transferred.
Wd...............................Wounded.

Tenth Infantry.

Company C.

Albert Stoddard Capt., Sep 6th, 1861, Com Sept 24th '61, m in Oct. 27th '64.

T. B. Martin 1st Lt, Sep 6th '61, Com Sep 24th '61, res June 26th '62,

G. H. Conant 1st Lt June 27th '62 from 2d Lt, killed at Mission Ridge.

T. W. Jackson 2d Lt Sep 6th '61, Com Sep 24th '61, pro Adjt Sep 24th '61.

G. W. Conant 2d Lt Oct 21st from 1st ser, pro Jan 27th 62.

Wm. H. Stoddard 2d Lt July 31st m in June 27th from pri Capt '65.

G. H. Conant 1st asst ser Sep 6th '61, pro 2d Lt, Oct 31st '61.

John M Stebbing 2d ser Sep 6th '61, killed Oct 4th '62 at Corinth, Miss.

K. Dexter 3d ser Sep 6th '61,? hon dis Feb 21st '63 at Davenport.

L. B. Nelson 4th ser Sep 6th '61, dis Aug 23d '62 at St. Louis. Mo.

Dorson Chase, 4th ser July 31st, 61 dis Feb. 13th 62 from pri at Birds Point.

J. W. Jones 5th ser, Sep 6th '61.

Frank W. Crosby 1st Cor, Sep 6th '61, pro Quarter Master, Sep 31st '61.

J. B. Hancock 2d Cor, Sep 6th '61, killed May 16th '63 at Champion Hills, Miss.

Wm. J. Carson 3d Cor, Sep 6th '61, hon dis Sep 27th '62 at St. Louis.

A. Davis 4th Cor, Sep 9th '61.

John R. Lux 5th Cor, Sep 6th '61,

N. P. Gray 6th Cor, Sep 6th '61, wd May 16th '63 at Champion Hills, Miss.

Joseph Kellogg Cor, July 31st '61, from private.

Angello Myers 7th Cor, Sep 6th '61, wd Jan 8th '62, near Charleston Mo., hon dis July 25th '62. at Corinth Miss.

N. P. Stephenson 8th Cor, Sep 6th '61, wd May 16th '63, Champion Hills, Miss.

E. A. Jeffreys Cor, July 31st '61 from private, hon dis at St. Louis Mo.

C. L. Palmer muscian, Sep 6th '61.

C. W. Woodward musician. Sep 6th '61.

Wm. Watts wagoner, Sep 6th '61.

J. W. Appelgate pri, July 31st '61, m in Sep 5th '61. died April 24th '63 at Memphis, Tenn. of small pox.

Wm. Appelgate pri, July 31st '61, m in Sep 6th '61, wd May 16th '63 at Champion Hills, Miss, and again Nov. 25th '63 at Missionary Ridge, Tenn.

Charles Bailey pri, July 31st '61, m in Sep 6th '61, taken prisoner June 25th '62.

O. Baldy, pri, July 31st '61, m in Sep 6th '61,

Truman Bixby pri, July 31st '61, m in Sep 6th '61, died at Mound City Ill. Nov. 27th '61.

Thomas Brannan pri, July 31st '61, m in Sep 6th '61, wd May 16th '63 at Champion Hills,

Charles Bunce pri, July 31st '61, m in Sep 6th '61, hon dis at St Louis.

E. B. Bailey pri, July 31st '61, m in Sep 6th '61.

Joseph Budka pri, July 31st '61, m in Sep 6th 61, killed May 1st '63 at Champion Hills, Miss. in battle.

Wm. H. Bryon pri, July 31st m in Sep 6th '61, died July 26th '62 at Clear Creek, Mississippi.

Dorson Chase pri, July 31st '61, m in Sep 6th '61, pro to 4th Sergeant.

Eli Clark pri, July 31st '61, died of disease at Farmington, Miss. May 30th '62.

Thomas Clem pri, July 31st '61, m in Sep 6th '61.

J. W. B. Cole pri, July 31st '61, m in Sep 6th '61.

James Connor pri, July 31st '61 m in Sep 6th '61, transferred Feb. 15th '64 to invalid corps.

R. D. Crosby pri, July 31st '61, m in Sep 6th '61.

Benjaman Dunbar pri, July 31st '61, m in Sep 6th '61, wd May 16th 63 at Champion Hills, Mississippi.

James Fairbank pri, July 31st '61, m in Sep 6th '61.

A. J. Filloon pri, July 31st '61 m in Sep 6th '61, wd May 6th '64 at Vicksburg, Miss. and died July 25th '63 at Milliken's Bend, La, of typhoid fever.

Thomas S. Free pri, July 31st m in Sep 6th '61.

Geo. W. Guilford pri, July 31st '61, m in Sep 6th '61, wd May 16th '63 at Champion Hills and again Nov 25th '63, at Missionary Ridge, Tenn.

Andrew Goodwin pri, July 31st '61, m in Sep 6th '61.

Geo. M. Gray pri, July 31st '61, m in Sep 6th '61, died at Cape Girardean Nov 2d '61.

T. Griffin pri, July 31st '61, m in Sep 6th 61, hon dis Jan 8th '63 at St Louis.

A. B. Harman pri, July 31st '61, m in Sep 6th '61, wd May 16th '63 at Champion Hills.

Solomon Haworth pri, July 31st '61, m in Sep 6th '61, hon dis Dec 8th '62 at Mound City, Ill.

J. P. Henry pri, July 31st '61, m Sep 6th '61, hon dis at St. Louis, Mo Dec 8th '62

C. J, Herrick pri, July 31st '61, m in Sep 6th '61, killed May 16th '63 at Champion Hills in battle.

Peter Higgins pri, July 31st '61, m in Sep 6th '61.

John Hillmon pri, July 31st '61 m in Sep 6th '61.

B. F Howard pri, July 31st '61, m in Sep 6th '61.

Wm. T. Hiatt, private, July 31st '61, m in Sep 6th '61. dis November 28th '62 at Davenport.

E. A. Jeffreys, private, July 31st '61, m in Sep 6th '61, hon dis Oct 22d, '62 St. Louis.

A. H. Kellogg pri, July 31st '61, m in Sep 6th '61, wd Jan 8th 62d near Charleston Mo. and hon dis Nov 30th '63 at Cairo, Ill.

James H. Lorimer pri, July 31st '61, m in Sep 6th '61, wd May 16th '63 at Champion, Hills.

Thomas Laughlin pri, July 31st '61, m in Sep 6th 61. captured Dec 12th '61, on the Cairo and Fulton R, R. and died Jan 22d '63 a prisoner of war.

Jacob Lux pri, July 31st '61, m in Sep 6th '61, died March 27th '62, near Madrid Mo. of typhoid fever.

Henry Levin pri, July 31st '61, m in Sep 6th '61, transferred Dec 1st '63 to invalid corps.

Cyrus Maholm pri, July 31st '61 m in Sep 6th '61, wd Jan 8th '62, near Charleston Mo.

Geo McCall pri, July 31st '61, m in Sep 6th '61, hon dis at Davenport, Iowa Oct 15th '62.

Jasper Misner pri, July 21st '61, m in Sept 8th '61, transferred July 25th '64 to invalid corps.

M. M. Myers pri, July. 31st '61, m in Sep 6th '61, died May 18th '64 at Madison, Ind of disease.

Geo. Newport pri, July 31st '61, m in Sep 6th '61, died Dec 3d '61 at Mound City Hospital Ill,

S. D. Newton pri, July 31st '61, m in Sep 6th '61, wd Nov 25th '61 at Missionary Ridge, Tenn.

F. Omwake pri, July 31st '61, m in Sep 6th '61, hon dis Feb 1st '63, St Louis.

C. W. Peck pri, July 31st '61, m in Sep 6th '61, killed May 16th '63, Champion Hill, Miss. in battle.

H. R. Pugh pri, July 31st '61, m in Sep 6th '61, died of disease, Birds Point Jan 15th '62.

Phillip Ramsey pri, July 31st '61, m in Sep 6th '61, killed in battle at Champion Hills May 16th '63

Wesley Randall pri, July 31st '61, m in Sep 6th '61, wd Oct 4th '63 at Corinth Miss and died Nov 8th '62.

Wm. W. Reed pri, July 31st '61 m in September 6th '61

Jacob Reinig pri, July 31st '61, m in September 6th' 61,

M. Rhoades pri, July 31st, '61, m in Sep, 6th '61 wd Nov. 25th '63, Missionary
  Ridge, Tenn. in the hand.
J. H. Richardson pri, July 31st '61, m in Sep, 6th, 61,
A. M. Roberts pri, July 31st. '61, m in Sep. 6th '61 wd Oct. 4th '62, Corinth, Miss.
  in the shoulder.
J. C. Rouse pri, July 31st '61, m in Sep 6th '61 killed May 16th '63 at Champion
  Hills, Miss. in battle.
C Ronband pri, July 31st '61, m in Sep, 6th '61 died Nov. 15th '62 at Davis Mills
  Miss. of accidental shot.
John Sawyer pri, July 31st '61, m in Sep. 6th '61.
J. H. Smith pri, July 31st '61, m in Sep. 6th '61.
James Smith pri, July 31st '61, m in Sep. 6th '61 died at St. Louis, Mo.
E. A. Southard, pri, July 31st '61 m in Sep. 6th '61 hon dis, Feb 3d '62 at Birds'
  Point Mo.
E. M. Stevens pri, July 31st '61, m in Sep 6th '61, hon dis Nov 11th '64 at Car-
  tersville Ga.
R. N. Stevens pri, July 31st '61. m in Sep 6th '61, hon dis Feb 5th '62 at Birds
  Point. Mo.
Wm. H. Stoddard pri, July 31st '61, m in Sep 6th '61, pro to 2d Lieutenant
  June 27th '62.
F. Tice pri, July 31st '61, m in Sep 6th '61.
A, Tice pri July 31st '61, m in Sep 6th '61 wd in action near Charleston, Mo,
  Jan 8th '62,
S. W. Tompkins pri, July 31st '61, m in Sep 6th '61, died at St Louis. May 24th
  1862.
James Turner pri, July 31st '61, m in Sep 6th '61, hon dis Jan 29th '62 at St.
  Louis, Mo.
N. Van Horn pri, July 31st '61. m in Sep. 6th '61 killed May 16th '63, Cham-
  pion Hills. Miss. in battle.
Geo. Van Riper pri, July 31st '61, m in Sep 6th '61.
Samuel Walker pri, July 31st '61, m in Sep 6th '61.
James Walton pri, July 31st '61, m in Sep 6th '61, wd May 16th '63 at Cham-
  pion Hills.

Wm. W. Yarham pri, July 31st, 61, m in Sep 6th '61,
James Young pri. July 31st '61, m in. Sep 6th '61. dis Jan 24th '63 at St. Louis.
Joseph Kellogg pri July 31st '61 m in Sep. 6th '61.
James Newport pri July 31st '61 m in Sep. 6th '61 died at Mound City, Ill,

Chas. D. Bailey pri, Sep 11th '61, m in March 1st '62, joined from Co D,
D. B. Mason, pri. Sep 11th '61, m in March 1st '62, joined from Co D.
Van Buren Rugg, pri, Sep 9th '61, m in March 1st '62, joind from Co D, died
  Clear Creek Miss. July 14th '62.
Charles T. Davis pri, Sep 5th '61, m in March 1st '62, joined from Co D died
  May 12th '62, at Toledo, Tama County. Iowa.
M. B. Myers pri, Sep 7th '61, m in March 1st '62, joined from Co D hon dis at
  Corinth Oct 28th '62,
Luke Camp pri, Feb 14th 62, m in March 1st 62, died Aug 27th '63 at Vicks-
  burg, Miss.

Wesley Camp, pri, Feb 14th '62, m in March 1st '62, hon dis Feb 20th '63 at St Louis, Mo.

E. Evans, pri, Feb 14th '62, and hon dis at Davenport May 6th '64,

H. R. Free, pri, Sep 2d '62, enlisted for 9 mo. dis at Corinth Oct 31st '62.

Fourteenth Infantry.

Company G.

W. H. Stivers Capt. Nov 6th '61, com Nov 4th '61, resigned Jan 24th 62.

Wm. Gallagher 1st Lt, Jan 25 '62 from 2d Lt.   missing at Shiloh April 6th '62,

S. F. Eccles 2d Lt, Oct 9th '61, m in Jan 25th '62 from 1st Ser, prisoner at Shiloh died at Madrid, Ga Aug 26th '62.

Simon F. Eccles 1st Ser, Oct 9th '61, m in Nov 2d 61, pro to 2d Lt Jan 25th '62.

J. A. Shanklin 1st Ser, Oct 9th '61, m in Jan 25th '62, from 2d Cor, missing at Shiloh.

G. A. Walroth 1st Ser, Nov 9th '61 from 4th Ser, dis at Danville, Miss, August 20th '62.

E. G. Oldroid 3d Ser, Nov 8th '61, m in Nov 2d '61, wd April 6th '62 at Shiloh, hon dis June '63,at Toledo.

G. A. Walroth 4th Ser, Oct 9th '61, m in Nov 2d '61 ,pro to 1st Ser, hon dis Aug 20th 1862 at Danville, Miss.

Peter Wilson 1st Cor, Oct 9th '61, m in Nov 2d '61.

B. F. Thomas 3d Cor, Oct '61 m in Nov 2d '61, captd April 6th '62 a, Shiloh.

John Maholm 4th Cor, Oct 9th '61, m in Nov 2d '61, hon dis April 25th '63 Benton Barracks, Mo.

Wm. Breese 4th Cor, Oct 9th '61, m in Dec 14th '61, from private.

J. A, Pope 6th Cor, Oct 10th '61 from pri, captd April 6th '62 at Shiloh and died July 11th '62 at Mound City of fever.

John Gaston 8th Cor, Oct 9th '61 from pri. dis at Corinth July 17th '62.

James Fox musican, Oct 9th '61, m in Nov 2d '61, captd April 6th '62, Shiloh.

L. Brannan pri, Oct 9th '61, m in Nov 2d '61 captd April 6th '62, Shiloh.

L. Bowen pri, Oct 9th '61, m in Nov 2d '61, died of measles at Benton Barracks Dec 22d '61.

J. Burright pri, Oct 9th '61, m in Nov 2d '61, captd April 6th '62, at Shiloh, Tenn trans Sep 3d '63 to invalid corps.

C. Burright pri, Oct 9th '61, m in Nov 2d '61.

S. Burright pri, Oct 9th '61, m in Nov 2d '61.

S. Clark pri, Oct 22d '61, m in Nov 2d '61.

M. Clark pri, Oct 9th '61, m in Nov 2d 61 captd April 6th '62, at Shiloh.

R. F. Clark pri, Oct 9th '61, m in Nov 6th '61, captd April 6th '62 at Shiloh and died May 15th '62, at Mobile, Ala.

E. Dykeman pri, Oct 9th '61, m in Nov 2d '61, died July 19th '63 at Columbus,Ky.

J. R. Edwards pri, Oct 9th '61, m in Nov 2d '61, captd and wd April 9th '62.

Charles Edwards pri, Oct 11th '61, m in Nov 4th '61,

R. Fitch pri, Oct 22d '61, m in Nov 2d '61, captd April 6th '62, at Shiloh, dis Dec '62 at St Louis, Mo.

J. R. Felter pri, Oct 22d '61, m in Nov 2d '61, captd April 6th '62 at Shiloh, Tenn.

M. Grubbs pri, Oct 9th '61, m in Nov 2d '61, captd April 6th '62 at Shiloh.

John Gaston pri, Oct 9th '61, m in Nov 2d '61, pro to 8th Cor, dis July 17th '62 at Corinth, Miss.

Wm. L. Goit pri, Oct 9th '61, m in Nov 2d '61, captd April 6th '62 at Shiloh, dis Dec '62 at St. Louis,

J, Hunnicutt pri, Oct 12th '61, m in Nov 2d '61, captd April 6th '62. at Shiloh,

Geo. Heimlick pri, Oct 6th '61 m in Nov 2d '61.

G. Hiatt pri, Oct 9th '61, m in Nov 2d '61, captured May 6th '61, at Shiloh and wd May 18th '64, at Buyan DeGlaize, La.

A, Kellogg pri, Oct 22d '61, m in Nov 2d '61, dis at Corinth Miss, July 8th '62.

J. H. Luke pri, Oct 9th '61, m in Nov 2d '61, captd April 6th '62. Shiloh.

Henry Loomis pri, Oct 9th '61, m in Nov 4th '61, wd April 6th '62 at Shiloh and dis August 25th '62.

J. Miles pri, Oct 9th '61, m in Nov 2d '61, wd April 6th '62, at Shiloh.

David Miles pri, Oct 9th '61, m in Nov 24 '61, captured April 6th '62 at Shiloh, died May 27th '62, at Montgomery, Ala, while a prisoner of war.

J. R. Myers pri, Oct 9th '61, m in Nov 2d '61, captd April 6th '62 Shiloh.

J. E McKune pri, Oct. 9th '61, m in Nov 2d '62 captd April 6th '62, at Shiloh, died August 9th '62 at Macon, Ga, while a prisoner of war.

J. B Overturf pri, Oct 9th '61, m in Nov 2d '61, captd April 6th '62. at Shiloh, dis March 27th '62 at St Louis.

L. Powell pri, Oct 9th '61, m in Nov 2d ,61, dis Feb 5th '61 at Davenport.

J. A. Pope pri, Oct 10th '61, m in Fov 2d '61, pro to 6th Cor, captd April 16th '62, at Shiloh, died July 11th '62. Mound City Ill. of fever.

E. Stokes pri, Oct 29th '61, m in Nov 2d '61, captd April 6th '62 at Shiloh, dis Nov 8th '62 at St Louis.

D. Southwick pri, Oct 29th '61, m in Nov 2d '62, captd April 6th '62 at Shiloh, died Aug 20th '62 at St Louis.

J. B. Wineman pri, Oct 29th '61, m in Nov 2d '61, captd April 6th '62 at Shiloh.

H. H. Williams pri, Oct 29th '61, m in Nov 2d '61, captd April 6th '62 Shiloh.

D. S. Young pri, Oct 20th '61, m in Nov 2d '61, captd April 6th '62 at Shiloh, dis April 7th '63.

E. S. Young pri, Oct 12th '61, m in Nov 2d '61, dis April 6th '62, at Cincinnatti, O.

David Zehrung pri, Oct 12th '61, m in Nov 2d '61, captd April 6th '62, dis March 31st '63.

Twenty-Fourth Infantry.

Company E.

Leander Clark Capt, Aug 21st '62. m in Sep 18th '61, Maj June 9th '64.

S. S Dillman 2nd Lt, Aug 21st '62. m in Sep 18th '61.

James Rokes 2nd Ser, Aug 18th '62 m in Sep 18th '62, 1st Lt Sep 20th '62. Capt Nov 19th 1864.

M. Mefford 4th Ser, Aug 21st '62. m in Sep 28th '62.

J. S. Edmonds 1st Cor, Aug 21st '62, m in Aug 28th '62. died Sep 22d '63.

E. S. Edwards 1st Cor, Aug 23d '61, m in Oct 3rd '61 from pri.

T. N. Perkins 3d Cor, Aug 21st '62, m in Aug 28th '62, died April 21st '63 Helena, Ark, of disease.

Geo. W. Stoddard 5th Cor, Aug 21st '62, m in Aug 28th '62, killed May 16th '63, Champion Hills, Miss. in action.

J. H. Lewis 7th Cor, Aug 21st '62 m in Aug 28th '62.

G. Alexander pri, Aug 21st '62 m in Aug 28th '62.

E. Bailey pri, Aug 21st '62, m in Aug 28th '62.

Wm. W. Beatty pri, Aug 21st '62 m in Aug 28th '62 died at Keokuk, of disease Nov 13th' 62.

J. W. Conant pri, Aug 18th' 62, m in Aug 28th 62, captd April 8th '64 Mansfield, La

J. W. Coe pri, Aug 22d '62 m in Aug 28th '62.

S. Dykeman pri, Aug 21st '62, m in Aug 28th '62, died July 8th '63 St Louis, Mo,

A. J. Dew pri, Aug 21st '62, m in Aug 28th '62, died May 12th '62, St Louis, Mo.

W. Dobson pri, Aug 22d '62, m in Aug 28th '62, captd Sep 19th '64 Winchester, Va

E. S. Edwards pri, Aug 22d '62, m in Aug 28th 62, pro first Cor Oct 3d 62, trans Dec 15th '63, to invalid corps.

R. Filloon pri, Aug 21st '62, m in Aug 28th '62.

A. H. Feeler pri, Aug 21st '62, m in Aug 28th '62.

W. Gower pri, Aug 21st '63 m in Aug 28th '62.

George Hillmon pri, Aug 18th '62, m in Aug 28th '62, wd May 16th '63 Champion Hills, Miss in action, died May 21st '63.

George Hemstead pri, Aug 18th '62, m in Aug 28th '62, dis Feb 20th '63 Helena, Ark

Wm. J. Knight pri, Aug 21st '62 m in Aug 28th '62, died June 18th '63 near Vicksburg, Miss.

D. W. Laughlin pri, Aug 21st '62, m in Aug 28th 62, dis Jan 21st '63 St. Louis, Mo.

J. A. Lamm pri, Aug 21st '62, m in Aug 28th '62, captd May 16th '63 Champion Hills, Miss.

G. W. Lonthan pri, Aug 21st '63, m in Aug 28th '62.

N. B. Loomis pri, Aug 20th '62, m in Aug 28th '62, dis Feb 19th '63 Helena, Ark.

M. Mink pri, Aug 21st 62, m in Aug 28th '62, wounded Oct 19th '64 Cedar Creek, Va severely in left thigh, died Dec 7th '64, Winchester, Va, of wounds.

John Mubeah pri, Aug 20th '62, m in Aug 28th 62,

L. Mitchell pri, Aug 22nd '62 m in Aug 28th '62 died Sep 1st '63, Jefferson Barracks, Mo.

O. N. Mason pri, Aug 20th '62, m in Aug 28th' 62,

S. W. McGee pri, Aug 19th '62 m in Aug 28th '62, pied at Muscatine, Oct 28th '62.

C. F. McGee pri, Aug 15th '62 m in Aug 28th '62, trans April 30th '64 Invalid corps.

John Misner pri, Aug 20th '62, m in Aug 28th '62.

J. Pass pri, Aug 21st '62 m in Aug 28th '62 wd Sep 19th '64 Winchester Va.

Henry Philips pri, Aug 21st '62 m in Aug 28th '62 dis Aug 23rd '63 Corinth, La.

S. R, Rushton pri, Aug 20th '62, m in Aug 28th 62, wd and captd April 8th '64 Mansfield, La.

J. M. Snow pri, Aug 21st 63, m in Aug 20th '62.

E. O. Thomas pri, Aug 20th '62, m in August 28th '62, dis Feb 20th '63, Helena Arkansas for disibility.

I. Vorhes pri, Aug 21st '62, m in Aug 28th '62.

F. Vernier pri, Aug 21st '62, m in Aug 28th '62, captd May 16th '63 at Champion Hills, Miss,

W. T. Wilber pri, Aug 21st '62, m in Aug 28th, dis Aug 23d '63, Charlston, La.

E. Brewer pri, March 28th '64 m in April 18th '64, wd Sep 19th '63 at Winchester.

Va trans April 28th '65 to veteran reserve corps.

W. L. Conant pri, Jan 1st '64, m in Jan 28th '64, captd April 8th '64 at Mansfield

I. Donald pri, Jan 5th '64, m in Jan 28th '64.

E. H. Finch pri, Jan 23d '64, m in Jan 28th '64.

D. O. Gardner pri, Feb 29th '64, m in March 11th '64.

M. Harris pri, Jan 5th '64, m in Jan 28th '64, died June 30th '64, on hospital boat
on the Mississippi River,

B. C. Hayes pri, Feb 29th '64, m in March 11th '64.

A. B. Knight pri, Jan 1st '64, m in Jan 28th '64.

A. T. King pri, Jan 1st '64, m in March 22d '64.

W. S. King pri, Jan 1st '64, m in Jan 28th '64.

J. Lamm pri, Jan 5th '63, m in Jan 28th '64, died in hospital at New Orleans
May 11th '64,

H. Merrill pri, Jan 1st '64, m in Jan 28th '64,

G. Parcher pri, March 31st '64, m in April 18th '64, died Sep 28th '64, at Cen-
tralia, Ill.

A. J. Roberts pri, March 31st '64, m in April 18th '64, wd Oct 19th 64.

Philip Rheads pri, Jan 1st, 64, m in Jan 28th 64.

Allen Mason pri, Jan 5th 64, m in Jan 5th 64, dis May 30th 64. at New Orleans.

A. A. Swarthout pri, March 31st 64, m in April 18th 64, died before reaching the
company,

E. S. Beckley pri, Jan 8th 1864.

E. Granger pri, Jan 1st 1864.

James Young pri, Jan 1st 1864.

Twenty-Eigth Infantry.

Company F.

John A. Staley Capt, August 5th '62, m in Oct 10th '62, com Oct 10th '62.

T. Schaffer 1st Lt, Aug 8th '62, m in Oct 10th '62, com Oct 10th '62, Capt company
F. Jan 13th '62.

J. Myers 2d Lieutenant, Aug 13th '62, m in Sep 9th '62, com Oct 10th '62, died
Aug 14th '63, at Helena, Ark.

G. G. Edmond 1st Ser, Aug 5th '62, m in Sept 15th '62, Appointed Aug 15th '62,
2d Ser Nov 1st '62,

J. S. Ferguson 1st Ser Aug 9th '62, m in Nov 1st '62, from second Ser, wd and
captd April 8th '64, at Sabine Cross Roads, dis July 28th '65, at Keokuk.

Louis Lopee 3d Ser, Aug 12th '62, m in Sep 15th '62.

J. Casey 4th Ser, Aug 14th '62, m in Sep 15th '62, appointed Aug 15th '62.

H. A. Weaver Ser, Aug 8th '62, m in Sep 15th '62, appointed Oct 15th '62, taken
prisoner Aug 29th '62.

J. W. Hiatt 1st Cor, Aug 15th '62, m in Sep 15th '62, wd May 16th '63 at Champion
Hills, died at same place of wd June 7th '63.

J. W. Fielding 2d Cor Aug 13th '62, died Oct 24th '63, New Orleans La.

W. Nixon 3d Cor Aug 15th '62, m in Sep 15th '62, wd May '6th '63, Champoin
Hills, captd Sep 19th '64, Winchester, Va.

J. H. Davis 4th Cor, Aug 5th '62 m in Sep 15th '62.

P. H. Mason 5 h Cor, Aug 12th '62, m in Sep 16th '64, wd May 1st '63, Port Gibson, Miss, trans Apri 12th '64 to invalid corps.

John Myers 6th Cor, Aug 15th '62, m in Sep 15th '62, wd May 1st '63 at Port Gibson, died Aug 14th '63 Helena Ark of disease.

B. F. Hubbart 7th Cor, Aug 15th '62, m in Sep 15th '62, dis Jan 23d '63, Mound City

D. W Emerson 7th Cor, Aug 7th '62, m in Nov 1st '62, from pri, died March 19th '63 Helena Ark.

J. S. Bishop 8th Cor, Aug 15th '62, m in Sep 15th '62, died Sep 8th '63 at Penna Landing La of disease.

S. J. M. Bear, Musician, Aug 15th '62, m in Sep 15th '62, dis April 23d '63 Helena.

J. Spindler musician, Aug 14th '62.

J. B. Daily, wagoner, Aug 15th '62, m in Sep 15th 62, dis April 23d '63, at Helena.

S. W. Arbuthnot pri, Aug 15th '62, m in Sep 15th '62, wd May 16th '63 at Champion Hills, dis Feb 8th '64, at St Louis.

E. W. Bunce pri, Aug 15th '62, m in Sep 15th '62, dis Oct 16th '64, Cedar Creek, Va

A. L. Babb pri, Aug 15th '62, m in Sep 15th '62.

W. Beal pri, Aug 11th '62 m in Sep 15th '62, dis April 24th '63, St Louis, Mo.

B. F. Brannan pri, Aug 5th '62 m in Sep 15th '62, captd Dec 29th '62, Helena, Ark trans May '64 to invalid corps.

John Blair pri, Aug 9th '62, m in Sep 15th '62.

N. Bywaters pri Aug 15th '62, m in Sep 15th '62, captd Oct 24th, '63 at Opelousas.

J. S. Brants pri, Aug 13th '62, m in Sep 15th '62, dis Aug 17th '63 at Memphis.

J. Behonneck pri, Aug 15th '62, m in Sep 15th '62, wd Sep 23d '64 at Fishers' Hill.

J. Chess pri, Aug 15th '62 m in Sep 15th '62 captd May 16th '63, Champion Hills, Miss. also at Cedar Creek, Va, Oct 19th '64.

John Chess pri, Aug 15th '62, m in Sep 15th '64, dis Nov 8th '64, at Camp Russell.

J. Crawford pri, Aug 15th '62, m in Sep 15th '62, wd Sep 13th '64 Winchester, Va.

C. C. Collins pri, Aug 14th '62, m in Sep 15th 62.

P. Cass pri, Aug 15th '62, m in Sep 15th '62,

S. G. Clark pri, Aug 13th '62, m in Sep 15th '62, wd June 10th '63 at Vicksburg.

O. T. Clark pri, Aug 14th '62, m in Sep 15th '62.

L. D. Campbell pri, Aug 12th '62, m in Sep 15th '62.

F. M. Conner pri, Aug 13th '62, m in Sep 15th '62, taken prisoner Dec 29th '62 at Helena Ark, dis April 1st '64 New Orleans, La.

B. F. Davis pri. Aug 15th '62, m in Sep 15th '62, dis March 3d '63 at Helena, Ark.

D. W. Emerson pri, Aug 7th '62 m in Sep 15th '62, pro to 7th Cor Nov 1st '62, died March 19th '63 at Helena.

E. J. Eldridge pri, Aug 14th '62, m in Sep 15th '62.

J. Fouts pri, Aug 13th '62, m in Sep 15th '62.

D. Frun pri, Aug 14th '62 m in Sep 15th '62, dis Jan 14th '62, St Louis.

J. L. Fitzgerald pri, Aug 15th '62, m in Sep 15th '62, wd May 1st '63 at Port Gibson. Miss.

J. Freeman pri, Aug 9th '62, m in Sep 15th '62, died May 11th '63 on James' plantation.

G. C. Freeman pri, Aug 14th '62, m in Sep 15th '62.

J. W. Flathers pri. Aug 15th '62, m in Sep 15th '62, captd July '63 Jackson Miss.

J. Freedle pri, Aug 15th '62, m in Sep 15th '62.

T. S. Finch pri, Aug 15th '62 m in Sep 15th '62, died Feb 6th '63 St Louis.

D. E. Finch pri, Aug 14th '62, m in Sep 15th '62, dis Feb 19th '63 at St Louis.

A. S. Godfrey pri, Aug 15th '62, m in Sep 15th '62, died Aug 13th '63.

Wm. Grubb pri, Aug 15th '62, m in Sep 15th '62, captd Oct 24th '92, Opelousas, La. missing Sep 19th '64, Winchester, Va.

J. C. Hopkins pri, Aug 15th '62 m in Sep 15th '52, died Jan 29th '63, on steamer Emma, near Cairo.

J. Hillman pri, Aug 15th '62, m in Sep 15th '62.

S. Holacker pri, Aug 15th '62, m in Sep 15th '62, Sabine Cross Roads, La.

J. D. Hutchinson pri, Aug 11th '62, m in Sep 16th '62.

S. W. Hammitt pri, Aug 14th '62, m in Sep 15th '63, killed May 16th '63, Champion Hills,Miss, in battle.

W. Hanna pri, Aug 9th '62, m in Sep 15th '62, wd and captd Sep 19th '64, Winchester, Va

J. Hart pri, Aug 14th '62 m in Sep 15th '62, captd April 8th '64, Sabine Cross ing, La.

John Hate pri, Aug 15th '62, m in Sep 15th '62, died April 18th '65, Savannah, Ga.

H. Hate pri, Aug 9th ,62, m in Sep 15th '62.

A. Jack pri, Aug 15th '62, m in Sep 15th 62, killed April 8th '64.

L. A. Kirk pri, Aug 12th '62, m in Sep 15th '62, dis April 6th '63, Memphis. Tenn.

A. Kosta pri, Aug 5th '62, m in Sep 16th '62.

S. W. Myers pri, Aug 15th '62, m in Set 15th '62, captd Oct 24th '63, Opelousas, La

R. Metz pri, Aug 15th '62, m in Sep 15th '62.

H. M. Miller pri, Aug 14th '62, m in Sep 15th '63, wd May 16th '63 Champion Hills Miss, died June 7th '63, of wounds.

G. A. Moss pri, Aug 14th '62, m in Sep 15th '62, wd May 16th '63 Champion Hills, Miss.

C. L. McNair pri, Aug 15th '62, m in Sep 15th '62, died Jan 22d '63, Helena, Ark.

D. Nance pri, Aug 14th 62, m in Sep 15th '62, died June 30th '63, St Louis, Mo.

J. B. Nicodemus pri, Aug 15th '62, m in Sep 15th '62, died Aug 20th '64 Washington, D. C.

P. P. Nungesser pri, Aug 15th '62, m in Sep 15th '62.

J. B. Reed pri, Aug 15th '62, m in Sep 15th '62, died April 10th '63, Helena, Ark.

C. M. Reed pri, Aug 15th '62, m in Sep 15th '62.

Wm T. Richardson pri, Aug 14th '62, m in Sep 15th '62, dis April 4th '63, Helena, Ark.

B. W. Russell pri, Aug 7th '62, m in Sep 15th '62, killed May 16th '63, Champion Hills, Miss.

J. E. Rockenfield pri, Aug 15th '62, m in Sep 15th '62 wd May 16th '63, Champion Hills, Miss, dis Oct 21st '63, at Keokuk.

C. W. Sipes pri, Aug 13th '62, m in Sep 15th '62, missing Sep 19th '64 Winchester.

I. Spindler pri, Aug 13th '62, m in Sep 15th '62.

F. Schaeffer pri, Aug 14th, '62, m in Sep 15th '62, captd April 8th '64 at Sabine Cross Roads, La.

D. Shelton pri, Aug 10th '62, m in Sep 15th '62, taken prisoner Dec 29th '62 captd Dec 29th '62 at Helena, Ark, killed May 16th '63, Champion Hills.

F. Sheldon pri, Aug 13th '62, m in Sep 15th '62, wd Sep 19th ,64 at Winchester,Va died Nov 14th '64, at Philadelphia.

J. H. Scott pri, Aug 14th '62, m in Sep 15th '62, wd and captd April 8th '64, at

Sabine Cross Roads, La. dis May 23th '65.

T. Southern pri. Aug 24th '62, m in Sep 15th '62, killed May 16th '63. Champion Hills.

J. A. Snap pri. Aug 14th '62, m in Sep 15th '62, killed May 16th '63, Champion Hills.

Wm. Taylor pri. Aug 13th '62, m in Sep 15th '62.

W. W. Vandorn pri. Aug 15th '62, m in Sep 15th '62, dis Dec 8th '63 Benton Barracks, Mo.

D. Way pri. Aug 13th '62, m in Sep 15th 62, dis June 18th '63, Milligan's Bend.

G. Williams pri. Aug 15th '62, m in Sep 15th '62, killed May 16th '63 at Champion Hills, Miss.

H. J. Williams pri. Aug 9th '62, m in Sep 15th '62, dis March 1st '64. New Orleans

John Wilson pri. Aug 15th '62, m in Sep 15th '62, captd May 16th '62, at Champion Hills.

J. Wood pri, Aug 15th '62, m in Sep 15th '62, wd Oct 19th '64 at Cedar Creek, Va.

J. Bain Pri, Dec 26th '63, m in Jan 23d '64.

E. M. Bielby pri Jan 1st '64, m in Feb 2d '64.

E. S. Beckley pri, Jan 8th '64, m in Feb 2d '64, missed Sep 19th '64 Winchester.

G. W. Bricker pri. March 25th '64, m in April 6th '64, died Aug 1st '64, at St Louis

J. B. M. Bishop pri. Feb 13th '64, m in March 1st '64, wd Sep 19th '64, Winchester.

S. Bruner pri. Feb 22d '64 m in March 1st '64, dis Oct 3d '62.

Wm. C. Crawford pri. Feb 13th '64, m in March 1st '64.

J. A. Davis pri. Feb 11th '64, m in March 1st '64, wd Oct 19th '64 at Cedar Creek.

J. Davis pri. Dec 23d '63, m in Jan 23d '64,

H. D. Fuller pri. Jan 22d '64, m in Feb 22d '64, wd Oct 19th Cedar Creek.

E. Granger pri. Jan 1st '64, m in Jan 15th '64.

A. H. Hisey pri. Feb 3d '64, m in Feb 3d '64.

J. M. Hammitt pri. Feb 11th '64, m in March 1st '64, wd Oct 19th '64 at Cedar Creek, Va.

W. Heyer pri. Feb 3d '64, m in, Feb 3d '64.

N. Miller pri' Feb 29th '64, m in March 16th '64

C. J. Moyer pri. Feb 17th '64, m in March 1st '64.

H. T. Miller pri. Feb 11th '64 m in March 1st '64.

S. B. Overmire pri. Feb 11th '64, m in March 1st '64,

A. D. Olney pri. Jan 1st '64, m in Jan 19th '64, dis Aug 1st '64, New Orleans.

A. J, Plumer pri. March 24th '64, m in April 6th '64,

H. A. Read pri. Jan 5th '64, m in Jan 23d '64,

J. Reedy pri. Jan 15th '64, m in Jan 23d '64,

J. Young Pri, Jan 2d '64, m in Jan 19th '64, wd Oct 19th '64, at Cedar Creek, Va died Oct 20th, '64, Martinsburg, Va.

G. F. Crawford pri. Oct 1st '64, m in Oct 1st '64.

Fourteenth Infantry.

Company A.

J, Luke 3rd Ser, Dec 1st '63, m in Dec 1st '63, from Com G.

L. B. Hartman 5th Ser, Dec 30th '63, m in Jan 23d '64, from Com G.

J. W. McRoberts 3rd Cor, Jan 2d '64, m in Jan 23d '64, from Co G.

C. F. Alexander pri, Jan 10th '64, m in Feb 21st '64, from Co G wd April 6th '64 Shiloh, Tenn. died July 10th '64, of wounds.

J. C. Barrett pri, Deb 3d '64, m in Feb 3d '64, from Com G.

H. S. Cunningham pri. Feb 21st '64, m in Feb 25th '64, from Co G.

E. Gallion pri, Feb 18th '64, m in March 1st '64 from Co G, wd July 15th '64, Tupelo Miss.

P. E. Greenlief pri, Feb 11th '64, m in Feb 25th '64, from Co G,

Geo Helm pri, March 31st '64, m in April 9th '64, from Co G.

M. C. Ingham pri, Jan 23d '64, m in Jan 23d '64, from Co G.

J. W. Kresson pri, Dec 30th '63, m in Jan 23th '64, from Co G.

J. M. Letler pri Jan 26th '64, m in Feb 4th '64, from Co G.

W. Leach pri, Jan 4th '64, m in Jan 23d '64. from Co G.

J. Mills pri, Dec 1st '63, m in Dec 1st '63, from Co G, wd April 6th'62,Shiloh, Tenn

J. Morton pri, Dec 21st '63, Jan 23d '64, from Co G wd and captd April 9th '64. Pleasant Hill, La.

J Manerth pri, Jan 5th '64, m in Jan 23d '64, from Co G captd April 9th '64, Pleasant Hill, La.

D. Rosenberger pri. Jan 4th '64, m in Jan 23d, '64. from Co G.

J. Rosenberger pri, Feb 3d '64, m in Feb 3d '64, from Co G.

W. Rogers pri, Dec 23d '63,m in Jan 23d '64 from Co G.

A. Reins pri, Jan 4th '64, m in Jan 23d '64, from Co G.

G. W. Shiner pri, Jan 1st '64, m in Jan 23d '64, from Co G.

W. Spear pri, Jan 4th '64, m in Jan 23d '64, from Co G.

C. Vimpany pri, Dec 21st '63, m in Jan 7th '64, from Co G. captd April 9th '64, Pleasant Hill.

P. B. Willey pri Jan 5th '64, m in Jan 23d '64, from Co G.

J. H. Wilkins pri, Dec 21st '63, m in Jan 18th '64, from Co G. wd and captd April 9th '64, Pleasant Hill, La.

Geo. Yarham pri, Dec 30th '63, m in Jan 19th '64, from Co G.

Fifth Infantry.

Company D.

L. D. F. Lewis 6th Cor, July 1st '61, m in July 15th '61.

M. Carter pri, July 1st '61, m in July 15th '61.

A. D. Eaton pri, July 1st '61, m in July 15th '61, dis July 24th '62, Clear Creek Miss

Wm. L. H. Jack pri, July 1st '61, m in July 15th '61, dis at Syracuse, Mo, Jan 2d '62.

John O. Mathews pri, July 1st '61, m in July 15th '61.

F. E. Strong pri, July 1st '61, m in July 15th '61, wd Sep 19th '62, Iuka, Miss.

Riley Wescott pri, July 1st '61, m in July 15th '61.

David Sullivan pri, Jan 3rd '62, killed at the battle of Iuka Sep 19th '62.

Eighth Infantry.

COMPANY D.

Henry N. Tohmpson pri, Aug 14th '61, m in Sep 16th '61, wd and captd April 6th

'62, at Shiloh. Tenn.
John S. Hopkins pri, Aug 14th '61.

Ninth Infantry.

Company G.

James H. Sipe 1st Corporal. Aug 12th '61, m in March 11th '62, wd May 22d '02, at Vicksburg, Miss.
James H. Sipe pri, Aug 12th '61, m in Sep 24th '61, March 28th '62.
G. B. Sharp pri, Sep 18th '61. m in Sep 24th '61.
Samuel Sharp pri, Sep 18th '61, m in Sep 24th '61, wd March 7th '62 at Pea Ridge.
Joseph Vincent pri, Aug 18th '61, m in Sep 24th '61, killed in at battle at Pea Ridge, March 7th '62.

Tenth Infantry.

Company K.

T. Walter Jackson Adjt com, Sep 24th '61, 1st Lt Company C. res April 28th '62.
Frank W. Crosky Q M S Dec 31st '61, wd Oct 4th '62 at Corinth, Miss.
J. W. Paxton pri Feb 25th '62.

Tenth Infantry.

Company B.

W. H. Huff pri, July 23d '64, m in July 23 64.
J. W. Porter pri Aug 23d '61, m in Sep 6th 61.

Thirteenth Infantry.

Company G.

R. Billingham pri. Sep 27th '61, dis Jan 21st '62.
James Millage pri, Sep 27th '61, m in Oct 28th '61,died at Corinth July 26th '62.
Ward B. Sherman pri. Sep 27th '61. m in Oct 28th '61. Adjt Sep 14th '64. ninth cavalry.
G. B. Sharp 1st Lt company G Jan 1st .65.

Eighth Infantry.

Company G.

S. A. Dobson 7th Cor, Aug 12th '73, m in Aug 27th '62.
E. P. Allen pri, Aug 11th '63, m in Aug 27th '63 wd May 28th '64.
Wm. E. Appelgate pri, Aug 15th '63, m in Aug 27th '63.
John Lewis pri, Aug 25th '63, refused,

J. D. Fuller pri, Oct 18th '63, m in Nov 30th '63.

Ninth Cavalry.

Company G.

E. F. Morse pri, Sep 28th '63, m in Sep 27th '63.
Thomas Murphy pri, Sep 24th '63, m in Sep 24th '63.
J. Ray pri, Oct 19th '62, m in Oct 19th '62.
R. Robertson pri, Oct 24th '63, m in Oct 24th '63.
G. Watts pri, Oct 3d '63, m in Oct 3d '63.

Tenth Infantry.

Company D.

H. L. Bigg 8th Cor, Sep 19th '62, m in Sep 28th '61, died May 16th '63, Champion Hills, Miss.
P. Daily waggoner, Sep 5th '61, m in Sep 28th '61, from pri, dis Jan 26th '52.
C. L. Bailey pri, Sep 11th '61, m in Sep 28th '61, transfered to Co C, March 1st '62.
George Buchanan pri, Aug 18th '61, m in Sep 28th '61.
David Clement pri, Sep 18th '61, m in Sep 28th '61, dis at St Louis Oct 12th '62.
C. T. Davis pri, Sep 5th '61, m in Sep 28th '61, trans to Co C, March 1st '61.
P. Daily pri, Sep 5th '61, m in Sep 20th '61.
Francis Fee pri, Sep 13th '61, m in Sep 28th '61, killed May 16th '63, Champion Hills, Miss in battle.
J. H. Fee pri, Sep 10th '61, m in Sep 28th '61, wd May 16th '63, Champion Hills, Miss.
D. B. Mason pri, Sep 9th '61, m in Sep 20th '61, trans to Co C March 1st, '62.
B. S. Myers pri, m in Sep 28th '61.
D. N. Reedy pri, Sep 18th '61, m in Sep 28th '61, died at Birds Point, Dec 24th '62.
V. B. Rugg pri, Sep 9th '61, m in Sep 28th '61, trans to Co C, March 1st '62.
J. Walnut pri, Sep 9th '61, m in Sep 28th '61.
J. L. Croskrey pri, Feb 21st '62, m in Feb 21st '62, trans Feb 17th '64, Champion Hills, Miss to inv corps, wd May 16th '63, Champion Hills, Miss.
G. M. Cooper pri, Feb 10th '62, m in Feb 10th '62.
Henry Cooper pri, Feb 10th '62, m in Feb 24th '62, wd Oct 4th '62, Corinth Miss, dis April 1st '63, Memphis, Tenn.
C. Arnold pri, Feb 20th '62, m in Feb 20th '63.
W. J. Newport pri, Feb 17th '62, m in Feb 17th '62.
J. F. Bartlett pri, March 10th '62, m in March 10th '62, died July 6th '62.

Forty-Seventh Infantry.

Company G.

John Linsday pri, May 4th, '64, m in June 4th '64.

W. D. Williams pri, May 4th, '64, m in June 4th, 64.
J. Williams pri, May 4th, '64, m in June 4th, 64.

Light Artillery.

Chas. Andress 8th Cor. Oct 31st, '63, m in Nov 9th 63.
S. J. Chapman pri, Nov 6th '63, m in Nov 9th 63.
G. A. Worley pri, Nov 5th '63, m in Nov 9th, 63.

First Cavalry.

Company B.

West McDowell pri, Aug 31st, '64, m in Aug 31st, 64.
Peter Quinn pri, Aug 31st '64, m in Aug 31st 64.
J P Ross pri, Jan 1st '64, m in Jan 1st, 64.
John Wilson pri, Aug 31st '64, m in Aug 31st 64.

Second Cavalry.

Company H

W. H. Anderson pri, Feb 3d, '64, m in Feb 3d, 64.
J. A. Anderson pri, Feb 3d, '64, m in Feb 3d, 64.
A. Heath pri, Feb 3d '64, m in Feb 3d 64.
J. Long pri, Jan 18th '64, m in Feb 3d 64.
E. Pearson pri, Jan 24th '64, m in Feb 3d 64,
James Rogers pri, Feb 3d '64, m in Feb 3d 64.

Second Infantry.

Company I.

J. G. Bowen pri, Jan 26th '64, m in Jan 26th '64.

Twelfth Infantry.

Company E.

H. H. Crowhurst pri, Feb 26th '64, m in March 18th '64, wd at Tupelo, Miss July
    14th '64, died at Memphis Tenn. Aug 3d '64.
M. Copeland pri, Dec 26th '64, m in Dec 26th '64.
W. C. Shafer, pri, Dec 26th '64, m in Dec 26th '64.

Thirteenth Infantry.

Company G.

W. G. Bates pri, Jan 4th '64, m in Jan 23d '64, Co unknown. wd April 9th '64.
J. Brick pri, Jan 5th '64, m in Jan 23d '64, Co unknown. Died July 21st '64.
E. Kern pri, Jan 4th 64, m in Jan 23d '64, reported wd and, captd April 9th '64.
J. R. Thomas pri, Jan 1st '61, m in Jan 23d 64 died April 13th 64.
Wm. S. Townsend pri, Dec 23d '63, m in Jan 23d '64, killed in action April 9th '64
Wm. Wade pri, Dec 23th, '63, m in Jan 23d, '64, died April 1st '64.

Tenth Infantry.

Company C.

Wm. H. Stoddard 1st Lt, com Nov 26th '63.
J. H. Larimer Ser, Feb 1st '64, m in Feb 1st '64.
V. P. Gray Ser, Feb 1st '64, m in Feb 1st '64.
J. K. Lux Ser, Feb 1st '64 m in Feb 1st '64.
J. M. Hillmon Ser, Feb 1st '64, m in Feb 1st, '64.
A. M. Roberts Ser, Feb 1st '64, m in Feb 1st '64
J. H. Richardson Cor, Feb 1st '64 m in Feb 1st '64.
Thos. S. Brannan Cor, Feb 1st '64, m in Feb 1st '64
J. H. Smith Cor, Feb 1st '64, m in Feb 1st '64.
B. J. Howard Cor, Feb 1st '64, m in Feb 1st '64.
C. L. Bailey pri, Feb 1st '64, m in Feb 1st '64,
E. B. Bailey pri, Feb 1st '64, m in Feb 1st '64.
Thos Clem pri, Feb 1st '64, m in Feb 1st '64.
J. W. B. Cole, pri Feb 1st '64, m in Feb 1st '64,
G. W. Guilford pri, Feb 1st '64, m in Feb 1st '64.
P. Piggins pri, Feb 1st '64, m in Feb 1st '64.
C. Maholm pri, Feb 1st '64, m in Feb 1st '64.
S. D. Newton pri, Jan 1st ' 64, m in Jan 1st '64.
M. Rhoads pri, Feb 1st '64, m in Feb 1st '64.
John Sawyer pri, Feb 1st '64, m in Feb 1st '64.
E. M. Stevens pri, Feb 1st '64, m in Feb 1st '64.
U. P. Stevens pri, Feb 1st '64, m in Feb 1st '64.
S. Walker pri, Feb 1st '64, m in Feb 1st '64.

Forty-Seventh Infantry.

Company K.

C. L. Bailey 1st Lt, May 24th '64, m in June 4th '64.
J. D. Jackson 1st Ser, May 20th '64, m in June 4th '64.
Denton Camery 3d Cor, May 23d '64, m in June 4th '64, from 4th Cor June 4th.
O. H. Cobb 4th Cor, May 14th '64, m in June 4th '64 from 5th Cor.

John Aldrich pri. May 21st '64, m in June 4th '64.

L. Allman pri. May 12th '64, m in June 4th '64.

J. B. M. Bear pri. May 16th '64, m in June 4th '64.

F. M. Bricker pri. May 16th '64 m in June 4th '64.

H. A. Bunce pri. May 30th '64, m in June 4th '64, died at Helena Ark. August 7th '64.

J. F. Coff pri, May 9th '64 m in June 4th '64.

R. M. Coffin pri, May 11th '64 m in June 4th '64.

J. C. Flathers pri. May 23d '64, m in June 4th '64.

W. F. Hillmon pri. May 9th '64 m in June 4th '64.

G. M. Hall pri, May 9th '64, m in June 4th '64.

G. R. Hershey pri. May 13th '64 m in June 4th '64.

S. E. Hall pri. May 13th '64 m in June 4th '64 died at Helena Ark. July 1st '46.

R. Lotzenhizer pri, May 23d '64 m in June 4th '64.

W. McLawry pri, May 20th '64, m in June 4th '64.

H. W. Nungesser pri, May 19th '64 m in June 4th '64.

L. Park pri, May 23d '64 m in June 4th '64.

W. Rittenhouse pri, May 9th '64 m in June 4th '64.

O. H. Stewart pri. May 13th '64 m in June 4th '64.

C. Soleman pri, May 9th '64 m in June 4th '64.

C. E. Sullivan pri, May 13th '64 m in June 4th '64.

L. H. Stoddard pri, May 14th '64 m in June 4th '64.

J. S. Vancuren pri, May 16th '64 died at Helena, Ark. August 23d '64,

F. A. Vancuren pri, May 12th '64 m in June 4th '64 died at Helena Ark . Aug 12th '64

A. Zehrung pri, May 23d '64 m in June 4th '64.

Ninth Cavelry,

Company K.

J, H. Brush pri. Oct 6th '63, m in Oct 30th '63.

Tenth Infantry,

Company F.

J. N. Paxton pri. Feb 25th '62, m in Feb 25th '62,

Jacob Yeiser pri, Aug 22d '61, m in Sep 7th '61, wd Nov 28th '63 Missionary Ridge Tenn, dis Nov 23d '64, Chatanooga Tenn.

J. C. Kellogg pri, Feb 20th '62, m in Feb 20th '62, dis Sep 17th '62. St Louis, Mo,

Tenth Infantry.

Company H.

D. H. Anderson pri, March 10th '62, m in March 10th '62.

S. Shreeves pri, March 10th '62, m in March 10th '62, wd May 16th '63, Champion
    Hills, Miss.
B. F. Zeller pri, Feb '64, '62, m in Feb 24th '62, dis Sep '62, Corinth, Miss.
H. P. Strain pri, Aug 28th '61, m in Sep 7th '61, died Feb 7th '62, Birds Point,
W. Strain pri, Aug 28th '61, m in Sep 7th '61.

Tenth Infantry.

Company K.

P. Herrington pri, Jan 30th '62, m in Jan 30th '62, trans Feb 15th '64, to inv corps
J. N. Paxton pri, Feb 24th '62.

Eleventh Infantry.

Company B.

B. C. Stevens musician Sep 18th '61, m in Oct 1st '61, died June 30th '62,

Twelth Infantry.

Company E.

S. J. Crowhurst pri, Oct 15th '61, m in Oct 26th '61, wd at Ft Donaldson.
C. B. Hayward pri, Oct 21st '61, m in Oct 26th '61, dis May 16th '62, Pittsburg
    Landing, Tenn.

Sixteenth Infantry.

Company I.

H. Sipe pri, Dec 17th '61, m in March 24th '62, wd Sep 19th '62, Iuka, Miss, dis
    March 16th '63.

Eighteenth Infantry.

Company K.

B. F. Smith pri, July 7th '62, m in Aug 6th '62, captd April 13th '64, Poison Creek
    Ark.

Twenty-Eighth Infantry.

Company B.

B. W. Wilson Capt July 24th '62, m in Oct 10th '62, Com Oct 10th '65,

J. M. Brothers 2d Cor Aug 7th '62, m in Aug 19th '62.

B. Wilkins 8th Cor Aug 7th '62.

G. Crittendon wagoner. Aug 19th '62, m in Aug 19th '62.

N. Devore pri, Aug 19th '62, m in Aug 19th '62, died Aug 27th '63, Corinth, La.

A. Felter pri, Aug 6th '62, m in Aug 19th '62, wd May 16th '63, Champion Hills, Miss captd Sep 19th .64, Winchester, Va.

H. M. Howard pri, Aug 15th '62, m in Aug 19th '62, died April 3rd '63, Helena, Ark.

E. D. Howard pri, Aug 19th '62, m in Aug 19th '62, died Jan 15th '63, Vicksburg Miss.

G. T. James pri, Aug 12th '62, m in Aug 19th '62. wd May 16th '63, Champion Hills, Miss, died Aug 18th '63, Corinth, La.

G. R. Walton pri, Jan 5th '64, m in Jan 5th '64, wd Oct 19th '64, Cedar Creek, Va.

Twenty-Eighth Infantry.

Company I.

C. P. N. Barker pri, Aug 15th '62, m in Sep 10th '62.

Second Cavalry.

Company B.

Wm. F. Eshbaugh buglr, July 30th '61, m in Aug 19th '61, captd Boonsville, Miss July 1st '62.

T. J. Cady farr, July 30th '62, m in Oct 15th '61, from pri, wagoner July 31st '61,

Wm. F. Burley pri, July 30th '61, m in Aug 31st '61.

Wm. Paxton pri, July 30th '61, m in Aug 31st '61, killed in skirmish Monterey, April 29th '62.

Fourth Cavalry.

Company E.

A. Spade pri, Sep 24th '61, m in Nov 23d '61.

J. J. Toland pri. Oct 1st '61, m in Nov 23d '61, died West Plains, Mo '62.

Sixth Cavalry.

Company A.

T. C. Williamson pri, Dec 1st '62, m in Dec 1st '62,

Sixth Cavalry.

Company H.

J. Hunter 3d Cor Sep 26th '62, m in Jan 31st '62

R. Stevens sadler Oct 6th '62, m in Nov 14th '62.
C. S. Sanborn wagoner, Oct 1st '62, m in Nov 1st '62.
J. Middleton pri, Nov 1st '62, m in Jan 19th '62.

Sixth Cavalry.

Company I.

A. N. Dodd pri, Oct 31st '62, m in Feb 2d '63.
S. A. Lewis pri, Sep 27th '62, m in Feb 3d '63.
W. A. Morgan pri, Sep 27th '62, m in Feb 2d '63.
S. Peck pri, Sep 27th '62, m in Feb 2d '63.
J. A. Twogood pri, Sep 27th '62, m in Feb 2d '63.
O. A. Terpenning pri, Oct 28th '62, m in Feb 2d '63.
H. Terpenning pri, Oct 28th '62, m in Feb 2d '63.

Tenth Infantry.

Company D.

G. W. Buchannan pri, Feb 1st '64, m in Feb 1st '64.
J. N. Paxton pri, Feb 26th '64, m in March 30th '64

Tenth Infantry.

Company H.

D. H. Anderson pri, March 12th '64, m in March 12th '64.

Twelth Infantry.

Company D.

S. J. Crowhurst Cor, Dec 25th '64, m in Jan 5th '64.

Fourteenth Infantry.

Company G.

J. H. Luke pri, Dec 1st '63, m in Dec 1st '63, pro 5th Cor June 1st '64.
J. Mills pri, Dec 1st '63, m in Dec 1st '63.

Fifth Cavalry.

Company I.

John Mathews pri, July 1st '61, m in July 15th '63, vet Feb 8th '64, from Co D.

B, H, Martin pri, June 24th '61, m in July 15th '61, vet Feb 6th '64, from Co G.
J. G. Martin pri, June 21th '61, m in July 15th '61, vet Jan 5th '64 from Co G.

Twenty-Fourth Infantry.

Company D.

E. A, Burnham pri, Feb 26th '64, m in March 11th '64

Twenty-Seventh Infantry.

Company D.

N. Huff pri, Feb 26th '64, m in March 16th '64, dis Dec 8th '64.
J. B. Vanauken pri, Feb 26th '64, m in April 6th '64,

Sixth Cavalry.

Company F.

A. A. Myers 1st Ser Sep 15th '62, m in Dec 24th '62, dis July 25th '64.
B. B. LaDow 2d Ser Oct 23d '62, m in Nov 27th '62.
J. Smith 5th Ser Nov 13th '62, m in Nov 27th '62.
D. Rosenberger 3d Cor Nov 13th '52, m in Nov 27th '62,
J. O. Beadle 6th Cor Oct 9th '62, m in Nov 15th '62.
C. Roberts teamster Oct 29th '62, m in Nov 22d '62.
W. G. Armstrong pri, Oct 9th '62, m in Nov 12th '62, killed Sep 3d '63 White Stone
    Hills D. T. in battle.
W. H. Alden pri, Oct 18th '62, m in Nov 12th '62,
M. D. Betts pri, Oct 9th '62, m in Nov 17th '62, died Sep 8th '62, D. T. of wds,
J. Cunningham pri, Nov 14th '62, m in Nov 17th '62,
Z. Davis pri, Oct 9th '62, m in Nov 14th '62.
T. Everett pri, Oct 12th '62, m in Nov 12th '62.
F. Eshbaugh pri, Oct 9th '62, m in Nov 12th '62,
A. Fedding pri, Nov 8th '62, m in Nov 18th '52,
G. Fox pri, Nov 1st '62, m in Nov 14th '62,
J. Galaspie pri, Oct 19th '62, m in Nov 17th '62,
S. Hallett pri, Oct 4th '62, m in Nov 17th '62,
F. Hubell pri, Nov 10th '62, m in Nov 27th '62,
W. Hubell pri, Nov 13th '62, m in Nov 27th '62, dis Nov 31st '64, Ft Randall, D T,
J. Keuhn pri, Dec 6th '62, m in Dec 15th '62,
J. Kerns pri, Nov 13th '62, m in Nov 27th '62,
L. D. Knight pri, Oct 28th '62, m in Nov 12th '62,
N, McKune pri, Dec 4th '62, m in Nov 12th '62,
J. Muddel pri, Nov 14th '62, m in Nov 27th '62,
A. Palacheek pri, Nov 13th '62, m in Nov 27th '62,
E. A. Richards pri, Nov 25th '62, m in Nov 29th '62.

S. Strong pri, Oct 25th '62, m in Nov 17th '62, died June 8th '65, Crow Creek D T.

B. F. Sanborn pri, Oct 9th '22, m in Nov 17th '62.

J. Shaler pri, Oct 18th '62, m in Nov 15th '62, wd Sep 3d '63, White Stone Hills
    D T.

J. Sullivan pri, Nov 1st '62, m in Nov 12th '62.

J. Ghampron pri, Oct 4th '62, m in Nov 12th '62.

CHAPTER XVI.

BIOGRAPAPHICAL.

J. C. Vermilya, first Judge of Tama County, is a native of the State of Delaware and was born on the 11th day of Septem ber, 1802, his parents being Edward and Joanna, (Right) Ver milya. When but about six months of age his parents emigrated to New York settling in Putman County where they remained until 1818 when they emigrated to Indiana, and settled in Jackson County. Shortly after settling here his father and mother both died, leaving young Vermilya with but little means, nothing but a common school education, no home, to do and provide for himself. With a good will and a strong constitution he determined to learn a trade and immediately went to work as a hatter which business he followed eight years, when he went to farming. In 1852, Mr Vermilya came to Tama County and entered land on section 26, in Tama township, and commenced to improve the same, which business he has followed ever since.

Mr Vermilya was elected to the office of County Judge in the year 1853, and was the first one in Tama County. This office he filled with honor, and from that date has held a high reputation over the County as a man who is strickly honest, and one who works for the best interest of the community in which he lives.

Mr. Vermilya was first married in the year 1823 to Miss Catharine Murphy of Jackson County Ind., with whom he lived twenty three years when she passed to the other shore, one child accompanied her. After the death of his first wife he married a Miss Mary Ann Carter, by whom he had four children, two of whom are dead, the other two are married, one is the wife of J. G. Strong of Grundy Center, the other the wife of A. L. Brooks, of Tama City. In 1870 his second wife was carried off by disease leaving Mr. Vermilya again to mourn the loss of one whom he loved and cherished. Mr. Vermilya was again married to Miss M. A. Carpenter, with whom he is still living. His farm is located about one mile north east of Tama City upon which he has made some fine improvments. His house and out buildings are among the best in the County and Mr. Vermilya in his old age has a happy home with all the enjoyments of life.

CHARLES MASON.

Few men are better known in York township, than the subject of this brief sketch—Charles Mason—who for a period of sixteen years has made his home on section three. His parents were natives of New York, where Charles their son, was born in Oneida County, December 28th, 1829. Here he remained until eight years of age when his father and family moved to Marshall County, Indiana. After remaining a number of years in this State, he emigrated to Illinois, where he remained until the year 1865 when he settled in this County in York township. Mr. Mason now owns one of the finest farms in Tama County, consisting of two hundred and twenty acres in sections two and three all under cultivation, with the beautiful little village of Waltham on part of it. This town was layed out by order of Mr. Mason in the year 1868 by H. Jacobs, containing about fifteen acres. His house is located upon a slight elevation facing the south and is surround ed by a beautiful grove together with a fine orchard covering about four acres. In this grove we find the American and European larches, firs, chestnut, iron wood and several varieties of cherries, both wild and tame pears, peaches and the white and yellow willow, which makes it very beautiful and attractive. In his garden, he raises large quantities of small fruit consisting of Russell's Great Prolific, Wilson's Albany and many other kind of strawberries, all kinds of grapes, raspberries, etc, and is successfully raising the hucklebury which is a very rare fruit in this County. Mr. Mason is what we may call a "willow man" believing that they are the only successful hedge to be used in this country. His entire farm together with the edges of sloughs are surrounded by the white willow which besides making a splendid fence, beautifies the place and gives it a neat appearence, while for about twenty or thirty feet upon the inside he has tame grass and clover sown making it very convenient in cultivating the fields.

In 1850 when but twenty one years of age he led to the hymenial alter Miss Mary Ann Thompson. Today he has a family of nine children, two boys and seven girls. His oldest son Albert Mason, is married, and besides carrying on his own farm assists in carrying on that of his fathers.

ABRAM TOMPKINS.

The subject of this sketch is a native of New York, having been born in that State September 23rd, 1811. His praents K. and Catherine (Brown) Tompkins were also of the same State, and in very limited circumstances, so poor, in fact, that their son was only permitted to attend the common subscription schools, from the time he was five years of age until he was old enough to do for himself.

The father of Abram Tompkins was a God fearing man, and an earnest christian, one who endeavored to bring up his children in the "fear and admonition of the Lord," and when his son was yet an infant he carried him in his arms to the Sabbath School. Here and at the family alter, was sown the "good seed of the word" which in after years bore fruit, and we trust will continue to bear by the hundred fold.

After living at home until he was twelve years of age Abram decided on leaving home to seek his own fortune. He did not leave the vicinity of his old home immediately, however, but hired to the neighboring farmers, earning enough to supply his wants and save a little for a rainy day.

In 1831 he left the State of New York and went to Michigan where he enlisted in the Black Hawk war as a private and after receiving his discharge returned and was united in marriage November 20th, 1833, to Miss Mary A. Eatin, by whom he had ten children: G. W., born in 1835 and died at St. Louis in 1862; C. M., now living in Kansas, born January 14th 1838; B. T., now living in Iowa County, this State, was born January 2nd 1840; Catherine J., born January 22nd, 1842: S. M., born March 16th, 1844; A. E., born June 30th, 1846; M. T., born October 18th, 1848: Z. A. E., born December 19th, 1850; Sumner, born March 26th, 1855; Z. E., born July 12th, 1857.

Shortly after marriage Mr. and Mrs. Tompkins wisely came to the conclusion that the advantages enjoyed in that State was not such as they desired and therefore determined to seek a home and fortune in a better country where the advantages would be greater. They came to this County in the year 1853, when all was a blank wilderness and have lived to see it "blossom as a rose".

Abram Tompkins is a large man of splendid appearance, pleasant and agreeable in his intercourse with friends and neighbors. In the family circle, he is kind to his children. strict in discipline and teaches each member to know that his yea means yea, and his nay means nay, from which can be no appeal. In business with the world his word can always be relied upon, his promises always being held sacred, and invariably carried out to the letter. He is a good friend and neighbor, living at peace with all men and a hard working farmer.

In 1859 Mr. Tompkins received the nomination for Representative in the Iowa Legislature and was triumphant. In this capacity he served his constituents in a faithful manner, attending closely to the business for which he was elected and afterwards retired from office bearing the laurels that none but the faithful can bear. Taking all in all Mr. Tompkins is a man possessing such qualifications as to place him high in the niches of the history of Tama County.

WEST WILSON.

Among the early pioneer settlers, and one who has watched the growth of this populous County from a mere wilderness of but few inhabitants to its present proportions, and has seen it take its place among the most important of Iowa's Counties is the person which heads this sketch. Mr. Wilson is a leading farmer and stock raiser of Crystal township. He was born in Ayrshire, Scotland in the year 1820. His parents were James and Jane (Lusk) Wilson, who were both natives of that country. He had very little opportunity for education in his early youth but acquired a fair education at the common schools being at the same time engaged in aiding his father to carry on the farm. Leaving Scotland Mr. Wilson emigrated to Connecticutt where he remained until the year 1856, when he came to this State and settled in Crystal township, Tama County, on section 13. He has a beautiful farm consisting of six hundred and sixty-six acres, the most of which is under cultivation and pasture. Of late years Mr. Wilson has been paying considerable attention to the raising of fine stock and now he has a large number of the best blooded cattle. Mr. Wilson, besides carrying on this immense farms, is engaged in the grain business at Traer, where he handles thousands of bushels annually through his elevator and warehouses. He is also interested in a lumber yard at Morrison Grundy County. In all the various changes of an active life Mr. Wilson has gained the respect of a large circle of friends and the confidence of the community.

JASPER H. SCOTT.

This gentleman is a native of Ohio having been born in Highland County of that State, in the year 1820, and when but two years of age came with his parents to Columbus O. where they settled upon a small farm. His mother died when he was small leaving a family of six children. Jasper being the youngest, was bound out to one of the neighbors, who was poor and could not give him such advantages as they desired, he only having been permitted to attend the common subscription school; which was all the means of education that he enjoyed, but natural good sense and a determined will have in a measure overcome every difficulty in this respect.

When Jasper reached his 16th year, boy that he was, decided on leaving his adopted home and henceforth to do for himself. In his twentieth year Mr. Scott was married to Miss E. Hawkins. The young couple though poor in this world, but rich in faith, and with a will and determination to dare to do, shortly after marriage moved to Illinois and settled on a small farm in Ogle County, where they remained until the year 1859, when Mr. Scott and family moved to this County settling in Grant township where they have since resided.

As a citizen Mr. Scott stands high in the estimation of the communities in which he has lives or resided, being a good neighbor and a kind hearted, benevolent man, one who would be well received and trusted implicitly by stranger and friend.

In 1840 he united with the Methodist Episcopal Church; up to the present time, a period of thirty-eight years, has ever been a constant member of that branch of the Christain Church. We believe it will be written of him in that great day like one of old "He hath done what he could." No better epitaph could be placed upon the monument of any one than this.

JAMES B. MERRITT.

One of the leading and most highly respected farmers of Highland township, as well as the first settler, is James B. Merritt, who was born in Orange County, New York, on the 5th day of Aug., 1814. His father Daniel M. Merritt was a farmer. James spent the first nineteen years of his life at home attending school and helping to carry on the farm, after which he left his parents and learned the mason trade, at which he worked until the year 1855, when he came west and settled in this County,

Highland township. As already stated Mr. Merritt, was the first settler in the township. Without neighbors, with nothing but the tall prairie grass for miles around, and the prairie wolves to sing him to sleep night after night, for a number of years still remaining making for himself and family a home in this beautiful township, which to-day is thickly settled.

His farm is located near the center portion of the township and is nearly all under cultivation with all the conveniences of the modern farmer. In the year 1839, Mr. Merritt was married to Miss Laura Wing of Shram, Litchfield Co., Connecticut. Since their marriage he has been blessed with ten children, three of whom are still living and hold a high position in society.

J. G. HULL.

J. G. Hull, a pioneer settler in Tama County as well as a leading farmer, is a native of New York, and was born in Rensselaer County and town of Burling, on the 29th day of October, 1815. Here J. G. was reared, receiving a common school edcuation and at the same time assisting his father to carry on the farm.

In the year 1854 he removed from that state and settled in this County, on section 13, Spring Creek township. He was among the first settlers in the township hauling his first load of lumber, provisions etc., from Waterloo, a distance of nearly forty miles. Mr. Hull still resides upon his farm, located upon the beautiful stream of Wolf Creek where he has all the conveniences necessary for a comfortable and happy home. He has always been a straight-forward, square dealer, early securing and steadily retaining the confidence of the community. He has seen this County slowly expand from a mere wilderness to a thickly settled and prosperous County, and never shown any backwardness in trying to encourage its growth and assist in its prosperity. He has served in the various township offices, and has proven himself prompt, perfectly reliable and very efficient.

In the year 1845, he was joined in wedlock with Miss J. L. Thomas with whom he lived until 1873, when Mrs. Hull died.

HON. S. S. MANN.

The subject of this note was born in Sussex County, New Jersey December 13th, A. D., 1830, and moved to Delaware County, Ohio with his parents in the fall of 1834. He was raised on the farm and inured to hard toil. Received a normal and academic education and afterwards studied for the profession of law, but owing to the deleterious effect produced upon his constitutional health from sedentary habits he abandoned the idea and never made application for admission to practice. During many consecutive years subsequent to his twentieth year he worked on the farm during the spring, summer and fall months and taught school during the winter.

On April 6th, 1852 Mr. Mann started on a six months journey from Columbus, O., with an ox team across the plains to the golden lands of the Eldorado of the far west. Arriving at the mining camps in Navada, on the South fork of the Eula River on the 6th day of Oct., 1852. At that time it was a great undertaking because it was a long tedious, tiresome and heart sickening journey. His return was in the winter of 1855, on steamers, by way of the Isthmus of Panama.

In the spring of 1865 he came viewing through Iowa. After traveling by foot and stage from Gelena Ill., arrived, on March 7th, at an uncle's by the name of John Mills, twelve miles North of Cedar Rapids. Through his uncle's solicitation and the loan of a horse Mr Mann was induced to view Tama County, coming by the way of Yankee Grove, G. Taylor's and Mr. Felter's, the latter living about nine miles farther west and up Wolf Creek from Mr. Taylor's. From these gentlemen he learned of Union Grove and to visit it was the desire of our tourist. The journey to the grove was one which is often experienced by the frontier traveler. The prairie over which the traveler passed was beautiful, and was the pleasure grounds of the deer, antelope and other species of quadrupeds. Our tourist was led from his road by the desire to give the wild deer a chase which he per-chanced to meet and when he realized his whereabouts he was in the darkness of the western horizon without shelter or even a companion; but soon he came to a small log cabin in Union Grove and on inquiry found it to be the home of a hospitable pioneer, Mr. Fredricks', whose house he had sought through the dark and stormy night.

Mr. Mann purchased the land he now lives upon of the Government, on the 15th day of January, A. D. 1855, situated near Union Grove. Since that time he has added thereto 210 acres making in all 530 acres. On this land he, has erected a fine, if not the finest farm residence in the County, at a cost of $5,000. He is the architect of his own fortune; never expecting anything from any man only that for which he gives a full and satisfactory equivalent. Through economy and incessant toil he has managed to keep out of debt.

Mr. Mann was married in his 21st year, on the 15th day of August, A. D., 1851 to Miss Sarah Allen, of one of the most respectable families of Muskingum County, Ohio. He emigrated to Jackson County, Iowa, in April. 1856, and was elected to the office of Magistrate two consecutive terms. He moved into this County and settled on the land where he now lives, in the spring of 1866. Was elected to the office of Magistrate and served two terms.

On January 19th. A. D., 1877, he met with the sad misfortune of loosing an affectionate and confiding companion.

He was nominated as representative in the State Legislature in the fall of 1877, by the National Greenback and Democratic parties jointly. He made a strong and vigorous campaign and although ran against eleven-hundred majority it was reduced nearly seven-hundred He has always been found a defender of the interests of labor.

HON. W. G. MALIN.

The subject of this sketch was born in Bellmont County, Ohio, March 7th, 1833. His youth and early manhood were spent in his native County, his time being employed chiefly as a farm laborer.

His education was such as the common schools of the State afforded at that time.

At the outbreak of the rebellion he enlisted as a private soldier under Captain Frank Askew. The company was assigned, a place in the 15th O. V. T., then forming at Mansfield, Ohio.

He was with his regiment in all of the campaigns of Buell and Rosecrans, commanders of the army of the Cumberland, and was slightly wounded at the battle of Shiloh, and severely wounded at the battle of Stone River, and at Chickamanga. At the latter place he was taken prisoner, and conveyed to Richmond, from thence to Andersonville, Savannah and Milan successively. At the latter place he was released on parol after having been held a prisoner of war fourteen months. Returned home and was discharged from the service at Columbus O., Jan. 12th, 1865.

He emigrated to Iowa in the fall of 1865, settled in Tama County and engaged in farming. Was married in Jan., 1868. Was placed in nomination by the Anti-Monopoly party for the office of Representative in the State Legislature in 1873, and elected a member of the 15th General Assembly of the State of Iowa. Was renominated in 1875, and defeated by the Republican candidate. He was nominated by the Greenback party for the office of State Senator in 1877, and again defeated.

He still resides where he first settled in the state, four miles south of Tama City.

JOHN W. FLEMING.

John W. Fleming was born in Mitlin, County Pennsylvania January 12th, 1837. His parents were John and Mary (Wills) Flemings natives of that State. They were poor yet rich in faith and in their intercourse with the world ever endeavored to observe the golden rule.   His father was a farmer, and when John was but 18 years of age he left home that he might learn the carpenter and cabinet business. For a number of years he followed his chosen trade acquiring considerable skill in the work

His education was limited to that of common schools; poverty was the obstacle that prevented him from becoming an eminent scholar. John was not that kind to yield to trifles but improved every spare moment in acquiring knowledge.

On February 15th, 1866, Mr. Fleming was married to Miss Jane E. Fleming, his cousin, and in a short time after marriage moved to this County, settling on land belonging to his father in Grant township, where he remained until after the death of his father, May 25th, 1868, when he removed to Buckingham township settling upon a farm formerly occupied by P. Wilbur, near the town of Tracer. He is well known to all residents of the County especially the older settlers, and enjoys the respect and confidence of all alike. Like the rest of the family, in politics, he is a Democrat of the old school, the principles of that party are dear to him. Although never attaining any special prominence in political affairs, yet Mr. Fleming has been chosen at different times to represent his community as Supervisor, and other offices within the township. In every position he has endeavored to preform his duty faithfully.

MAJ. T. S. FREE

Among those who have been prominently identified in the history of Tama County none deserves more honorable mention than Thomas S. Free. He was born in Ohio, were he resided with his parents until the spring of 1853, when his father and family came west and settled in this County, near Toledo. At this time Thomas was a lad of but thirteen, and coming to a new country where schools were "like angels visits" few and far between, his opportunity for education was somewhat limited. Though by hard work he managed to keep himself at school, and in 1860 entered the Iowa State University. While attending school the President issued his call for one hundred thousand men to go to the front. Mr. Free, was among the first to respond to this call and immediately left school, came home to Toledo, and in August 1861, enlisted in company C, 10th Iowa as a private, and was immediately off for war. While in the service, we can safely say

that not many young men were promoted to positions of honor
as was Mr. Free.   He was first appointed Sergeant Major, of the
10th Iowa, afterwards, in order, to first Lieutenant Adjutant and
Major of the 49th U. S. C. I. Served on staff duty, as Judge Advocate of the district of Mississippi, afterwards assigned to duty
by order of the Secretary of war, as Assistant Inspector General of
the State of Mississippi. Discharged March 22d, 1866, after being in
the service of the United States over five years, engaging in all
the battles with the 10th Iowa, up to the battle of Champion
Hills, besides numerous others.

Two years after, Mr. Free, returned home he was elected
to the office of County Judge which he filled with honor.   And
afterwards the office of County Auditor two and one half terms
For a number of years Mr. Free, has been in active law practice
and is now, besides doing a large business at law, acting as
United S ate Indian Agent for the Sac and Fox Indians, which
appointment dates back to 1875.   Mr. Free is liberal, enterprising, and consequently successful, and stands among the leading
men of the County.

DR. H. WELTON

Was born in the State of Connecticut, town of Walcott, New
Haven County, and while quite young, become a member of the
Episcopalian Church.   Here he resided with his parents until
the year 1814 when they moved to Harpersfield, New York,
Delaware County, where they remained until the year 1817, when
they again moved going to Austinburg, Ashtabula County, Ohio.
After a few years his father changed in religious belief to that
of the Methodists and became a class leader.   His house was
a house of plenty for ministers, which gave his son Hiram an opportunity to inform himself concerning this branch of the Church
of Christ and together with the religions decipline of his parents
their son was taught the salvation of his soul.

When Hiram was 18 years of age he left home and spent three
years traveling in New York and Connecticut, and retu rned

home to Ohio. After a few years Hiram thought there was work for him in the vineyard of the Lord and accordingly devoted several years to this work.

In 1855 he moved to Coles County Ill., and remained several years near the head of the Little Wabash, six miles west of Mattoon. In the year 1857, moved to the State of Iowa and settled in Carlton township, Tama County, on section 34.

Mr. Welton has always been a hard working man, and is now carrying on a large farm, at the same time following the profession of a doctor. By economy and energetic labor he has placed himself in comfortable circumstances, so that in his declining years he can pass quietly along, and when the summons shall come he can answer "here Lord am I."

JACOB W. LAMB.

Among the successful young men of Tama County may fairly be placed the name of Jacob W. Lamb. It will be generally found that similar cases lead to like results in whatever branch of human activity a man's genius and enterprise may be employed. The essentials of success are courage, patience and perseverance. Success brings honor in every honest occupation, and when it is achieved by a young man it adds new pleasure.

The subject of this sketch was born in Columbus, Ohio, in 1849, and is the son of D. C. and Rebecca (Walters) Lamb, who came to Tama County from Ohio, in the spring of 1856 when there were few inhabitants and but little expectation that Tama County would be what it now is. Jacob's early life was that of a farm boy, and he attained only a common school education until 1869, when he developed a taste for study and the acquirement of knowledge and shortly after entered the Iowa State University, where he remained six years, receiving his degree of Bachelor of Philosophy, June 30th, 1875. After receiving his diploma his ambition led him to choose law for his profession, and to this end commenced his studies in the law department at Iowa City, remaining one year, June 20th, 1876, he received his degree of bachelor of Law, and was admitted to practice in all the courts of the State at the State House in Des Moines. From that date Mr. Lamb has been in the law practice at Toledo, Tama County Iowa, and has built up a fine business. His office is located on High Street over W. A. Fee's dry goods store, where he has nicely fitted up rooms and a large library. Mr. Lamb is known as a man of sterling integrity, decided character and untiring energy, and has every promise of a prosperous and honorable career.

ANTHONY WILKINSON.

One of the oldest families in the County is that of the Wilkinsons—living in the south eastern part. Although none have ever occupied high official positions, they still have traits of character which distinguish them from others and are as highly respected as any living in the County. Anthony Wilkinson, with his parents, emigrated to this County in 1849, having left his native country in 1834. He was born in Ireland, Donegal County on July 28th, 1817. He resided with his parents until he was 14 years of age then left and went to Maryland. Here he obtained a situation as clerk in a dry goods store, serving a number of years and from there went to Coshocton County, Ohio, and was apprenticed to the carpenter trade which he learned and followed until the spring of 1845, when he went south and while there enlisted in the Mexican war, was taken prisoner by the Mexicans at Encornation, and lay in captivity eight months; was liberated at Frankford. In 1849 he came to this State, stopping at Iowa City. Anthony and two brothers purchased an ox team and wagon, laid in a supply of provisions and come to Tama County, and settled in Salt Creek township. Here they entered a tract of land in section 20, and immediately set to work making for themselves a home.

In 1851, he returned to Ohio, and was married to Miss Sarah A. Graham, by whom he had seven children. The members of the family all fill honorable positions in society.

Anthony Wilkinson is a self-made man in every respect. With a very limited education obtained, from a common school, but with a determined will and strong heart and hands, he has pressed forward overcoming every obstacle that arose in his way. However great the difficulties with which he may be surrounded, he knows no such word as fail, and his example is worthy of emulation by the young men of to-day without a cent of capital. Through his own individual exertions, he has amassed a sufficient amount of this world's goods to enable him to live at ease until called away to join the loved ones that have gone before. He has always been a hard working, industrious man, having excellent physical powers and being capable of great endurance.

Farming has been the principal occupation of Mr. Wilkinson, and in this work he has been eminently successful. Through hard work and careful management he has from time to time added to his possession, until he now owns as nice a tract of land as can be found in Tama County. For many years he has devoted considerable attention to raising fine stock and in this has met with the same good success as in other operations of the farm. Although he may not have obtained the prominence of many others, Anthony Wilkinson is well known through out the County especially by the older settlers, while none know him but to respect the sterling worth of his character.

HON. WILLIAM HARTSOCK.

Early biographical history is largely filled with the struggle of farmer's sons in procuring an education and laying the foundation for future usefulness. The brief History of Willian Hartsock, is a fine illustration of what self-reliance can accomplish under discouraging circumstances. He was born in Knox County, Ohio on the 20th day of May, 1825, his parents being Henry and Ama (Cox,) Hartsock. They were both natives of Pennsylvania, and moved into Ohio at an early day, settling in Knox County, upon a farm. When William was twelve years of age his father realizing the fact that an old settled country is not the place for a poor man, very wisely concluded to emigrate to Illinois and settle in Green County of that State. William remained with his parents upon the farm, aiding in clearing and cultivating it, having only educational privileges of very inferior district schools during the winter months until the year 1841, when he came to this State and settled in Johnson County. Here he remained until the year 1853, when he sold out and moved to Keokuk County, and settled upon a farm.

While a resident of Keokuk County Mr. Hartsock made many friends, and in the fall of 1867, was elected by the Republican party to the office of Representative by a large majority; a position which he held one term, giving satisfaction to his supporters.

In the spring of 1870, Mr. Hartsock and family came to this County and settled in Columbia township. Since that time he has been engaged in farming.

Throughout his life he has maintained a high standing as a man of high moral tone, and in his habits have been strictly temperate and moderate having used neither tobacco or intoxicating liquors.

Mr. Hartsock, was first married to Miss Catherine E. Heaton, with whom he lived until Nov. 24th, 1868, when she died; and in 1869, he was married to Mrs. A. A. Biggs, a widow, who is his present wife. Mr. Hartsock has a happy home with all the conveniences of the modern farmer.

D. C. LAMB.

Among the early settlers of Tama County is D. C. Lamb a heavy farmer and stock raiser of Otter Creek township. Ohio is Mr. Lamb's native State having been born in that State on the 4th day of March, 1820. He remained there assisting his father in business and attending school until the year 1841. When he had attained a majority he quit home to attend school at Grandville, Ohio. Here he remained for several years after which he followed teaching.

In 1844 Mr. Lamb was married to Miss Rebecca Walters, with whom he lived until the year 1863, when she was called away by death. Four years after this Mr. Lamb was again married; Miss Mary Shenheit became his wife with whom he is now living.

In 1856, Mr. Lamb came to this County and settled in Otter Creek township where he has a beautiful farm of over one thousand acres, the most of which is under improvemnet.

Such farmers and citizens as Mr. Lamb are a credit to any County and with pride we note the success which he has attained through economy and good management. His dealings with men are of a strictly honest character, which has attained for him a wide and creditable reputation, such that none but the honest and upright can boast.

JAMES H. BROOKS.

James Harper Brooks comes of good patriotic fighting stock, both grandfathers were in the revolution. His grandsire Harper was a colonel; his grandsire Brooks a private. His parents were James Brooks, farmer, steamboat owner and contractor, and Mary Harper, industrious, well-to-do people residing at the time of the son's birth on the 3d of April, 1829, at Conneaut, Ashtabula County, Ohio. His father was a private under General Harrison during the second contest with the mother country. James Harper made Ashtabula County his home until past age, although he was absent, more or less, nearly every year after sixteen. He finished his education at Kingsville Academy, in his native County.

In his seventeenth year his father sent him to Illinois with two thousand sheep, the only assistance he had was a boy one year younger than himself. His eighteenth year he spent mainly on the farm at home.

During the seasons of 1848 and 1849 he acted as clerk on the steamer Ohio, owned by his father, and run on Lake Erie.

In the spring of 1851 Mr. Brooks moved to Kane County, Illinois; there farmed for three years, then took a contract on the Chicago & Northwestern railroad, furnishing the ties and some other wood-work for the track from the Junction to Dixon.

In the spring of 1856 he removed to Iowa, settling in Otter Creek township, Tama County, alternating between farming and railroading for ten or eleven years; most of this time, when off the farm, he was an employee rather than a contractor.

In the spring of 1866 Mr. Brooks moved his family into the new village of Tama City, then springing up on the Northwestern railroad, two miles south of Toledo. He went on the Union Pacific railroad and spent fourteen months there as a contractor, in company with Lewis Carmichael, the work done being largely between the Black Hills and Ogden. The operations of Mr. Brooks at this period were very successful.

Since leaving the Union Pacific Mr. Brooks has done some heavy work on the Chicago & Northwestern railroad in Monroe County, Wisconsin, on the Baraboo division.

Meantime he was also farming, merchandising and banking, mainly by proxy, and, strange to say, making a success of every branch. He has a thousand acres of land in this County, all under good improvement, most of it cultivated by renters. He is of the firm of Brooks & Holmes, dry goods merchants at Tama City; the business being managed principally by his partner, Ryland A. Holmes, a promising young man, son of Rev. O. A. Holmes. This firm was formed two years ago, and is one of the largest and best in the place.

Mr. Brooks has been in the banking business for seven years, and is of the firm of Brooks & Moore at Traer, Tama County, and of Brooks & Moore Brothers at Reinbeck, Grundy County, both places on the Pacific branch of the Burlington, Cedar Rapids & Northern railroad.

Mr. Brooks has great energy and pluck, usually pushing his business rather than allowing his business to push him. He has kept all the irons in the fire, but let none of them become overheated.

Laterly he has let others assume most of the labor, and having a competency, he lives very much at his ease. He has one of the most delightful residences in the County, located in a two acre lot most tastefully embellished. The house alone cost twenty-five thousand dollars, and the entire homestead, as it stands, must be worth nearly twice that sum.

Mr. Brooks was in early life a whig; since 1855 he has been a republican; is very decided in his political sentiments; is ready to help a worthy friend to office, but has no aspirations himself in that direction.

His wife was Miss Harriet Hartshorn, of Erie County, Pennsylvania. Married at Meadville on the 5th of December, 1850. Both are active members of the Baptist church, filling their places and generously responding to the calls and requirements of the church, and of religious charitable objects generally. Few kinder hearted men live than James H. Brooks. He not only pities the poor and unfortunate, but is always ready to help them.

Mr. and Mrs. Brooks have had two children, but lost one of them. Arthur Lee Brooks, their only living child, has a family, and is managing the home farm, paying particular attention to the stock department. He is energetic like his father, a hard worker and a young man of sterling worth.

GEORGE H. WARREN.

Among the younger class of men whose names appear in this book is George Henry Warren, who was born in Withingham, Vermont, on the 18th of December, 1844. His parents were Linus Austin Warren, a well-to-do farmer, and Sophronia Parker, both industrious, religious and much respected people. They had five children, three boys and two girls, and strove to bring up all of them carefully, early instilling into their tender hearts the pure principles of christianity. George was the fourth child. His parental grandfather, Deacon James Warren, moved from Conway, Massachusetts, to Withingham at an early date, settling in the wilderness, and residing in that town until old age, dying at Shelburne Falls, Massachusetts, where he lived a short time. The maternal grandfather of George H. was Captain Samuel Parker, of Whitingham, a revolutionary soldier, who, was detailed for special service under General Washington, with whom he was a favorite.   Both the Warren and Parker families were remarkable for their strength and longevity.

Mr. Warren had a pleasant home, affectionate parents, a love for books and an oportunity to gratify it.   He preferred mental to physical labor, and for that reason some of his bucolic associates called him "lazy," and that annoyed him; it was, perhaps, the sole grief of childhood years.   He had so much literary ambition that at fifteen he was prepared to teach, and commenced his first district school.   For three years he taught during the winter and studied in the summer.

At eighteen he entered the old and famous academy at Shelburne Falls, Massachusetts, paying his way by teaching a part of each day, while carrying on a regular and full course of studies At nineteen, owing to mental overwork, his health began to decline, and he gave up the idea, fondly cherished, of going through Brown University.   He became teller of the Shelburne Falls National Bank, and soon afterwards cashier of the same.   Prior to this period he had been looking to the law as his profession, but relinquished this hope and made up his mind to be a banker.

In the winter of 1868 he resigned his position in the bank at Shelburne Falls, came to Tama City and carried on a private banking business until October, 1871, when the First National Bank of Tama City was organized, of which institution he has since held the position of cashier, and has managed its business with a great deal of clerical and executive ability.

Since 1874 he has given a great deal of attention, and all the energy at his command, to the developement of the water-power on the Iowa river at Tama City.   He is deeply impressed with the importance of encouraging manufactures at the west, as a hand-maid of railroads in embracing the true interests of all classes.   The water-power enterprise, started here in 1874, has proven a grand success, several manufactories being already in operation.   In 1875 he formed the Union Plow Company, which bids fair to become one of the most successful enterprises in the interior of Iowa.

He joined the Freemasons in Massachusetts in 1867, and took the chapter degrees at Tama City, in 1870.

He has been a member of the Baptist church since ten years of age, and has been accustomed from youth to make every business enterprise, project or charge of any kind, a subject of especial prayer He is convinced that his petitions have been answered, and evidently believes his Heavenly Father regards the minutest as well as greatest interests of the trusting one's life. He is a Sunday School worker and aims to make himself useful in many ways.

Mr. Warren married his wife at Shelburne Falls, Massachusetts, on the 14th of April, 1866, she being Miss Kate Louise Gardner, only child of Joseph W. Gardner, a celebrated cutlery manufacturer of England, and is a man of wealth and high standing. Mrs. Warren is the mother of two children.

NATHAN C. WIETING.

The subject of this sketch was born in the town of Decatur, Otsego County, New York, June 8th, 1828. He is of German decent, his grandparents coming from Germany to the United States during the Revolutionary war. He is eldest son of John C. and Catharine Wieting, whose family consisted of nine children. His father was a farmer, and his son Nathan remained at home working on the farm until he was nineteen years of age, when he commenced teaching school to enable him to complete his studies at a Seminary near his home, in which manner, alternating in teaching and attending school, he spent his time until about February, 1856. On the 10th day of April 1856 he came to Toledo, and cast his lot with the early settlers of this County, and has had an unbroken residence since that time. At the first term of the District Court after his arrival he was admitted to the bar of Tama County and formed a partnership with T. Walter Jackson, in Toledo. At the fall election in 1856 he was elected Prosecuting Attorney for the County under the old law, and served during his term. In politics being an ardent

Republican, he signed the first call for party organization, and assisted in the organization of the party in 1856.

In the fall of 1858 he became proprietor of the "Toledo Tribune" and changed the name to the "Iowa Transcript" and ably conducted its columns until the fall of 1866, when he retired from the editorship of the same.

He was married to Miss Emily H. Muckler, of Toledo, on December 4th, 1858, and has one son, John Guy Wieting, born July 6th, 1873.

In the spring of 1867 he entered into the mercantile business in Toledo and, continued in the same until the fall of 1876, when he closed out his business. In January 1878 at the solicitation of many prominent Republicans he purchased the "Tama County Inpdependent" and changed the name to "Toledo Times" also the politics of the paper and is now conducting the same as a Republican organ in full sympathy with the principles of the party. The paper is one of the permanent institutions of the County, edited and owned by one who has watched the growth and progress of our County for years, and who has been fully identified with the interests of the people and as an editor shows a continuous series of more years in the County than any editor among us.

FRANK E. SMITH.

While it is true that some men inherit greatness and others have greatness thrust upon them, a large number are architects of their own fortunes. The man of this stamp, self-reliant and courageous, building on principal and not on pedigree, start out with the idea that God helps those only who help themselves. He who has faith in his own powers, who is dilligent in his calling and has his heart in his work, is on the road to success. By this direct rout the subject of this brief notice reached his present high position as book-keeper, and to a good degree, business manager in the Toledo City Bank. He is a native of Ohio, and was born in that State in Seneca County town of Republic, on the 17th day of May, 1848, and is the son of G. G. and A. Z. (Covey) Smith. His father was a mechanic and farmer.

Frank E. remained at home with his parents attending school until the year 1864, when he quit home and went to Sandusky Ohio, and enlisted as a private in the 191st Ohio, and went to the army—though but sixteen years of age, by his earnest solicitation he was permitted to enter, after which he was with his regiment from 1864 until the close of the war.

In the fall of 1865, Mr. Smith emigrated to this State and settled in Garden Grove, Decatur County. From that time to 1867 he spent his time attending school and teaching. During the next four years he clerked for D. & A. B. Stearns, and in 1871 he attended the Commercial College at Pittsburgh, graduated and received his diploma. During 1872 he was book-keeper for the firm of Boyle, Woodbury & Boyle. In 1873 he taught the Intermediate Department of the school at Garden Grove. He lived in Garden Grove until the year 1874 when he moved to Toledo, Iowa, where he remained in the Land and Loan office of Nelson & Barker, as book-keeper, until May, 1878, when he relinquished his position in that office to accept the place of assistant cashier of the Toledo City Bank, of Toledo Iowa. In so doing he gave up one of the best clerkships in the County, and one which he filled for several years. The proprietors of the City Bank have good reason to congratulate themselves on securing the services of so competent an assistant. In his business transactions he has shown himself to be a man of first-class business qualifications, and an indefatigable worker. As a book-keeper he has earned the enviable reputation of being one of the best in this part of the State. His books are models of neatness and accuracy.

HON. GAMALIEL JAQUA.

The subject of this brief note is a native of Ohio, and was born in that State, Preble County, December 30th, 1828. His parents were both natives of New York and emigrated to Ohio at a very early day settling upon a farm.

Gamaliel remained at home with his parents assisting in farming and attending district school until eighteen years of age. At this age he had acquired a sufficient amount of knowledge to make school teaching his business during the winter months, attended school during the summer until he had attained his majority Mr. Jaqua was appointed County Examiner of teachers of Preble County, Ohio. This position he filled with honor to himself and the County. Shortly after this he was elected County Superintendent of public schools, and filled the office for several years.

In the year 1856, Mr. Jaqua emigrated to this State and located in Buckingham township, this County. For a number of years after locating here, besides attending to the duties of his farm, he was engaged in teaching the Buckingham schools.

In the year 1866 he was elected a member of the Board of Supervisors filling the office for a number of years giving satisfaction to all, and besides this Mr. Jaqua has filled several of the various township offices.

In the year 1875 Mr. Jaqua was elected a member of the House of Representatives by the Republican party, and filled the office two terms, to the satisfaction of his numerous friends and supporters.

Since Mr. Jaqua has been a resident of this County, he has gathered about him a host of friends and has proven himself in the eyes of the people, an honorable and valuable citizen. His farm is located about one mile north of Traer, where he has one of the finest and most convenient homes in the County.

CHAPTER XVII.

NEWSPAPER ENTERPRISE.

A history of the County without mention of its newspapers would be incomplete—like the play of Hamlet with the part of Hamlet left out. We therefore make mention in our history of such as were easily obtainable. The first paper in the County was

The Toledo Tribune.—This paper was established in the year 1856, the first issue making its appearance April 21st, with M. V. B. Kenton, editor. In politics it was independent, though leaning somewhat toward Republicanism, and in size was a six column folio. Mr. Kenton remained connected with the paper only a short time, when he disposed of it to H. T. Baldy, and T. W. Jackson, and returned to Ohio, from whence he came.

The paper had a growing circulation and the merchants of the town done all in their power, in the way of advertising, to make it a success. On August 23d, 1865, the paper passed into the hands of George Sowers, now one of the proprietors of the "Marshall Times" and E. B. Bolens, who run the paper until Oct. 28th, 1858, when the paper again changed hands to N. C. Wieting the present editor of the "Toledo Times" who changed its name to the *Iowa Transcript.* After publishing but a few issues, Mr. Wieting disposed of one half interest to J. T. Staley. The paper was run with good success for a number of months under their management when Staley disposed of his interest, and J. F. Farley became partially interested, remaining but a short time. In Nov., 1866, Mr. Wieting removed the office to Belle Plaine, Ia., where he disposed of it shortly afterwards to Nixon & Yarham who after running it about eight months sold it to S. S. Farrington, who published it for a while; then the material passed into the hands of D. H. Frost, the present proprietor of the *Belle Plaine Union* where no doubt some of the material is used to this day.

The Tama County Republican.—This paper was established at Toledo in 1867, by J. T. Rice, who published it a short time when J. T. Stewart bought an interest. Stewart however did not remain connected with the paper very long. He disposed of his interest, and on July 17th, 1867, M. B. C. True became interested. The paper was run under the management of these gentleman but a few months, when Mr. True became sole proprietor. In 1870 Mr. True leased the office to Warren Harman, who changed its name to the *Toledo Chronicle*, and ran the paper until Jan. 1st, 1874, when J. B. Hedge, its present proprietor, bought the office of Mr. True. We now find it in the beginning of the year 1878, a large nine column paper filled with interesting and profitable reading matter, and with an advertising patronage that betokens prosperity, and that the family of its editor can have and enjoy a little more than the bare necessaries of life.

The *Chronicle* has lately added to its office a new job press, and now boasts of doing its work a little faster and a little better than its neighbors. The job office is complete, and work of all kinds, from a visiting card to a mammoth poster or a large book, can be printed in the best style. Mr. Hedge is determined not to be out-done in any way, and will not rest until he is in advance of all his neighbors in that which goes to make a first-class printing office, and a neat readable paper. It is Republican in politics.

Orford Weekly Ledger—Established in the year 1868, and was the first paper published in the town of Orford, now Montour. It was edited and published by W. M. Patrick, and was a lively little paper, well printed, and an honor to the town. The first few issues show that its editor was very sanguine of success. Of course no paper could live in as small a town as Montour was then and naturally met the fate of the frog in the fable that endeavored to swell its proportions to the size of an ox, and in doing so burst itself; we therefore learn that in a short time it ceased to exist.

The Tama County Liberal.—A nine column paper established during the campaign of 1872, and run in the interest of the Demo cratic party, with L. G. Kinne as editor. This paper was print ed at Marshalltown, and had only an existence of 5 or 6 months. Its editor, Mr. Kinne is one of the best local and plitical writers in the State, and while it existed done good work for the party.

The Tama County Independent.—This was an Independent eight column paper established by R. Reichman. July 4th, 1874, it made its first appearance. It supported the anti-monopoly party, and contributed largely to the election of the candidates on that ticket in Tama County, that fall. Mr. Reichman managed the paper up to August 1st, 1877, when it went into the hands of S. W. Grove, now editor of the *Tama County Democrat* who leased the office and run it a few months, when it again passed into Mr. Reichman's hands who shortly after sold the office to N. C. Wieting. The office of the *Penmans Help,* owned by Mr. Will Clark, was then united with it and a partnership formed by Messrs Wieting & Clark, and the name changed by them to the *Toledo Times.* After the office passed into Messrs Weiting & Clark's hands it was largely restocked with new type, etc., and to-day is a forty-eight column quarto always clearly and neatly printed. It enjoys a large circulation, and is a welcome visitor in many a home in the far west, where it is eagerly read by former inhabitants of this County. The proprietors claim to have three hundred subscribers more than any other paper in the County and to be unexcelled in any class of job work.

The chief feature of this paper is its excellence as a local and family newspaper. Nothing is ever permitted to appear either in its editorial or advertising columns which may not be read by any family circle or at any fireside.   It has a good advertising patron-age and stands on its own merits.   It is well known for its short and spicy paragraphs, and is more widely quoted from than any paper in the County.   In politics, Republican.

The Tama County Union.—By Cyrus B. Ingham, was established in the year, 1866, the first issue making its appearance April 26th, of that year.   It was devoted to home interests, literary, agricultural and general news, free from party cliques.   This paper was the first one published at the town of Iuka, now Tama City, with C. B. Ingham and C. E. Heath, editors.   The following motto appeared under its head.

> "O seize on truth where'er its found,
>   Among your friends, among your foes,
>   On christian or on Heathen ground,
>   The plant's divine where'er it grows".

The paper was a six Column folio, and while under their management met with good success, both in advertising and in circulation.   In the first issue appears the names of many who are still in business in Tama City.   Among them we can mention Thomas Murray, dry goods; M. C. Murdough, agricultural implements, dry goods etc; James Brice Jr., groceries; Thomas Whitaker, produce dealer and Wm. Corns M. D.   The paper was conducted by them some two years then went into the hands of W. G. Cambridge, who changed the heading of the paper to *The Tama Citizen.* and enlarged it to an eight column paper. During his management the paper was well supported, having a good circulation both in the County and out.   After running the paper until the latter part of 1875, Mr. Cambridge stopped issuing it on account of ill health, and a few months after the material was sold to F. J. M. Wonser, and on October 8th, 1875, the paper was enlarged to nine columns and issued under the head of *The Tama Herald.*   The paper at present is managed by Mr. Wonser, he being the editor and proprietor, and receives good support both at home and abroad.   From time to time Mr. Wonser has added to the material new styles of type, until now he owns a very fine office.

The Tama City Press.—In consequence of the expression of the political views of the Republican papers in the County, the Democrats in Tama City and vicinity were desirous of establishing a Democratic paper, and S. M. Chapman, father of the publisher of this work, was persuaded to embark in the enterprise, and under the above name the first number was issued, January 1st, 1874.

After publishing but a few issues the paper was turned over to J. B. Spafford and W. S. Mesmer, who issued it for a number of months, but, on account of want of capital these gentleman soon withdrew, and the paper went back into its first owners hands, who again resumed the responsibility of publishing it. He afterwards sold an interest to S. W. Grove, the present editor of the *Tama County Democrat*, and the paper was enlarged to a six column quarto, published every Friday morning by Chapman & Grove, with good success having a large circulation and advertising medium, until in the latter part of 1875, when it passed into the hands of J. B. Chapman, son of S. M. Chapman; who run the paper, making it one of the official papers of the County, until the latter part of 1877, when the material was sold to J. G. Strong and removed to Grundy Center.

The Tama County Democrat.—This paper is published every week by S. W. Grove. The first issue made its appearance April 12th, 1878. The paper is a six column folio, well printed and newsy sheet. Its editor, Mr. Grove is a spicy local writer and his paper is read by many. In politics it is Democratic and works for the advancement of that party. Connected with the office is a job department, from which is turned out good work.

The Traer Star.—This paper was established at Traer in 1878, by Elmer E. Taylor, and its first issue made its appearance May 1st, of that year. It is a five column folio, filled with interesting and profitable reading matter, and with an advertising patronage that betokens prosperity. Its editor though young in years, is a public spirited and enterprising young man, and deserves success.

The People's Friend.—We have been unable to find a copy of this paper, or learn any special information in regard to it, further than it was published by an erratic genius, who knew more about "table-tipping" than running a newspaper. The *Friend* only lived a few months, the people of Chelsea and vicinity failing to render it the neccessary aid to keep it before the people.

The Dysart Reporter.—This is a seven column folio established in 1878, by T. N. Ives, and is the first paper published in the town of Dysart; the first number of which bears date of March 20th, 1878. Its editor and proprietor, Mr. Ives, is publishing one among the finest papers in the County, is well printed and is an honor to the town. It has a good advertising patronage and a large circulation for the time it has been in existence. It is an Independent advocator.

The Penman's Help.—This paper was established at Toledo, in March, 1877, and is devoted to the interests of penmen, and penmanship, by Will Clark. In April, 1879, the name was changed to *Album of Pen Art*, improved in appearance and is now an eight page semi-monthly, a well printed and edited sheet. Mr. Clark informs us that its circulation extends to thirty-two States of the Union, as well as to Canada, New Brunswick and Nova Scotia.

The Traer Clipper,—Was established by Bernard Murphy, in 1874. Mr. M. being a fine editor and a printer met with good success and his paper was liked by all. He had a good advertising patronage, and done much in building up the place. It was an eight column folio, and made its first appearance, January 1st 1874. Mr. M. managed the paper until August 16th, 1876, when it passed into the hands of Averill Bros & Beatty, who enlarged it January 1st, 1877, to nine columns and printed it all at home. In the fall of 1878, Averill Bros bought Beatty's interest and published the paper in their own name making it one of the official papers of the County.

Like many other newspapers, the *Clipper* has had its ups and downs, its seasons of prosperity and seasons of adversity, but it continued to toil on looking forward to the better day coming until the night of December 24th, 1878, when from some cause it was destroyed by fire. Its proprietors though somewhat discouraged soon had new presses and material on hand. The paper continued under their management until July, 1879, when it passed into the hands of Hon. James Wilson, James Morrison, and R. H. Moore, the present managers.

CHAPTER XVIII.

In seeking a new home at the present day the question is almost invariably asked as to what are the religious influences in the community to which it is desired to emigrate. A community in which the school house and the church find a special recognition will always be selected in preference to the one in which these are not found. Men of the world recognize the fact that educational and Christian institutions are the hand-maids of general thrift and prosperity. Improvements in the manners, tastes and moral status of the people, follow closely the preaching of the gospel. The following, says Ford in his history of Illinois, and it is the same everywhere:

"As to the practice of attending church on Sunday, I am confident that it produces these effects, the improvement in dress, manners, etc. I have observed very carefully in the course of thirty-five years spent upon the frontier, that in those neighborhoods where the people habitually neglect to attend public worship on Sunday, such improvements rarely, if ever, take place. In such places, the young people feel no pride, and do not desire improvement. They scarcely ever throw aside their every-day rough apparel to dress up neat and clean on Sunday.

On that day the young men are seen with uncombed hair, unshaved beards, and mashed linen, strolling in the woods hunting,

or on the race course, or at a grocery contracting habits of in-
toxication, or lounging sullenly and lazily at home. The young
women, in appearance, dress, manners and intelligence, are the
fit companions for their brothers. Sunday to them brings no
bright skies, no gladness, no lively or cheerful thoughts, no
spirits renovated by mixing in the sober, decent, quiet, but gay
assemblage of youth and beauty. Their week of labor is not
cheered by anticipations of the gay and bright fête with which it
is to close. Labor through the week is to them a drudgery, and
is performed with surliness and grudgery, and their Sabbaths are
spent in heedless, sleepy stupidity. The young people of both
sexes are without self-respect and are conscious of not deserving
the respect of others. They feel a crushing and withering sense
of meanness and inferiority, mingled with an envious malignity
towards all excellence in others who exhibit an ambition for improvement. Such neighborhoods are pretty certain to breed up
a rough, vicious ill-mannered and ill-natured race of men and
women."

The early settlements of this County were especially blessed
in respect to religious influences. The sound of the hammers
used in the erection of the first cabins had hardly died away before the minister of the gospel made his appearance. As recorded elsewhere a few families settled in the neighborhood of the
present town of Traer in 1852; here Rev. S. W. Ingham, a Methodist
minister, in May, 1853, effected the first religious organization, at
the house of Normon L. Osborn, in Tama County and preached
the first sermon at that time. This organization was called the
Tama Mission, with Ira Taylor as class Leader. Their first
quarterly meeting was held on November 26th, 1853 at the house
of Zebedee Rush, near Toledo. They built the first church in
the summer of 1857 at Toledo.

Elder Ingham is still a resident of this County and is a hard
working, zealous Christain, who has spent much time in laboring
for his Master. For many years he traveled from settlement to
settlement in this County, preaching the gospel of Jesus Christ.
He was instrumental in organizing many of the Methodist

churches in this County and his name is held in greatful rememberance by all who has had the pleasure of forming his acquaintance.

METHODIST EPISCOPAL CHURCH.

While other denominations lagged in the work, the Methodist have pushed boldly on, holding their meetings in public halls, school houses, private dwellings or any place where the people could be brought together to hear the proclamation of the gospel. Whatever may be said of the religious views of this denomination its zeal is to be commended, and the fact that its members are zealous workers.

The first church was built in Toledo, at a cost of nearly $3,200 and a membership of thirteen. The church from that time to the present has been in a very prosperous condition and at this writing, February 12th, 1879, its members number one-hundred and twenty. The church building a few years ago was partially rebuilt and refitted at a cost of $1,500, and now the members worship in a vast and commodious chapel.

The pastors in charge, since 1857, have been Revs. D. H. Peterfish, W. N. Brown, S. Dunton, C. Babcock, J. J. Kelly, S. W. Ingham, B. Swearinger, D. C. Worts, D. H. Mallory, S. A Lee, J. S. Eberheart, R. N. Earheart, F. M. Roberts, W. B. Frazelle and the present pastor H. H. Green, who is now serving his third year here. The church stands upon the corner of Broadway and Ohio Streets, and in connection with the church is a beautiful parsonage, in the same yard, built of brick, two stories high, with eight fine rooms, wardrobes etc., which is occupied by the pastor.

METHODIST EPISCOPAL CHURCH OF TAMA CITY.

The first meetings of this branch were held in Iuka, at the old school house in the north part of town. These meetings were conducted by Rev. D. M. Mallory. In 1865 a society was organized with the following members: W. T. Hollen and wife, Mrs. M. Soleman, F. J. M. Wonser and wife, J. W. McIntire and wife, C. King and wife, L. Merchant, and Mr. Grist. The next year a church structure was erected in the north west part of town on the corner of Eighth and Seigel Steets, at a cost of $4.200. It was a good frame building, thirty feet wide and fifty feet long, with a basement which was used for school purposes.

In 1862 the building was removed from this site to its present location on the corner of State and Sixth Streets. After the building was moved it was rebuilt and refitted at a large expense and now is a large and commodious place of worship. The growth of the society has been moderate, and at present the membership numbers one hundred. The following are those having served as pastors: Revs. D. M. Mallory, J. Todd, R. M. Wade, A. Critchfield, J. G. Wilkinson, M. T. Smedley, L. Catlin, E. S. Bargelt, S. B. Warner, and the present pastor is B. C. Barns. A good Sunday School is held in connection with the church, with Mr. Mahana as Superintendent, and an average attendance of one hundred and forty.

METHODIST EPISCOPAL CHURCH OF TRAER.

This Church was organized in 1853, with a small membership, at Buckingham. After which services was held in the school house, at Buckingham until the year 1868, when a church house was erected. This denomination continued to hold services at this place, building up the cause and doing a good work for the master until the year 1874, when the church was moved to Traer. After the church was moved it was greatly improved, and to a good extent rebuilt, and now the people of Trear and vicinity worship in a fine church house, with Rev. M. H. Smith, as their pastor. The present membership is about one hundred and twenty. There is a fine Sunday School in connection which num bers about one hundred and fifteen scholars.

METHODIST EPISCOPAL CHURCH OF MONTOUR.

In the year 1854, this society was organized at Indiantown, by Rev. S. Dunton, an old pioneer preacher. Services were held in the school house at Indiantown, until the town of Montour was located where it afterwards met. From this date services were held in the Town Hall until the year 1874, when a church house was erected at a cost of $3.000. The building is a fine frame structure thirty-two feet wide and sixty feet long. On July

26th, 1874, it was dedicated by the Rev. J. W. Clinton. The Church is now in good standing with a membership of forty-seven and Rev. S. N. Howard, pastor. In connection with the it there is a fine Sunday School with an average attendance of eighty. L. Bingham, Superintendent.

METHODIST EPISCOPAL CHURCH OF DYSART.

This organization is also quite old, it being organized before the town was laid out. When the town was established, the denomination having no church, services were held in a wagon shop in the north west part of the town. In the year 1874, a church was erected and dedicated by Rev. E. Holland, assisted by Rev. A. R. Shinner. A good Sunday School is held in connection with the Church.

METHODIST EPISCOPAL CHURCH OF HOWARD TOWNSHIP.

This society has been in existence for a long time, and until quite recently has been without a house of worship, hold ing their services in the various school houses of the township. At present the people of this township have a neat and commodious house of worship, with a fine Sunday School in connection.

PRESBYTERIANS.

This eminent respectable body of evangelical christians were the third to establish its cause in this County.

A sufficient number of former members of this body having settled in Crystal township, in the early part of the year 1855, it was determined to effect an organization, and the Rev. W. J. Lyons, of Blackhawk County, was invited here for that purpose. A meeting was called at the house of J. S. Townsend, where he organized the first Presbyterian Church in the County, with fifteen members. Mr. Lyon continued laboring with this congregation for some years preaching frequently in various parts of the County.

Although not an aggressive body, the Presbyterians in this County have continued steadily to grow, until they now number several hundred. In the order of their organization we append sketches of each congregation, beginning first with Salem Church of Crystal township.

SALEM CHURCH.

The Presbyterian Church of Crystal township was the first of that denomination in the County, and was organized in 1856, three years after the County was organized. The organization took place at the residence of J. S. Townsend, who is yet a resident of the township. At this time fifteen persons became members of the society. Services were held at different places in the neighborhood each Sunday, for a number of years until a church building was erected and given the above name. The society at this writing is in a prosperous condition, with Rev. James Stickle as pastor. The membership at present numbers fifty-six.

TOLEDO CHURCH.

This Church was organized about the year 1859, with fifteen members, by Rev. L. Dodd. In the year 1862, a house of worship was erected at a cost of $1,600. From time to time the church has been repaired and refitted until now it is a neat place of worship. This organization is also under the care of Rev. James Stickle. The present membership is fifty-two. A large Sunday School is held in connection with the society.

ROCK CREEK CHURCH.

At an early day services were held at the residence of James Laughlin, by Rev. J. S. Mason, although no permanent organization existed until a church building was erected in the year 1865. This church is located in Carlton township, and is known as, the Rock Creek Church. The present membership is forty. A good Sunday School is in connection with the Church which averages about thirty members.

DYSART CHURCH.

The Presbyterian society of this place was organized at Yankee Grove, Benton County, in the year 1860. When the town of Dysart was established the congregation changed its place of worship to that town. In the year 1873 a church was built at a cost of $3,000, which was dedicated by Rev. S. Phelps, assisted by Rev. D. L. Hughes, who has labored with the congregation from that time to the present, and is a well known and well educated minister of that denomination. A Sunday School which averages about forty members is in successful operation with the Church, and has Rev. Mr. Hughes as Superintendent.

TRANQUILITY CHURCH.

This church is located in the south western corner of Perry township in a fine Scotch settlement. In the year 1874-5, the congregation erected a frame church at a cost of about $1,200, and was dedicated by Rev. L. Dodd. A Sunday School is connected with the Church which is in successful working order.

CONGREGATIONAL CHURCH OF TOLEDO.

The first Congregational Church of Toledo was organized in December, 1854, with eleven members. Three years after, a fine church was erected on the corner of East and State Streets, 30x45, with a large basement which for a number of years afterwards was used for school purposes. It was in this basement the publisher of this work learned to read and write. The building when completed cost $3,000. The first pastor, Mr. Woodward was among the pioneer ministers of the County, and did much to establish the good cause here. It is but a few years since this eminent minister passed to the other shore, and left many sorrowing hearts and the seed of his good works which have sprung up a monument to his name.

The membership, at present numbers seventy-five. In connection with this is a prosperous Sabbath School.

MONTOUR CHURCH.

The Congregational Church of Montour was organized at Indiantown, June 10th, 1855, by Rev. T. M. Skinner, with the following members: J. M. Bradley and wife; J. E. and O. Cunningham, Mrs. Abbott, Miss Lucy and Carolina Helm and J. Moore. Services were held in the school house at this place until a church building was erected at Montour, in 1868, when the society changed their place of worship to the new building. The society now numbers sixty-two members. Rev. C. C. Adams is the present pastor, and also superintendent of the Sunday School which is a good one.

TRAER CHURCH.

In 1857 the settlers of this part of the County, feeling the need of divine worship, obtained the assistance of Rev. J. R. Upton, a minister of this denomination who labored with them for two years, and was followed by Rev. Emerson who remained until September, 1863, when he was succeeded by Rev. Mr. Roberts who labored with the congregation for a number of years. In 1866-7 a church was built an Buckingham, which cost about $5,000 and was dedicated in June, 1867, by Rev. D. Myers. When the town of Traer was established the church was moved to that place in September, 1874. After the building had been moved and fitted up Rev. C. H. Bissell became pastor and still remains with the congregation. The membership at present is about one-hundred.

BAPTIST CHURCH OF TAMA CITY.

This society was organized in 1869 by Rev. L. L. Gage, with the following members: L. Carmichael and wife, Miss Ella Carmichael, J. H. Brooks and wife, J. H. Lewis and wife, C. R. Veber and wife, J. Herbage and wife, S. W. Cole, G. H. Warren and G. E. Maxwell. The next year, 1870 a fine brick church building was erected on the corner of State and Seventh Streets, forty feet wide and fifty feet long, at a cost of $6,000. The house at present is in good repair and affords a neat and commodious house of worship. The membership is now one hundred and fifty. The following persons have served as pastors since the organization: Revs. L. L. Gage. T. W. Powell and the present pastor Rev. O. A. Holmes. Mr. Holmes has labored with the congregation nearly nine years. He is a zealous christian and is doing much for the cause of christianity. In connection with the Church is a large Sunday School that has an average attendance of about one hundred and twenty-five, with G. E. Iligley, Superintendent.

BAPTIST CHURCH OF TOLEDO.

The first Baptist Church of Toledo was organized January 18th, 1856, with fourteen members, by Rev. G. G. Edwards. About the year 1860 a church house was built at a cost of nearly $2,000.

At present there are eighty persons in full connection with the Church, with Rev. H. A. Brown as their pastor. Mr. Brown has been at the head of this society ever since the year 1865 and his labor in Toledo has been blessed with the richest tokens of divine favors.

UNITED PRESBYTERIANS AT TRAER.

In the year 1878, this denomination erected one of the finest churches in the County. The building is a brick structure valued at $7,000. A very tall and beautifully proportioned steeple arises from the front end, towers far above the surrounding buildings and within hangs an immense bell. The audience room is neat and commodious, well furnished and artistically painted, with a capacity of seating several hundred people. The present pastor is Rev. Livingston.

CHRISTAIN CHURCH OF TOLEDO.

This organization was effected in 1865, and had six members. Rev. A. Cordner as pastor. In the following year a good frame building was erected at a cost of about $1,700. The various pastors employed by this congregation from time to time have been Rev. A. Cordner, E. J. Stanley, A. H. Mulkey, J. A. Wilson, O. H. Derry, L. Lane and the present pastor Rev. A. Cordner, of Tama City. The present membership is about sixty-five. A good Sunday School is in connection with the church, averaging about forty scholars.

CATHOLIC CHURCH OF TAMA COUNTY.

Five congregations exist in this County, viz; at Toledo, Tama City, Chelsea and two in Otter Creek township. In these congregations there has been a special effort made to build up their cause, and at present there are over one hundred and fifty families, at an average of five persons to the family, making seven hundred and fifty members in connection with their Churches. The first society was organized at Toledo, with twenty members. In 1861, a church was built at the same place, and now the membership is over one hundred.

TAMA CITY CHURCH.

The Catholic Church of Tama City was organized in 1874, by

Rev. Father McCabe, and the following year a fine church was built in the northeast part of town, where services are held every two weeks. Rev. Mr. McCabe officiated for about three years and was succeeded by Father O'Tarrell who remained one year. The present pastor is Rev. Father Meagher. The church financially is in good condition; the whole property is valued at $5,000 The average attendance in the Sunday School is about eighty.

CHELSEA AND OTTER CREEK CHURCHES.

These congregations are officiated over by Rev. Father Zleipsic. The churches are well attended and good Sunday School in connection.

UNION CHURCH.

This Church was built at Eureka, in the year 1866, by the people of Richland township, and given the above name. As its name signifies it was not built for one special denomination but holds its door open for all that are of the true christain religion.

FREE WILL BAPTISTS OF TOLEDO.

This society was organized in 1865, and this same year a church building was erected. For a while the Church was quite prosperous having a large membership, but at present the membership is but thirty. There is no regular pastor at present.

UNITED BRETHERN OF TOLEDO.

In the year 1873, this society was organized at Toledo, by Elder M. Bowman, who preached the first sermon. In 1874 a magnificent church edifice was erected on Church Street near the business portion of the town, at a cost of nearly $6,000. Many interesting and profitable meetings have been held at this church. The present membership is sixty, with Rev. J. P. Wilson leader. A large Sunday School is held in connection with the Church which is in a prosperous condition. The following named persons have served as pastors: Revs. M. Bowman, C. Kephart, M. R. Drury.

BADGER HILL CHURCH.

This Church was organized October 22nd, 1877, and in 1879

a fine church building was erected at that point. The attendance is large.

CHURCH OF GOD.

The Church of God was organized at West Irving, October 13th, 1877, and a church building was erected the same year at a cost of about $2,000, and is beautifully located. The membership is large.

There are other temporary organizations which we might mention, but space will not permit.

CHAPTER XIX.

EDUCATIONAL.

The progress in this County is nowhere better illustrated than in connection with our public schools. In the early day good schools were like "angels visits, few and far between" and it was considered very fortunate indeed if an opportunity was offered for obtaining even the rudiments of a common school education. A person competent to teach the three branches commonly and sarcastically spoken of as "Reading 'Riting and 'Rithmetic," could seldom be obtained. Some of the few scattered settlements could not afford to employ a teacher, and were therefore compelled to do without, or send their children through the timber, or across the prairie to some more fortunate settlement where a school was in operation. The writer is personally acquainted with some who were sent a distance of four to six miles, walking the entire distance, morning and evening, of each day, in order that they might avail themselves of the opportunity of acquiring a little knowledge of their mother tongue, and thus fit themselves for the duties of life. How different now, in every township there are from seven to nine schools in successful operation; competent teachers are employed, many of whom have spent years in fitting themselves for their vocation, and who make teaching a profession, by preparing themselves as thoroughly for this work as the lawyer, doctor, or divine are presumed to do.

In those days a log house or shanty was erected, on some of the settlers land probably 10x12, with but one window, a small door way, cut through the logs at the most convenient place for the teacher and scholars to come in at, while the furniture consisted of slab seats for the scholars, a three legged stool and a hazel or hickory rod for the teacher. As for books, but few were needed the less the better; as the teacher could get along the more readily. The walls of the school room were decorated by the artistic hands of the scholars, with drawings of the teacher, instead of being hung with such beautiful and instructive maps, as are now found in all our school buildings.

Instead of the beautiful specimens of penmanship now-a-days set for children to copy, teachers were then employed who in many instance, could scarcely write their own names. Altogether in the light of to-day, the schools of twenty and twenty-five years ago were very dreary affairs.

By law the sixteenth section of every township was to be used for school purposes, but there being little or no sale for land, and the government price of $1.25 per acre, being all that could be realized from its sale, the income to be derived from them, amounted to but little. Subscription schools, therefore, had to be depended upon.

Among the first schools opened in the County, was one in Buckingham township, in the summer of 1854, and taught by Mrs. Rachel Wood. The first school house paid for from the public treasury was built in the spring of 1856. From this time forward the people began to avail themselves of the privileges of the school law, but not until the last few years was any remarkable progress made.

The school statistics of the County are an interesting study. We find there are, between the ages of five and twenty-one years, 7,379 persons. There were enrolled during the year 1878, 6,067 pupils in the various schools, showing that 1,712 of the number of those of school age, were kept altogether from the schools; but notwithstanding there are but eight females and seven males between the age of twelve and twenty-one that are unable to read or write.

There are 172 school houses having a total value of $139,538. There was raised for all school purposes during the year 1878 in tax, and from other sources $86,360.46 of which $23,736.40 were paid teachers; $14,202.13 paid for school houses and sites; rent and repairs $5,085.65; fuel $4,730.77; records, dictionaries and apparatus $244.82; insurance $356.60; janitors $773.43; for other purposes $3,960.13; on bonds and interest $2,327.05; and some other expenses which added to the above will make a total expenditure for school purposes of $53,416.98 with a balance on hand of $32,943.48. The average wages paid male teacher out side of Tama City, Toledo, Traer, Dysart, and Montour, are about $30 per month, and female teachers $24.37. The highest salary paid any male teacher was $111.10 per month, the lowest salary, $25. The highest paid any female teacher was $50 lowest $20 per month. The number of first grade certificates granted during 1878, were ninety-four; second grade 198; third grade 86; There were 278 applicants for certificates, of whom 157 were females.

There are now some fine schools in Tama County, among which are the graded schools of Tama City, Traer, Toledo, and Montour all of which are in fine operation and doing much for the cause of education, and many young gentlemen and ladies have graduated from these institutions, who are now occupying honorable positions in life. The public schools at Toledo are under the management of Prof. J. J. Andrews; at Tama City, Prof. F. B. Gault; at Montour, Prof. W. H. Black. and at Traer, Prof. W. H. Brinkerhoff. All of these gentlemen are men of rare educational ability, and are doing much in their individual schools for the education of the young and are making Tama County's graded schools as fine as any in the State of Iowa.

In the year 1878 a fine school house was erected at Dysart and ere long this school will rank with the rest.

THE NORMAL INSTITUTE.

In 1874 the Normal Institute of this County was organized at Toledo, for the benefit of those engaged in teaching, by Prof A.

H. Sterrett. This year the Normal Institute opened August 11st, by order of H. A. Brown, County Superintendent, in the public school building at Toledo, continuing until September 7th, with a fine corps of teachers consisting of Prof's, J. J. Andrews, W. H. Black, C. A. Wessell, F. B. Gault, and Mrs. A. N. Sterrett. The institution has a valuable reputation and great pains are taken to make it a thorough work, and of lasting benefit to the teachers.

CHAPTER XX.

Ever since the organization of the County, the unfortunate, the infirm and the poor have been generously and humanely provided for by the County under the management and direction of the County Supervisors. When the management of County affairs passed into the hands of Supervisors, they with the township Trustees became agents for the care of the poor with power to provide for their wants, and supply them with all needed necessaries. The accounts for which were submitted to the full Board at stated periods, duly audited and ordered to be paid out of the proper funds.

At the general election 1875, the proposition was submitted to the voters for the purchase of a poor farm and the erection of necessary buildings, etc. At this election, the proposition prevailed by a large majority and the Board of Supervisors proceeded to purchase, of A. J. Wheaton, a tract of one hundred and fifty acres of land on section two, township eighty-three, range fifteen, and pay therefor the sum of $6,750, to be paid out of the Poor Farm fund as follows: $500 upon the execution and delivering of a good warrantee deed from A. J. Wheaton and wife, to Tama County, Iowa, and $3,125, on or before the first day of March, 1877, and $3,125 on or before the first day of November, 1877, and the County Auditor was authorized to draw warrants on the Poor Farm fund to pay for said farm as above stated. The contract for re-moddling and enlarging the building was awarded to the Tama Hydraulic and Builders Association of Tama City, for $4,084.65, while Kent and Conklin, were the architects. The entire building is in height two stories; the architectural design is modern and very neat, giving the building an appearance of beauty and comfort, with an eighty-four foot front, and large wings upon the north and west. Upon the second floor, or sleeping department, are twenty pleasant rooms with closets, wardrobes and halls, while the first floor contains the dining hall, a large and pleasant room, situated in the south east corner with a large kitchen upon the west; and upon the north connected with a large hall leading from the dining room and kitchen, are the rooms occupied by the overseers, Mr. and Mrs. Childs. This appartment contains a parlor or sitting room, several bed rooms, with wardrobes etc., making it a pleasant home for its occupants, while in the entire building there are thirty-six rooms.

The building is built upon a high elevation and stands in a beautifully decorated yard, enclosed by a neat and substantial fence. From this point a fine view of the surrounding country can be obtained. The farm is well fenced, and stocked in good style, and has all the latest improvements. No doubt, ere long, this will be a self supporting institution. January 1st, 1879, Tama County was supporting twenty-six paupers at the Poor Farm, under the supervision of A. Child, who took posession December 1st, 1876.

THE FARMERS' MUTUAL AID COMPANY

This company is a County organization formed for the purpose of protecting its members against loss of property by fire or lightning. At a meeting held at White Pigeon School House in Carlton township, March 11th, 1873, a company was organized known as the Farmers' Mutual Aid Company of Tama County, Iowa, offering insurance to all in the County, with the exception of towns and houses in the immediate vicinity of towns. The business headquarters are at Toledo.

March 11th, 1873, L. F. Hammitt was elected President; D.

H. Patterson, Secretary and Samuel Giger, Treasurer. These gentlemen served one year, when their successors were elected.

The company has been in successful operation from the time of its organization, and on December 31st, 1878, it was carrying risks to the amount of $1,032,141.00 which speaks well for the organization. In the year 1878 the company paid losses to the amount of $1,816.55. Total expense for the year, including the expenses of running the company, losses paid etc., $1,992.51.

This is a home institution and one that should meet the approval and support of every inhabitant of Tama County. Persons wishing to carry insurance can do so in this company much less than in other companies, and by doing so support a home institution. The present officers are Franklin Davis, President; D. McCormick, Secretary; J. B. M. Bishop, Treasurer.

POLITICAL.

Politically, Tama County has always been classed among the Republican Counties. During the exciting Presidential campaign of 1856, party lines were distinctly drawn. The Republicans remained in power, filling the various County offices, until 1873, when the anti-Monopoly party sprang into existence and by uniting with the Democrats, they elected all their ticket but one officer. In 1874, there was a triangular fight; three parties in the field, Democratic, Republican, and Independent, the organization known as the anti-Monopoly party having been abandoned or merged into the Independent. About seven-eighths of the regular vote was polled, the Republicans for most of the County offices being successful. In 1876 success in various States gave the Democracy increased hope and being thoroughly organized came out under the old name. Certain abuses in the administration of the civil service of the country gave the party a chance to demand a change, and under the cry of "Reform" they went into the canvass with a determination to win, and joined in a union ticket with the third party which was now known as the Greenback party.

The tickets were good ones. The union ticket elected their candidate for Sheriff and the Republicans the balance.

For the past few years in consequense of closeness the different canvasses have been very warm, and in general men of unquestionable personal character have been nominated, each party trusting the personal popularity of its nominee would insure success.

CHAPTER XXI.

When Peter McRoberts erected his log cabin near the present site of the school building on the corner of Green and Carlton Streets in Toledo, little did he think there would spring up around it a busy little city with all its various industries. Time in its unceasing round brings many changes, and the wild prairie land, with its beautiful flowers watting their sweet perfume upon every breeze, is now dotted over with home-like residences, from the lowly cottage to the stately mansion. Elegant buildings, filled with products gathered from the entire world, surround a beautiful temple of justice, while the sound of the hammer and hum of the machinery are heard upon every hand.

Having a population which entitled them to the benefit of the act which authorized the organization of counties, in the year 1853 the citizens of Tama County petitioned for an organization and in the fall of this year, Hon. James P. Carlton, District Judge, of the Fourth Judicial District, appointed J. M. Furgerson of Marshall County and R. B. Ogden of Poweshiek County, commissioners to locate a seat of justice for this County. They met at the house of J. C. Vermilya, on October 20th of that year and proceeded to choose a suitable location. They first examined a quarter section near Bruner's Mill, adjoining Monticello, a village in Howard township, but not receiving sufficient inducement in donation of lands, they concluded to look farther. The next place they examined was a part of the farm surrounding the residence of Mr. Franklin Davis, a half mile north of its present northern boundary. The location being a very fine one they offered to take less land for its location here than they demanded before. Mr. Davis not being inclined to donate any of his land for that purpose, thy next came and located it upon its present site, receiving donations in land for that purpose as previously described in a former chapter of this work.

The first sale of lots in the town were made very soon after (and quite a number reserved for donation,) from which was realized a a large sum of money. The erection of business and dwelling houses immediately commenced. In the fall of this year John Zehrung erected the first store building in the place, on the lot now occupied by J. W. Coe as a shoemaker and harness shop. The building was a small frame affair about 18x20. The stock, says our informant, contained in that store was a wonder to behold! A conglomeration of almost everything that could be thought of in the mercantile trade, and still added to its mess was the post office in the same room. John Nixon and Lewis Merchant shortly after erected a building to be used for general trade. About this time a Mr. Mitchell opened a tavern a little south of E. E. Stickney's present hotel. This was a small log house with but two or three rooms and they poorly furnished. The culinary department was well represented with various wild meats and good wholesome food.

As time passed the place rapidly increased and every one was looking forward to a bright future. During court week the settlers would gather in the town, and of course, as it was customary in those days upon the frontier to drink, many would indulge, just for a little fun.

In 1866 the town of Toledo was incorporated as a city of the third class, and at the first election the following gentlemen were chosen for officers: Mayor, W. F. Johnston; Recorder, S. C. Rogers; Marshal, S. O. Bishop; Attorney, A. Stoddard; Assessor, A. H. Lawrence; Treasurer,———- Trustees, D. D. Appel gate, N. Bates, W. H. Harrison, G. W. Free, Sr. and L. Wells. These gentlemen were elected for the term of one year. It has now been thirteen years since its organization, and in that time no city of its size has made more permanent improvement and none enjoy a better reputation. Its credit has always been at par and its bonds would doubtless command a premium. This shows conclusively that the financiering of the city fathers has been excellent. A glance at the list of officers given in this article, will show a good reason for this state of affairs.

Notwithstanding the city has never been prodigal in its expenditures it has yet never been niggardly. Improvements are constantly being made. During the past year, (1878) several fine buildings have been erected, and numerous other minor improvements such as decorating yards, erecting street lamps, etc. which add largely to the beauty of the place. There is also a well organized fire department. It has so far in its existence been very fortunate in escaping the ravages of the fire fiend, but there is always danger and that danger we can say, is well guarded against, with an excellent and well conducted fire company, with an engine and a large amount of hose. The town also has built three very large cisterns and an unusually large well, to use in case of fire.

The sanitary condition of the city has always been excellent. The Board of Health, has always consisted of the best physician, representing various medical schools, with the Mayor as an ex-officio member.

In relation to the financial standing of the city, we may say it never has to go abroad for aid, capitalists at home are ever ready and willing to advance all that is needed.

The town is not on any direct railroad, but connected with the Chicago & Northwestern by a branch road running from Tama City, two and one-half miles south, operated by the Northwestern company. This gives an outlet for transportation and tends to make Toledo a good trading ·point. No town in the County can boast of finer public buildings. Among which we

mention the Court House, Public School building, business blocks
jail, churches, etc.

The new school house, built in 1878, is the pride of the city,
It is a large and handsome structure, with accommodations for
about eight hundred pupils. It is situated on the corner of
Green and Carlton Streets, and known as the Toledo Public
School. When completed and furnished it was estimated to
have cost about $20,000. It is 71x72 feet on the ground ex-
clusive of the old part or wing. It is three stories high, besides
the basement, and is built of brick, with a stone foundation.
The first and second floors contain three school-rooms each.
There is also a room in the tower for the Principal in which is
kept the apparatus. The third floor contains a large hall, which
is used as a society room, or other purposes as may be seen fit.
There are also on the first and second floors good roomy closets
or wardrobes provided with hooks for hanging clothes, packages,
etc. The basement is fitted up for a play room with the exception
of a room large enough for the fuel.

The entrance is made at the tower, through two large double
doors, and also another at the end of the wide hall extending
through the building from north to south. The stairs leading to
the second floor are double, one flight on both north and
south side of a small hall running east and west. The roof is
entirely covered with slate and tin. The rooms and halls are all
wainscoted with Georgia pine—a specie of pine which is almost
as hard as oak.

The school is now made up of six departments First, Second
and third Primary, Intermediate, Grammar, and High School.
This is a matter in which the citizens of the town take an special
pride. For many years there has been employed by the Board
of directors none but teachers with first class certificates. On
the completion of the school building in the fall of 1878, Prof.
Andrews, who has been in the employ of the Board, took charge
of the schools in the new building and since that time he has
made some changes for the good of the school. The course of
study has been as thorough as in any of the academies of the

State. Prof. Andrews still continues as superintendent and has succeeded in a perfect organization of every department, giving entire satisfaction to the people.

The following is a complete list of those filling the various city offices from its organization up to the present year 1879:

1866.—W. F. Johnston, Mayor; S. C. Rogers, Recorder; S. O. Bishop, Marshal; ———— Treasurer; A. Stoddard, Attorney; A. H. Lawrence, Assessor; D. D. Appelgate, N. Bates, G. W. Free, Sr., L. Wells, Wm. H. Harrison, Trsntees.

1867.—P. B. McCullough, Mayor; T. S. Free, Recorder; S. O. Bishop, Marshal; J. H. Struble, Treasurer; T. J. Rice, Attorney; T. H. Graham, Assessor; J. N. Springer, E. Gallion, Geo. W. Free, C. G. Buttkereit, J. S. Moore, Trustees.

1868.—J. N. Springer, Mayor; J. R. McClaskey, Recorder; R. C. Wilson, John Thede, Marshals; ———— Attorney, Silas McClain, Assessor; Geo. W. Free, Jr., H Galley, P. G. Wieting, J. Q. Clark, D. Stoner, Trustees.

1869.—H. Galley, Mayor; J. D. Newcomer, Recorder; John Thede, Marshal; Wm. H. Allen, Treasurer; ———— Attorney; Silas McClain, Assessor; C. C. Guilford, C. G. Buttkereit, Smith Newcomer, L. Clark, L. B. Nelson, Trustees.

1870.—Alford Phillips, Mayor; J. D. Newcomer, Recorder; C. S. Bailey, Marshal; A. J. Free, Treasurer; C. H. Crawford, Attorney; Wm. Reickhoff, Assessor; W. N. Brown, W. H. Harrison, J. N. Springer, N. C. Wieting, C. W. Hyatt, Trustees.

1871.—Alford Phillips, Mayor; J. D. Newcomer, Recorder; C. S. Bailey, Marshal; L. Wells, Street Commissioner; A. J. Free Treasurer; L. G. Kinne, Attorney; J. H. Struble, Assessor; C. W. Conant, R. H. Frazee, H. Galley, L. B. Nelson, N. C. Wieting, Trustees.

1872.—L. B. Nelson, Mayor; J. D. Newcomer, Recorder; W. E. Appelgate, Marshal; Luke Wells, Street Commissioner; H. Galley, Treasurer; G. H. Goodrich, Attorney; C. W. Conant, Assessor; J. Q. Clark, L. G. Kinne, A. J. Free, Benj. Stone, P. G. Wieting, Trustees.

1873.—L. B. Nelson and L. G. Kinne, Mayors; G. L. Bailey,

Recorder; W. E. Appelgate, Marshal; N. C. Wieting, Street Commissioner; Smith Newcomer, Treasurer; J. W. Willett, Attorney; W. H. Alden, Assessor; J. Q. Clark, P. G. Wieting, B. Stone, J. G. Salley, C. W. Conant, Trustees.

1874.—Thomas S. Free, Mayor; Geo. L. Bailey, Recorder; B. B. Houghkirk, C. S. Jerome, Marshals; J. H. Bates, Street Commissioner; Geo. M. Berger, Treasurer; J. W. Willett, Attorney; E. M. Bielby, Assessor; J. G. Salley, R. H. Frazee, C. W. Conant, W. C. Walters, N. Fisher. Trustees.

1875.—D. D. Appelgate, Mayor; H. S. Bradshaw, Recorder; J. H. Bates, Marshal; J. H. Bates, Street Commissioner; C. E. Olney, Treasurer: J. W. Willet, Attorney; E. M. Bielby, Assessor; David Arb, G. H. Goodrich, W. N. Brown, S. Stiger, P. G. Wieting, Trustees.

1876.—E. C. Ebersole, Mayor; H. S. Bradshaw, Recorder; J. W. Coe, W. H. Blakely, Marshals, J. H. Bates, Street Commissioner; C. E. Olney, Treasurer; M. Austin, Attorney; O. F. Elmer, Assessor; G. M. Berger, H. Galley, J. M. Camery, J. S. Moore, S. Stiger, Trustees.

1877.—E. C. Ebersole, Mayor: J. W. Willett, Recorder; J. H. Bates, Marshal and Street Commissioner; A. H. Sterrett, Treasurer: H. S. Bradshaw, Attorney; O. F. Elmer, Assessor; J. S. Moore, Louis Loupee, J. M. Camery, D. Spayth, Jas. B. Hedge Trustees.

1878.—L. G. Kinne, Mayor; T. E. Smith, Recorder; J. H. Bates, Marshal; A. H Sterrett, Treasurer; M. Austin, Attorney; O. F. Elmer, Assessor; J. Q. Clark, G. M. Rogers, H. Wagner, B.Stone, J. S. Moore, Trustees.

1879.—L. G. Kinne, Mayor; H. J. Stiger, Recorder; E. J. Cannon, Marshal; C. E. Olney, Treasurer; M. Austin, Attorney; E. M. Bielby, Assessor; W. C. Walters, L. Loupee, R. S. Clark, B. Stone, H. Wagner, F. Junker, Trustees.

The following are among the leading business men of the place.

Dr. H. W. Boynton, Physician and Surgeon.—This eminent physician is one of Toledo's successful men, and is having a successful practice in medicine and surgery. By close study and thorough practical demonstrations he has attained that skill which marks him master of his profession. He can always be found at his residence on Church Street, Toledo, Tama County, Iowa. Below will be found a short but creditable biography of his progress through life.

Mr. Boynton is a native of the State of New York. He came to Iowa in the year 1861, and in the same year began the study of medicine and surgery in the office of Dr. John Conaway, a prominent physician of Brooklyn, Poweshiek County, Iowa. In August, 1863, he left his studies, went to Iowa City and enlisted for the war as a private in the 28th Iowa Infantry, Volunteers, which was fully organized in barracks at Camp Pope awaiting orders to move south. Shortly after enlistment he was promoted to Hospital Steward of his regiment, which position he held until the regiment was discharged at the close of the war. After discharged from services he pursued the study of medicine and surgery until he graduated at the Albany Medical College, New York, December 24th, 1866. Immediately after finishing his studies he returned to Iowa where he practiced his profession nearly four years at La Porte City, Iowa, then moved to Toledo, Tama County, Iowa, in 1870, where he has since followed his profession with ability and success making Surgery a speciality. In 1872, he was appointed United States Examining Surgeon for Pensions for Tama County, which appointment he held until he resigned in 1876, on account of temporary absence from the County. He is a member of the Iowa State Medical Society and President of the Tama County Medical Association.

J. W. Kreminak, Boots and Shoes.—This gentleman has been a resident of Toledo but a short time coming here in 1878, and yet by energy, good management and skillful work has already built up an extensive business and has gained a good name for integrity and is classed among the liberal merchants of the city. He is located on Broadway, where he has one of the neatest stores and stocks in the town. He is a practical workman, having followed the trade since a boy, and meets with a large patronage from all classes of citizens in custom made goods of which he makes a speciality.

J. M. Camery & Son, Hardware and Agricultural Implements.—In 1870, these gentlemen established themselves in Toledo, and during the past nine years have met with more than average success. Their machinery in which they deal consists of all kinds of farm implements, Deere &Co's., plows and cultivators Keystone plows, Buckeye seeders, for which they are agents. They also handle all kinds of field and garden seeds, and are doing an extensive business in hardware, carrying one of the largest stocks in the County. We may also say in this branch of their business they handle the best quality of goods. Store at the corner of High and Main Streets.

Homer S. Bradshaw, Law and Collection Office.—For the past eight years the above named gentleman has been well known to the citizens of Toledo, and vicinity, and in fact, over the entire County. In the year 1871, Mr. Bradshaw came to Toledo from Mechanicsville, Iowa, where he had been employed for a number of years as principal of the public schools, and engaged in the practice of law; since which date he has been having a comparatively good practice and has proven himself of more than average legal ability and is now ranked among the leading practitioners of the County. His office is in Nelson & Barker's Real Estate and Loan office, where he has a good library. He has a legal knowledge that only can be attained by close study and large practice.

B. Stone, Grocer etc.—This gentleman's success goes to show what may be attained by the majority of persons if they are industrious, persevering and enterprising. Mr. stone has been in this city for a great many years, and since 1872, in the grocery business, during which time he has been cautious and careful, and always attending to the wants of his customers, ever striving to please those from whom he receives patronage. This is the correct method of conducting business, in our opinion, and has proven successful in most cases when closely followed. It has, however, in the case of Mr. Stone as to-day he is rewarded with a large and growing business. Store on the corner of High and Broadway.

W. W. Souster, M. D.—One of the leading and largely patronized medical practitioners of Toledo is the above named gentleman. He practices Homœpathy fully believing that this system of practice is the right one for the successful treatment of the various ills which flesh is heir to. His business was established in this city in 1873, shortly after graduating. Since this date he has succeeded in securing a large profitable practice being a gentleman of acknowledged ability and well educated in the medical profession. He enjoys the confidence of the community in which he resides and follows the profession of his choice and we may say truthfully that it would be difficult to find a more genial, and social gentleman than Mr. Souster. Office over Mr. Stigers drug store.

William Reickhoff, Abstracter.—This gentleman is one of Toledo's most respected citizens, and one who has the confidence of the people in business transactions. He is classed among the oldest inhabitants, having resided in the place since 1862. For a number of years after Mr. Rieckhoff came to Toledo he was engaged at blacksmithing, which business he followed until 1872 when he sold his shop and engaged in the law and real estate business. In the fall of 1875, began abstracting and still continues at that business. Mr. Rieckhoff has a fine set of abstract books, and any one wishing anything in his line will do well to call on him at his office in Toledo.

Bailey & Austin, Attorneys at Law and Loan Agents.—Although the above firm has not been established as long as some others in the city, yet all will admit that each member has become popular and proven himself well posted in the intracacies of law. The former gentleman is well known in the County having resided in the vicinity of Toledo for a great many years, while the latter has resided in Toledo since 1874. They form a valuable copartnership, and we have no hesitation in saying that they are classed among our most reputable lawyers. They do a general practice, but from what we can learn, Mr. Austin has principally shown his aptitude for criminal law.

H. Galley, Dry Goods.—One of the foremost dry goods houses in Toledo is that conducted by the above gentleman, on the south side of High street. It was established in 1871, and since then has held a leading position. Mr. Galley handles all kinds of dry goods and notions, oil cloths, upholstery goods, boots and shoes. In every article he holds a leading position, and has become well known for his fine quality of goods. Mr. Galley is one of the oldest settlers of Toledo settling here in 1858, and ever since that date has been in the dry goods trade, and is well known all over the County as a straight forward and honorable citizen and tradesman.

G. H. Goodrich, Attorney at Law.—In 1869 this gentleman came to Tama County from Essex County, Mass. and in the following year established business at Toledo. From that time he held an extensive practice, both at Toledo and various other towns in the County, until a few weeks ago when he moved to Marshall County, and settled in Marshalltown. Mr. Goodrich, is a well educated gentleman and thoroughly understands law in all its branches; his gentle manners and reliable character makes it very pleasant to do business with him. Persons wishing anything in his business will do well to call upon him.

J. N. Springer, Drugs and Medicines.—The above named gentleman has now been in our midst for fourteen years and has been in the drug business since 1870, and has become one of our permanent business men. He is located on High Street south of the Court House where he has built up a large and increasing business. Drugs, medicines, perfumeries, toilet goods, fancy articles, cigars, tobacco are among his stock, and in which he does a large business. Mr. Springer is also a practicing physician and is well known throughout the County, as one of our best read and educated physicians.

Henry Wagner, Harness Manufacturer.—For the past ten years this gentleman has been well known to our citizens, having been a resident of Toledo during that time, hence takes rank as one of our leading business men.   Since 1872, he has been in business, and is the largest manufacturer and dealer in harness, collars, trunks, valises, lady's side saddles, horse brushes etc., of any firm in the County.   He is a practical workman, and during his business career has distinguished himself for selling a good quality of goods.   All persons will do well to call upon Mr. Wagner when in need of any thing in his line at his store on High Street.

T. K. Armstrong, Drugs and Medicines.--Every dispenser of drugs should, to our mind, be a cautious and well educated person to avoid the very serious and often times fatal mistakes that may occur by incompetent individuals.   In the above named gentleman, Toledo has a cautious dispenser of medicines, and one whose education eminently qualifies him for this position. Mr. Armstrong has been a resident of Toledo since 1860, and from that date has been in the drug business.   He deals in the best goods and is practically and well known as a leading dispensing druggist.   His store is located on Broadway, east of the Court House, where he may always be found ready to wait upon you.

J. S. Moore, Photographer.—This gentleman came to this County and settled in Toledo in 1857, which makes him one of Toledo's old settlers. and one who, since becoming a resident, has done much for the building up of the town.   In 1860 he established himself in the above business in which he still continues, giving entire satisfaction to all his patrons.   His work is of the finest quality and it is really a treat to take a look through his gallery, examining the various specimens of work on exhibition; whether a card photograph or one of life size, excellence is written thereon.   Those desiring this class of work should call and see specimens and learn prices.   Gallery, on Broadway just north of E. E. Stickney's Hotel.

Smith & Lee.—An indispensable institution that deserves favorable mention is the store of Messrs Smith & Lee.   These young gentleman are an important acquisition to any community. Both are graduates of Cornell College and are men of culture and good citizens. In commercial circles they stand high. In their chosen vocation they have met with the success that good business ability, fine address, and fairness in dealing always secure. Their stock of miscellaneous books is large and select, while their stock of school books, blank stock, stationery, inks, &c., including the celebrated "Red Line Series" of school blanks, are complete in every particular.

The city and country schools and County stationery supplies are procured of this firm. In their news department is constantly found all the leading daily and periodical publications.

Their stock of boots and shoes is unequaled by any in the County. It is select and first-class in every particular. They make a specialty of fine goods and always have on hand the leading brands of goods for ladies, gentlemen, and children.

W. S. Johnston & Co.--On High Street, is located one of the oldest dry goods houses in Tama County, being established in the year 1858, by Galley & Johnston, who managed the business ten years when Mr. Galley sold his interest, and Wesley Johnston, and C. C. Guilford, became interested. After the firm changed hands it done business under the firm name of W. F. Johnston & Co, until the spring of 1879, when it passed into the above named gentleman's hands. The firm now consists of W. S. Johnston, and J. A. Owen. Who are both young men of good reputation and during the present proprietors ownership, we are happy to state, that they have not allowed any of the former prestige of the store to wane, but have rather increased its former business. They keep a full line of staple dry goods and dress goods, making a specialty of fancy goods, notions, embroideries, laces, etc.

Appelgate & Leland, Attorneys at Law.--Among the oldest practicing attorneys, and honorable citizens of the County, we can mention D. D. Appelgate, of the above firm, who became a citizen in the year 1851. When Mr. Applegate, first came to the County he took up a claim twelve miles north west of Toledo; worked his land till the fall of 1854, when he moved to a place near where Toledo now stands, he having been chosen County

Clerk, which office he held by re-election from May, 1853, to the first of January, 1869, making a faithful and efficient officer. He has also held other prominent offices, that of Supervisor, Mayor, and member of the School Board at sundry times, being quite active in educational matters and in whatever tends to the mental or moral good of the community. In 1868, was admited to the bar, and law practice has since been his business. After being alone one year he became the partner of L. G. Kinne, this firm continued from November, 1869, to December, 1876, when Mr. Kinne retired after which Mr. Appelgate practiced alone until September 1878, when S. C. Leland, became his partner. Since that time they have been doing a good collection business as well as court practice, and in all respects they are safe, true and reliable men, and are both respected and honorable citizens. Office on High Street.

Winn & Free, Abstracters, Land and Loan Agents.—The abstract business now owned by the above gentlemen was establishrd in 1866 by Lawrence & Free, consequently their books which cost between three and four thousand dollars are very reliable. Abstracting is a business, the importance of which the people in general do not fully understand, and still it is one that is very important to those buying and selling real estate. It gives a condensed history of all recorded transactions in any manner affecting the title thereto, and when written out in a proper form shows all conveyances, mortgages, bonds, leases, tax deeds etc., all of which can be filed away for future reference, so that the purchaser of a piece of land is perfectly safe in buying and selling and in many cases avoids an expensive law suit. These gentlemen also carry on a land and loan office in which they are doing an extensive business.

A. J. Burtlett, Bakery and Confectionary.—This business was established by L. Wentz in 1874, and conducted by him with good success until March 1st, 1879, when it changed hands to the above named gentleman, who after taking posession refitted the building and added largely to the stock and now he has one of the finest stocks, and doing as large business in his line as any one in the town. Mr. Bartlett, besides carrying on the bakery, which is conducted by the skillful hands of J. T. M. Glenn, carries a full line of confectionaries, cigars, tobaccos, nuts, etc., which he sells with small profits. Mr. Bartlett is a young man who was raised in Toledo and is well known, as a straight forward business man and there is no doubt that he will meet with unbounded success.

Stickney House, E. E. Stickney Proprietor.—This hotel has been under the management of this gentleman for a number of years. He became sole proprietor in the year 1874. Since then he has remoddled and refitted it at a great expense and now his hotel ranks with any first-class hotel of the County. The house is located south of the Court House on Broadway, where all travelers and those wishing board and lodging will find a neat and comfortable stoping place, and one of those jovial good landlords who has had years of experience in hotel keeping and who always makes it pleasant for his patrons.

L. H. Cary, Physician and Surgeon.—Among the physicians who hold a prominent position in the profession of medicine, we mention L. H. Cary whose office is at his residence on Main Street south of the public square or Court House. He has practiced medicine for the past twenty-five years, having graduated at Willoughby Medical College, Ohio, and after graduating attended a course of studies in New York City. Since locating in Toledo in 1858, he has met with success, especially when we take in consideration the great number of practitioners in this place. He is recognized as one of the reputable, permanent and leading physicians of the town.

Struble & Kinne, Attorneys at Law.—It is an acknowledged fact that the legal profession is well represented in Toledo, its talent being above the average in a city of two thousand inhabitants. One of the most prominent and most thoroughly educated firms of this County is the above, whose establishment dates back to November, 1877, since which date the firm of Struble & Kinne has had a large and profitable practice, and has proven to numerous clients, and in fact, to the entire County their legal ability. The firm is composed of G. R. Struble and L. G. Kinne, the latter has been a resident of Toledo since 1869, having come here, from Mendota, La Salle County, Illinois, where he had been in active practice for many years. Since becoming a citizen of Toledo, Mr. Kinne, has done much for the upbuilding of the place, and donating liberally to every good enterprise whereby the town or County would be benefitted. He is an acttive worker in politics and for the past few years has had a large influence in the Democratic organization of the County, and has made many warm friends in that party. The former, Mr. Struble, is an old settler in the place. He came from Chesterville, Morrow County, Ohio, to Toledo, in the year 1857, since which date he, also, has been in active practice, and has made many friends throughout the County. Mr. Struble politically, is a Republican and in 1870 was appointed by the Governor to the office of Circuit Judge, which office he filled with honor giving satisfaction, to all and discharging his duties faithfully as an officer.

We regard this firm as one of the strongest and most successful law firms in the County. They are located upon the south side of High Street over the Toledo Saving Bank, in rooms belonging to Mr. Struble. Their Library is one of the finest, largest and most complete in the city and numbers over one thousand volumes. They are not only well educated lawyers but honorable and reliable gentlemen, with whom any legal business may be safely placed, as they rank among the leading professional men of the County.

Stoner & Jones, Hardware.—The business of these gentlemen has been established many years and owned and ably conducted by A. Bartlett until February, 1879, when it passed into the hands of the above named gentlemen. Ever since that time they have taken a leading part in the hardware trade of this County. Their store is located on Broadway, and is large and well filled with first-class goods consisting of every article kept in a first-class hardware store. These gentlemen are among the leading merchants of the city, and have established a name and

trade of which they may be justly proud. Mr. Stoner is an old
settler in the place and Mr. Jones is a young man formerly of
Marshalltown, Iowa.

Louis. Sime, Clothier.--Among the important institutions of
the town worthy of special mention, is the clothing establishment
of L. Sime, on the corner of Broadway and High Streets, in the
Toledo House building. This business was established in 1877
by Sime & Solomon, and conducted by them until March 10th
1879, when Mr. Solomon sold his interest and moved to Tama
City. Since Mr. Sime . became sole proprietor he has added
greatly to his stock of clothing and now carries a full line of
ready made clothing, hats and caps, boots and shoes, trunks,
valises, etc. which he offers cheap.

Stivers & Bradshaw, Attorneys at Law.—This firm is composed of W. H. Stivers and C. B. Bradshaw, the former has been
a resident attorney of Toledo since the year 1856, and the latter
since 1867. In speaking of these gentlemen we can say that
they compose one of the strongest law firms in the County, and
since its establishment their business has constantly been on the
increase. In regard to Mr. Stivers we can truly say as the author of the United States Biographical Dictionary says in an
article referring to him. "One of the best examples of a self-
made man in the State of Iowa, is Wm. H. Stivers, who never
went to school ten weeks after twelve years of age, who worked
at the blacksmith trade until twenty-six years old and who is now
a leading man at the bar of Tama County. Mr. Stivers besides
being a prominent attorney, has since residing in the city done
much for the building up of the place and always donated liberally to every good enterprise. The same can be said of Mr.
Bradshaw. Their office is located on High Street over H. Wagner's harness shop, where they have nicely fitted up rooms and
a splendid library.

B. L. Knapp, Grain and Stock Dealer.—This gentleman has
been a resident of Tama County since 1866, settling in Otter
Creek township, upon what was known as the Staley farm. When
Mr. Knapp came to the County he brought with him a large herd

of sheep, intending to go into that business but owing to the cold winters shortly after disposed of his herd of sheep and went to farming. Since 1877, besides carrying on his farm he has been engaged in the above business at Toledo, since which date he has been doing a large busines always paying the highest possible price for grain and stock.

J. A. Merritt, Attorney at Law.—Although his business is classed among the most recently established in the city, yet all will admit that Mr. Merritt, has become popular and proved himself well posted in the intricacies of the Law. In the first place, he has good natural ability and having studied under the guidance of experienced attorneys, is a well qualified young lawyer and has already gained a gratifying success. Mr. Merritt is well known, having been raised in Highland township, and is respected by all who has formed his acquaintance. His office is on High Street over Clark Bros. store.

H. T. Baldy, M. D.—The oldest physician in Toledo is Henry T. Baldy, a graduate of the Rush Medical College of Chicago, and a man of good reputation both personally and professionally. In 1854 Mr. Baldy located at Toledo, where he is still found in good practice. His calls are both numerous and profitable extending over the entire County. The Doctor is well known in nearly every township, and the respect shown him is as wide as his acquaintance. He is kind to the poor and has ridden hundreds of miles to administer to their necessities without expectation of any compensation. Years ago he was very active in politics, but of late years has done but little more than vote. In 1856 he published the "Toledo Tribune," the first paper in this County, and in which he published the first delinquent tax list in the County. Since locating in Toledo, Mr. Baldy has been very active, enterprising and useful to the place, and has donated liberally to every good enterprise. His office is at his residence on Broadway Street, Toledo.

L. Loupee, Blacksmith.—This gentleman came to Toledo from Cass County, Michigan, in the year 1865, and established himself in the blacksmithing business. His shop is in the northwest

part of town near the depot. Since locating here he has succeeded in building up a large run of custom in all branches of
business connected with the blacksmith trade. Mr. Loupee is a
fine workman and we take pride in recommending him to the
public, and if you have any thing in the shape of blacksmithing to
be done he is the man that can do it in good style.

Union Stoner, Confectionaries.—This gentleman established
business in this city in the year 1877 and is well known as a
young man of high reputation and good business talent. He
carries a fine stock of goods consisting of every article in the confectionary line, cigars tobaccos etc., and commands quite an extensive trade in Toledo and surrounding country. His store is
located upon the south side of the public square on High Street,
where he may always be found ready to wait upon patrons in
good style, and when you buy goods of him you will get your
money's worth. Give him a call.

Ingersoll & Fisher, Blacksmiths.—This firm is composed of
G. W. Ingersoll and H. L. Fisher, the former of which has been
a resident of Tama County since 1868, and the latter since 1867.
In the year 1873, these gentlemen established business together
in the shops formerly occupied by W. Bradbrook and continued
together until 1877, when Mr. Ingersoll, disposed of his interest
and moved to Tama City, where he remained until 1879, when
he bought back one half interest. At present Messrs. Ingersoll
& Fisher are doing business under the old firm name, and are
giving satisfaction in all branches of their business, which consists
of all kinds of blacksmithing, carriage and wagon making, together with all kinds of reparing. Call and see them.

Stoner & Emmerling, Painters.—In the year 1876 these gentlemen established themselves in the above business at Toledo open-
ning a paint shop on State Street where they are doing all kinds
of painting. They are skilled house, sign and carriage painters
as their work plainly shows. Mr. Stoner has lived in Toledo
since a mere boy and is known to be a man of sterling worth.
Mr. Emmerling came here in 1876 and has since been a member

of the above firm. He is a promising young man of good business qualifications.

Ebersole & Willett, Attorneys and Counsellors at Law, Tama City and Toledo.—E. C. Ebersole, Toledo, Office in Galley & Johnston's block, West rooms, Second floor. J. W. Willett, Tama City, Office Front rooms, over First National Bank.

These gentlemen do a general law and collection business in the State and Federal Courts. The firm was established at Toledo in August, 1873, and at once entered upon, and has since maintained a good and growing business. Both members have devoted themselves exclusively to the ligitimate practice of the law, and have refused to divide their attention with speculations out side of their professions; and their course in this respect has justified them, for few firms have in the same length of time built up so fair a reputation and business so flourishing. Their offices are always open during business hours, their motto being "Business first and pleasure afterwards." They have been for three successive terms the official attorneys for Tama County, and are now serving their fourth term in that capacity. For the better accommodation of their clients, they have just recently, May 1st, 1879, opened an additional office in Tama City, at which place all business pertaining to the South part of the County will hereafter be transacted.

E. C. Ebersole, was born at Mt. Pleasant, Westmoreland County, Pennsylvania, October 18th, 1840; was educated at Otterbein University, Ohio, and Amherst College, Mass., graduating at the latter institution in 1862; served in the Union Army; was several years Professor of Mathematics in Western College, and afterwards President of that institution; was two years one of the Professors of Ancient Languages in the Iowa State University. After five years private preparation was admitted to the bar at Iowa City, in 1870, and at once entered upon the practice there. Removed to Toledo in 1873, where he has resided ever since, and been twice Mayor of that City.

J. W. Willett, was born in Mercer County, Illinois, in March, 1846. Served in the United States Navy during the late civil war. Received a commercial education and graduated at Pough-keepsie, New York, in 1868. Came to Toledo, Iowa, in February, 1871, and entered upon the study of law with Messrs Stivers & Salley; was admitted to the bar in 1872, and has remained in the practice ever since.

BUSINESS DIRECTORY.

Groceries.

O. F. Elmer, Broadway and High St.

B. Stone, Broadway and High St.

W. C. Walters, High St.

B. F. Page, State St.

C. W. Conant, High St.

Dry Goods.

J. W. Youngman, High St.

W. S. Johnston & Co., High St.

H. Galley, High Street.

Clarke Bro's High St.

W. A. Fee, High St.

F. Salasek, High St.

Clothing.

Louis Sime, High Street.

Confectioneries.

U. Stoner, High Street.

A. J. Bartlett, High St.

Drugs.

T. K. Armstrong, Broadway Street.

S. Stiger, High Street.

J. N. Springer, High St.

Agricultural.

Camery & Son, High Street.

Harness.

H. Wagner, High Street.

J. W. Coe, State Street.

Attorneys.

Stivers & Bradshaw, High St.

T. S. Free.

J. W. Stewart.

Ebersole & Willett.

J. W. Lamb.

H. S. Bradshaw.

Appelgate & Leland.

Bailey & Austin.

G. Raines.

Struble & Kinne.

W. Reickhoff.

Furniture.

D. Arb & Co. High St.

Abstractors.

Winn & Free, High St.

William Reickhoff, High St.

Justices.

J. R. McClaskey, High St

N. Fisher, High St

Photographer.

J. S. Moore, Broadway.

Tailor Shop.

W. Hayes, Broadway St.

Physicians.

W. W. Souster.

H. T. Baldy.

J. N. Springer.

W. H. Boynton.

J. H. Fletcher

L. H. Cary.

Hotels.

Stickney House, Broadway.

Toledo House, Broadway and High.

Shoemakers.

M. Reusch, Broadway.

J. W. Kremenak, Broadway.

J. Junkers, Broadway.

J. W. Coe, State Street.

Painter.

Stoner & Emmerling, State Street

Boots and Shoes.

Smith & Lee, High Street.

Book Stores.

T. W. Nash, High St.

Smith & Lee, High St.

Post Office.

Mrs. E. L. Dillman,

Express.

Smith & Lee.

Banks.

Toledo Savings Bank, High St.

Toledo City Bank, Broadway.

Papers.

Chronicle, High St.

Album of Pen Art, Broadway.

Toledo Times, Broadway.

Dentists.

C. W. Miller, High St.

S. G. Bruner, High St.

Millinery.

Mrs. E. B. Coats, High St.

Mrs. E. Nash, High St.

Mrs. E. J. Cannon, High St.

Mrs. A. M. Reynolds, State St.

Loan Agencies.

Nelson & Barker, High St.

Winn & Free, High St.

Yeiser & Sterrett, High St.

Jewelry.

R. H. Frazee, High St.

B'acksmiths.

Fisher & Ingersoll, High St.

L. Loupee State St.

Wm. Ferris, High St.

G. W. Lacy & Son, State St.

Hardware.

A. J. Hassell, High St.

Stoner & Jones, Broadway.

Camery & Son, High and Main St.

Flour and Feed.

E. E. Ramsdell, High St.

E. Irish, Church St.

Meat Market.

Jons & Tode, Broadway.

Livery.

McGee, Appelgate & Ross, Main and High Streets.

C. D. Terry & Co.

J. L. Bracken.

W. C. Walters.

Stoner & Bielby,
L. Mathews.

S. J. Wilson.

Lumber.

J. P. Henry & Co.

Grain.

Coal.

C. D. Terry & Co.

Carpenter Shops.

H. B. Belden.

Barber Shop.

CHAPTER XXII.

TAMA CITY.

When the beautiful town of Tama was first laid out it was called Iuka,* but soon changed to its present name Tama City. In 1862, at which time the extension of the Cedar Rapids and Missouri, now known as the Chicago & Northwestern Railroad reached this point, it was first founded and being for a considerable time the terminus of the road, the place was soon established in the minds of men of good judgment, as one destined at an early day, to be what it has since proven, a town of no inconsiderable importance.

At this time, B. A. Hall and J. H. Hollen were virtually monarchs of all they surveyed, being the only residents, and each possessing large and finely located farms. Of the latter the railroad company purchased a tract of land; Mr. Hollen also generously donated several acres to secure the location of the station on the spot where it now stands. Among the first who came here for the purpose of establishing themselves in business were Col. C. K. Bodfish, M. C. Murdough, and W. P. Browne. Mr. Bodfish engaged largely in the shipment of grain and produce, and also opened a dry goods and grocery store in a small frame building, which stood on the lot now occupied by the First National Bank building, owned by Mack &

*So named in commemoration of the battle of Iuka, Mississippi, in which many of the brave boys of Iowa participated.

Little and was known as the pioneer business building of the town. This building was also used for a long time as a hotel; and, says our informant, it was kept rather on the European plan, as meals only were furnished its patrons, who obtained their lodging principally in the store rooms where not more than "four-in-a-bed" were ever allowed. Two grain warehouses were soon erected, which shortly after were occupied by M. C. Murdough and C. B. Barnard, and filled for months to their utmost capacity, which at last proved inadequate for handling the increasing shipments and P. K. Hayden commenced the erection of an elevator, which was a great benefit to the town. Shortly after finishing the building Mr. Hayden disposed of his interest to Wm. P. Browne who continued its management until the fall of 1865, when he sold out to Messrs. J. D. Merritt & Son. In 1872 this elevator together with one owned by C. H. Kentner was destroyed by fire, but shortly after new ones were built.

Mr. Murdough, came here from Toledo, and engaged extensively in the shipment of grain and live stock, and in the following year 1863, erected the building now standing on the corner of Seigel and Third Streets in which he commenced the dry goods and grocery trade, and still continues at this busines. To the gentlemen above mentioned is due a great degree of credit, for by their unceasing efforts and enterprise, the town to a large extent is what we see to-day.

The growth of the town was very rapid. The railroad being completed and the people accustomed to pushing things through with lightning speed, and as the sound of the locomotive's whistle could be heard in the distance, they began to pour in; and by the time the merry call of the conductor's "all aboard," was heard the town was fairly alive, and the spirit of "Young America" seemed to pervade every citizen of the little village, and dreams of future growth and greatness pervaded the minds of all. A class of citizens came to the village full of perseverance and grit, and a determination to make the town one of the best in the State of Iowa. The city at present is a flourishing manufacturing and commercial town, of nearly two thousand inhabitants, located one-fourth of a mile north of the Iowa River, surrounded on all sides by a remarkably rich and productive country.

The city was incorporated in 1869, having for its first Mayor, M. A. Newcomb. From this date the place advanced in all those natural interests that go to make up a thriving city, yet nothing in particular occured in its history until of late years to attract those from the over crowded east to its advantages to any remarkable degree. Time passed, however, and the city became supplied with good schools, churches, fine streets, public buildings etc., together with one of the finest water powers in the State of Iowa. Afterwards Tama City began to attract special attention and since the year 1875, her prosperity has been encouraging to the inhabitants.

The water power above spoken of propels quite a number of mills and manufactories, yet not half the available power is utilized. On either side of the race many others factories might be erected and conducted with profit, especially as great inducements are being offered by the company, to those wishing to locate here. During the past few years many and various kinds of enterprises have been established and it has been abundantly demonstrated by their success that this is a desirable point to locate. The city is situated in the midst of a very fertile agricultural region and draws a retail trade for many miles, while the products of her manufactories are being extensively shipped over a large portion of the west.

Among the fine buildings of the city, we refer with pride to the residences, of J. H. Brooks and L. Carmichael, located in the northwestern part of the city, each erected at a cost of many thousand dollars; the Harmon House, Murdough's block, the First National Bank building, Bank of Tama, Empire block, First Baptist and Catholic Churches and Public School buildings.

The various benevolent and reformatory societies are well represented, there being flourishing lodges of Masons, Odd Fellows and United Workmen. All of these organizations have as neat lodge rooms as any in the County. Tama City has many live firms in her midst of which special mention is made further on in this chapter.

At an election held July 23d, 1869, for or against the adoption of a city Charter, there were polled 105 votes for, and 5 against the proposition. At the first annual election for city officers, held at the office of F. J. M. Wonser, September 4th, 1869, the following named persons were elected:

M. A. Newcomb, Mayor; James H. Brooks, Thomas Murray, James Brice, Jr., S. W. Coles, and J. B. Spafford, Trustees; G. W. Walton, Recorder. Since 1869 the officers have been elected as follows:

Mayors.—E. Harmon, J. B. Spafford, W. H. Tiffany, C. H. Kentner, M. Bostwick, E. G. Penrose and O. H. Mills.

Trustees.—L. Carmichael, O. Parks, C. H. Kentner, A. W. Wells, J. R. Smith, R. H. Ryan, G. W. Coles, O. J. Stoddard, S. Patterson, R. Harris, J. F. Hegart, L. Merchant, C. R. Palmer, H. Soleman, E. Parks, S. M. Chapman, S. Bruner, J. McClung, B. Thompson, C. L. McClung, B. F. Crenshaw, M. Bostwick, C. Homan, O. H. Mills, E. G. Penrose, G. V. Goodell, J. H. Smith, Wm. Cummings, W. Blodgett, D. W. Bressler T. Whitaker, W. A. Sharp, G. W. Ingersoll, G. E. Higley, R. Forker. The present Councilmen are H. Soleman, W. H. Cummings, E. G. Penrose, T. H. Bruhn, B. Thompson, and F. B. Ramsdell.

Treasurers.—G. H. Warren, J. D. Laudi, M. Levi, L. Carmichael, James McClung and F. R. Holmes.

Recorders.—J. L. Bracken, G. E. Maxwell, B. W. Homan, R. H. Moore, J. McClung, W. Maxwell, G. D. Sherman, F. N. Warren, and the present T. E. Warren.

Marshals.—H. Day, W. T. Hollen, T. Avery, J. F. Ward, D. W. Bressler, R. Harris, L. V. Kellum. The present Marshal is W. L. Brannan.

TAMA CITY UNION SCHOOL BUILDING.

This building was erected in 1769, at a cost of nearly $20,000. It is located in the north-eastern part of town and stands in the center of a beautifully decorated yard, comprising a whole block and is enclosed by a neat and substantial fence. The architectural design is plain throughout, yet neat and well proportioned. The plans ware drawn by Mr. George Kline, of Marshalltown. The brick work was done by G. H. Clark, and the carpenter work was done under contract of Thomas Horsefall and George Crabtree. The building is in height three stories, with a finely proportioned belfry surmounting the main part, in which is placed a bell weighing about 700 pounds. The foundation is built of stone, while the main walls are built of red brick. The building contains five rooms which are used for school purposes besides recitation and library rooms, closets and halls.

The main enterance to the building opens into a large hall from the west; from this hall a stairway leads to the second and third stories. The building is capable of accommodating with convenience, seven hundred pupils. In addition to this, the city has two other buildings, used for school purposes. The city of Tama deserves great credit for the erection of this building which is a fine one indeed. With a full corps of efficient teachers in every department; with a school board alive to the best interests of education. the schools of this place will rank with any in the County or State. The following named gentlemen have served on the School Board since 1870: B. A. Hall, L. Carmichael F. J. M. Wonser, S. W. Cole, C. E. Heath, T. Parks, C. E. Hibbard, S. Patterson, H. Day, J. B. Tims, A. Cordner, J. McClung, B.F. Crenshaw, J. B. Spafford, R. H. Ryan, J. H. Hollen, A. W. Guernsey, W. E. Newcomb, C. B. Bentley and E. G. Penrose. The present Board consists of J. Nicholson, J. W. Coburn, E. G. Penrose, W. E. Newcomb, C. B. Bentley and A. Cordner.

TAMA CITY HYDRAULIC WORKS.

Many years prior to 1874, Charles Irish, then a citizen of this County, while surveying in company with J. H. Hollen, in the bottom near where the water works has since been constructed, made the discovery of the fact that there was fall sufficient in the river to render possible an extensive water power. His plan was to dam the river near where the present dam is; bring the water along the base of the bluffs and use Deer Creek as a tail race. This was before the town was laid out and consequently before there was any special reason for extending the work to its present limits. But the undertaking was too large for the ability of those then interested, and nothing was done with it. For many years, after the town had been established the water power was a subject that enlisted a good deal of attention from the people; not only in Tama City, but for many miles in the surrounding country. In Tama City and vicinity water power improvement excitement would break out every once in a while, and spread its eruptions through the vicinity; meetings were called, resolutions adopted, committees appointed, petitions drafted and great flames inaugurated for this purpose. And indeed, it seems almost a pity that after so much time, money and labor spent in this direction, the efforts were not rewarded as the majority of the people hoped.

Time passed and nothing of any consequence done until the winter of 1872–3, when the matter was brought promptly before the people. The services of Mr. Irish, now of Iowa City, were secured for the purpose of making a survey. The result of Mr. Irish's examinations was to establish the fact that by a sufficient out-lay of means, Tama City could have a water power second to none in the State, and scarcely equaled by any in the West. He recommended the construction of the works entirely upon the south side of the railroad track as the most possible plan, which a more thorough examination subsequently proved to be the best course to pursue.

As time passed the opposers of the water power, were not idle, but used every means in their power to influence the people against it. But the presistent efforts of the company were not to be blasted and the work was finely accomplished by their efforts and expenditures, and to-day, Tama City has large manufacturing establishments and extensive railroad communications with the commercial world.

G. H. Warren, who had been instrumental in securing the survey by Mr. Irish, had become possessed of the idea that the power could and would be improved, and while others were faithless and indifferent in regard to it, he, with that persistence and determination so characteristic to him, continued his efforts to keep the project before the people. Finally Mr. D. B. Sears, of Rock Island, a man of large experience in hydraulics both in Indiana and Illinois, whose judgement in a matter of this kind is entitled to all respect, was invited to Tama City to render his judgement in relation to it. He came, and was at once impressed with the feasibility of the undertaking and was enthusiastic in his expressions of confidence in it. At this instance, Mr. J. D. Arey, an hydraulic engineer of Illinois, was engaged to make a thorough survey and plat of the contemplated work, which he at once proceeded to do; fully corroborating the survey made by Mr. Irish, and disclosing the fact that with the completion of this work, Tama City would have a magnificent water power at her door of at least one thousand horse power, which would make it one of the best manufacturing towns in the West.

A company was at once organized under the general laws of Iowa, for the purpose of improving and utilizing the power of the Iowa River at Tama City, with a capital stock of $100,000; the following gentlemen constituting the company:

B. A. Hall, President; G. H. Warren, Secretary; Thomas Murray, James McClung, John Ramsdell, Lewis Merchant, M. C. Murdough, B. A. Hall and Eli Harmon, Directors. At the very first these men had to face the unwelcome and stubborn fact, that about $100,000 would be required to carry the work through. Of course it was a giant undertaking for so small a town as Tama City, even though assistance was rendered by the citizens of the surrounding country. But the same indomitable persistence of which we have before spoken, upon the part of Mr. Warren and the directors, soon secured stock enough in cash and property subscription, to justify letting the contract for the entire work, which was immediately done to Mr. D. B. Sears and Mr. M. C. Orton, the latter of Sterling, Illinois, and the former of Rock Island, Illinois. The services of Mr. Arey were secured as engineer.

The confidence of these gentlemen in the enterprise is shown in the fact, that though they were strangers, and in no way interested in the destinies of the town, the former invested $15,000 in stock, and the latter, Mr. Arey, took his entire wages in the same. These men afterwards sub-contracted the entire earth work to Messrs. Judd and Joslin, who sub-let parts to others; all pushed their work on rapidly.

The work was completed the first of November, 1874, and on the thirteenth of the same month a grand celebration was given on the fair grounds at Tama City over the completion of the works. The *Tama City Press* had the following to say of the jubilee:

"Friday, the 13th, was the day set for a jollification by the people over the Water power prospects, and large numbers of the good friends of Tama City came in from neighboring towns and country, determined to partake of the roasted ox, and join in the general festivities.

The immense reservoir in front of town had commenced filling the evening before and on Friday a broad sheet of water lay there, sullenly tossing and surging under the prevailing heavy winds, like a very lake, indeed.

Many were present from abroad; some of the speakers expected were, for one reason or another, deterred from coming, but when the throng assembled within the fair ground there were excellent and encouraging speeches made by Rev. G. F. Magoun, President of Iowa College; Hon. James Wilson, M. C.; E. A. Chapin, Esq., editor of the Marshalltown *Times*, and others. Rev. O. A. Holmes read a Historical Essay and O. H. Mills, Esq. read that which the *Inter-Ocean* Reporter styled "The event of the day"—a first-rate poem.

Then after music by the Cedar Rapids Cornet Band, and the Tama City Brass Band the people repaired to Floral Hall, enlarged and well fitted for a dining room, and ate roasted ox and cake, and chicken fixin's, and drank hot coffee and tea, till hunger and thirst were things of the past and the possible future only, and not at all of the present time.

Taken altogether, notwithstanding the very unfavorable weather, the people who came were well contented and Tama City enjoyed a new evidence that the masses of her neighbors in town and country, take pride in her enterprise, and rejoice over her success.''

"How the Water came down, at Tama," by O. H. Mills; read at Tama City, November 13th, 1874, on the occasion of the grand jubilee at the completion of the Tama Hydraulic Works:

You've undoubtedly heard of the "Falls o' Lodore!"
How the water came down with a rush and a roar—
With a dash and a bound—a lull and a swell:
Such circles and whirls—'tis a wonder to tell!
But the way it comes down through the "Tama Hydraulic"—
(The name seems an odd one, but that's what they call it.)—
Is another, a different, and separate fall;—
(It can't fail to remind of the "Raging Kanawl."

On the river, at "The Narrows," 'twas oftentimes said:
"Were the water only here, 't were twenty feet head!"
But how could we get it?—the project seemed rash;
'T would take months of hard labor, and mountains of cash!
But a handfull of men whose watchword was "Pluck!"
Who never by trifles were hindred or "stuck,"
Said, "The work must be done, whatever's to pay,
The funds shall be raised and the ditch dug straightway,"

So a meeting was called, to have a good talk;
But little was said, but Lord! how the stock
Of the "Tama Hydraulic" was taken that night!
And the water (to the brave) seemed plainly in sight!

There were men who were poor and of money had none,
Said; "We'll work on the ditch, and when it is done,
Just give us our time, be it ever so small,
And stock we'll receive in this "Hydraulic Fall."
And one had a farm—he made us a deed:
"Here, take my broad acres, the work must proceed!"
There were cattle and horses, they all were put in:
In fact, all we could spare was put into "tin."

And good Tama City, the mother of all,—
Woman-like, she wanted a good "waterfall!"
She wanted the hum of machinery to hear;
She wanted factories and mills by her side to appear;
She wanted more thrift, more labor for all;—
So she expended twelve thousand in this "Hydraulic Fall."

Unheeding the jeers of the doubting ,and wiseacres too,
With a might and a will we've put the work through;

We've dammed the broad river with wood and stone;—
A glorious old guard-lock, 'tis finished and done.
We've cut through the hills, and filled up the sloughs,
And made a rugged, hard bank for the water to use.

We've got a nice lake as clear as the sky,
Whose blue waves forever will dance merrily
And make our hearts glad, our souls to rejoice,—
For they speak with a sure, unmistakable voice:
" 'Twas that watchword of yours—that gritty word. "Pluck!"
('Tis worth a million such words as "Fortune!" and "Luck!")—
'T was that union, that might, that effort si: cere,
That make us so happy in our cosy banks here.
And the whirl of my wheels will be merrier still;
I will factories build, and a glorious mill;
And business shall come and nestle by me.—
I'm a nice little lake, and happy I'll be!"

So forget all your troubles and now we'll rejoice,
And make the air ring with jubilant voice;
United we were—still "Union" is our song;—
That's how the water in the Hydraulic came down!

The dam is built across the Iowa River at a place called the "Narrows," three and one-half miles west of Tama City, with a head of six and one-half feet added to the natural fall of the river, which between the town and the dam is sixteen feet, giving a head of twenty-two and one-half feet. There are seven miles of back water above the dam; three miles of canal; and forty-seven acres of reservoir; thereby giving an immense storage of water, practically a pond of ten miles in length. Of course the volume of power attained under these conditions is immense.

The race has an average width of near one hundred feet, and a a sufficient depth to carry at low water, nearly all there is in the river. For about the first mile it is dug in the natural ground. The rest of the way it is made by heavy banks of earth, which at the lower end of the race are about seven feet high. The inside of the banks are thickly set with water willows, which effectually prevent the action of the water from reducing them

The reservoir covers forty-seven acres of land, mostly within the town plat of Tama City. The water in this reservoir, when full, will average about six feet deep. The banks are made of earth, very heavy, about seven feet high, and like those of the race are set with willows, which are growing luxuriantly. This reservoir having water running constantly in and out, having no shallow water, and being within a few rods of the business portion of the town, forms one of the most attractive features of the place, and is used largely for a skating, boating and fishing park.

Bulk-head and aqueduct, are substantially constructed of timber and piling, at a great cost, and control the high water, letting into the race and reservoir no more than is wanted at any time. The aqueduct is constructed for the purpose of carrying the water over Deer Creek, and is arranged with waste gates on each side by which the race can be drained without letting water into the reservoir.

The tail race is about thirteen hundred feet long, and thirteen feet deep—even with the bottom of the river. On both sides of it, for its entire length, are the building lots, commodiously laid out for any kind of factories, being about three hundred feet deep. Land for a rail road track across the ends of all the lots, on the west side of the tail race is reserved.

If time and space allowed we would love to do honor to all those who have contributed to this result, but where all have done so well, such a service is impossible. We can and should say however, that the members of the Board of Directors have been untiring in their efforts, and have displayed business tact and administrative ability, such as to justify the confidence reposed in them by the company. But it is just to say, as the author of the Biographical Dictionary of the United States says in an article referring to this work "of all those who have labored for the accomplishment of this work, G. H. Warren is deserving of the highest credit. It is safe to say, only for Mr. Warren it would not have been undertaken, and no one but he would have carried it through. It is his strong faith, his dogged persistence, that did it. Some men do not know when they are defeated, and will always manage to turn a defeat into a victory, such a man is G. H. Warren."

The work is done, tried and proven a success, and there are

already large manufactories run by this vast power; among which
we can mention the Paper Mill, the Hydraulic Flouring Mills,
the Union Plow Company's Foundry and Machine Shops, Wind
Mill and Pump Factory, Sash and Door Factory, Pearl Barley
Mills, Manufacturers and Builders Association's Shops and Butter
tub Factory. The present officers are B. A. Hall, President;
G. H. Warren, Secretary; B. A. Hall, J. Ramsdell, F. E. Ramsdell,
L. Carmichael, T. Murray, G. E. Higley, J. McClung, and
Directors.

Among the live and most enterprising firms in the city we
would call attention to the following:

E. G. Penrose, Hardware.—This gentleman first established
himself in business in this city in 1872, and is the largest and
most reputable and successful hardware merchant in the city,
and holds a position for business integrity, above an average
character. In 1872, Mr. Penrose came here from Grand Junction, Greene County, and engaged in business; he has been oper-
ating here ever since, and has exhibited distinguished energy and
enterprise in business. He has increased his trade until now it
extends throughout the County. He is neatly located in a large
brick building at the corner of Third and McClellan Streets. It is
one of the finest and largest in the city, being 25x76 feet, two
stories above the basement. The entire lower floor and basement is occupied by his business. Each department is filled
with an admirable stock of goods consisting of the various articles
belonging to the trade. These are purchased direct from first
hands and therefore he is enabled to successfully compete with
any in the County. General shelf and heavy hardware, carriage
and wagon stock, Burnett's steel and barbed wire, iron, stone,
tinware, cuttlery, wooden and willow ware, is found in his immense stock. Mr. Penrose has always taken a deep interest in
the up-building of the city, and but few if any enterprises of
merit are started unless aided by him. He was Mayor of the
city in 1878, and is at the present time serving as a member of
the City Council to which office he has been several times elected.
He is classed among our esteemed and leading business men.

He is also a member of the School Board and is doing all in his power for the advancement of educational interests of the city.

James M. Burge, Cigar Manufacturer.—This gentleman, since establishing himself in this choice business has met with splendid success, which has been his marked feature, and the fine cigars issuing from his manufactory meet with an extensive sale. This arises from the fact that the proprietor has become thoroughly acquainted with the tobacco trade, and understands the quality of leaf to perfection. He manufactures quite a number of different brands, each and all are of choice tobaccos. Mr. Burge also has in connection with his factory a retail department, in which he keeps all of the best brands of chewing and smoking tobaccos, pipes, pipe stems, and in fact, everything pertaining to the smoker's wants. Factory and retail rooms on Third Street, Tama City.

Madison Bostwick, Carpenter.—Mr. Bostwick is an old settler in this County and has made Tama City his home a large portion of the time. Carpentering is his chosen trade, and he is one among the best in the County. He has been Mayor of this city several terms and has held other offices of trust and proven himself a man who does more thinking in private than talk in public, and can always be relied upon for prompt attendance and solid work in business affairs. He has the best interests of his community at heart. His parents were natives of Connecticut. Madison was born in the year 1812, his parents were poor and consequently his education was somewhat limited, enjoying only such as a common school affords. While yet quite young, Mr. Bostwick concluded to learn a trade, and immediately went to work with a Mr. Leet, a carpenter, of Middletown, Penn., with whom he continued until he had accomplished his aim. On December 18th, 1833, he was married to Miss Amanda Griffis, by whom he had four children, three boys and one girl.

Mr. Bostwick continued at the carpentering trade, in Pennsylvinia, until the death of his wife, when he sold his property there and came west; spent sometime in Wisconsin and af-

terwards came to this County.   Since he came to Tama City he
has been engaged in contracting and building.   Mr. Bostwick is
capable of doing any work in his line, and is ever willing to work
at a reasonable price, believing in the motto "Live and let live."

Bostwick House.—This house was erected by its owner M.
Bostwick, in the year 1868, and since that date has been a pleasant resort for the traveler.   The house is located on corner of
State and Fourth Streets, two blocks from Chicago & Northwestern depot.   The building is frame, large and commodious.
Mr S. Russell has the house in charge and commands a large
patronage.

C. C. Harris & Bro., Painters.—This firm opened business
in this city, in the month of April, 1878, in the building known
as the "Pioneer building of the city," located on McClellan,
Street, now owned by S. C. Brown, and have been doing a
thriving business in house, sign, buggy, wagon and ornamental
painting.   The work turned out of their shop gives evidence of
skillful workmen.   They came here from Pennsylvania where
they followed the same business, and came well recommended.
They have had over twenty years of experience in this business.
These are good reliable gentlemen and work left with them will
promptly receive attention.

C. Homan, Steam Saw and Flouring Mills.—In 1868, these
mills were established by Bodfish, Homan & Co.   In 1869, they
changed hands to C. K. Bodfish & Co., in 1871 they passed back
into Mr. Homan's hands who assumed their management to the
present time.   The flouring mill is a large structure, two stories
and one-half high, and is equipped with superior machinery, having three run of stone, which enables him to manufacture large
quantities of that excellent quality of flour which is so widely
known throughout this section.   Since Mr. Homan took charge
of the mills he has done an extensive business, and has added
largely to the value of them.   He is a prominent citizen of Tama
City and takes an active part in the up building of the place.

Thomas Whitaker, Produce dealer.—The above named gentleman ranks among our oldest citizens, having been a resident of

Tama City since the town was located. Mr. Whitaker came to this place from Toledo and established himself in the produce business, and from the earliest period he has been constantly engaged in buying and shipping all kinds of produce, for which he pays the highest possible price. His store is located on the corner of Fourth and McClellan Streets, where you can always find him ready for a bargain. Mr. Whitaker is a property owner and a successful business man.

E. H. Price, House Contractor.—It is very important in a town the size of Tama City, that every business be well represented and that the public should have pointed out those who are known to be reliable. In undertaking this task we take pleasure in saying that the above named gentleman has proven himself an experienced workman and in all branches of his business he ranks among the first. Mr. Price is among the old settlers of this County, and is nicely located in the Empire Block, on Third Street, where he manufactures wood work for wagons, sleighs, and repairs all kinds of implements. He has also a steam planing mill in his shop where all kinds of turning is done in any shape required.

L. A. Graves, Harness Manufacturer.—Every manufactory is of advantage to a city, therefore ought to be encouraged by each citizen in every possible way. The above gentleman's institution is no exception to this rule, as it sends out wares over a large territory. Mr. Graves is a practical workman of life-long experience and after working at the trade in this city from 1875 to 1877, he began on his own account. He is located on Third Street near the post office, where he manufactures and deals in all kinds of light and heavy harness, saddles, collars, whips etc. Mr. Graves is building up a large business and is deserving of success. He is honorable and always among the first to help forward the enterprises of his growing city to the full extent of his ability. He is also interested in the harness business at Union Grove, managed by L. V. Kellum.

William Richards, Boots and Shoes.—The subject of this sketch has been a resident of Tama City since the year 1872.

During this time he has been in business and gained a good name for integrity; and is classed among the liberal merchants of the city, while the stock is not as extensive as some others yet it consists of an excellent assortment of boots, shoes, gaiters, slippers and rubber goods etc. He is a practical workman, having been brought up to the trade and meets with a large patronage from all classes of citizens. In ready-made goods as well as in his costom department he makes a specialty.

John F. Hegardt, Meat Market.—This gentleman is among the old settlers in the place, and conducts an extensive meat market on Third Street where he does a very creditable business. During the time he has been identified with the city he has done much to develop its interests. Mr. Hegardt deals in hides, tallow, lard, fresh and salt meats, oysters, fish and game in their seasons. He is well known by nearly every one in the County, respected by all and has a large trade. Few men in the city have a firmer hold upon the good will of the people, than Mr. Hegardt, and when in nomination for office he invariably runs ahead of his ticket.

John Nicholson, Dentist.—Every one will concede that it is of great importance to have pointed out a thorough practical dentist and one whose reputation is above reproach in faithfully attending to dental operations. In pointing the public to John Nicholson, we have no hesitation in saying that he is a well experienced dentist of more than average ability. He is located on the corner of Third and McClellan Streets, over Penrose's hardware store, where he has nicely fitted up rooms and every appliance known to the profession of dentistry. He has had years of experience and stands high in his profession.

W. H. Hawk, Agricultural Implements.—This gentleman established himself in Tama City in 1877, and during the past two years has met with good success. The machinery in which he deals consists of all kinds of farming implements, from a hoe to a threshing machine. He is agent for the Champion Reaper and Mower, Wood's Mowers, and J. I. Case's Threshing Machines, a great number of which have been sold from his depot on the south side of Third Street where those wishing any kind of farming implements may rely on good bargains.

W. H. H. Tiffany.—First having received a scientific and literary education studied law with Judge Tiffany, and F. C. Beeman, of the city of Adrian, Michigan, and at the Ann Arbor University likewise. He was admitted to the Supreme Court of New York held at Syracuse, to practice as an attorney at law and solicitor in chancery in all the Courts of that State, and, he is also, admitted to practice in all the Courts of Ohio and Iowa. He has been practicing in said Courts for the last twenty-four years and has always sustained a fine reputation as a gentleman of good character, sound legal ability and strict integrity. He came to Tama City in the year 1870, and is one of the most reliable and successful lawyers in Tama County. He has been Mayor and City Attorney of Tama City, and we insert the following sentiment as expressed in the Martindale United States Law Directory. "We take pleasure in recommending W. H. H. Tiffany, as a gentleman of sound legal ability, assiduous, reliable and of strict integrity, fine reputation and good character and competent to attend to any business intrusted to his care. He refers to

G. E. Maxwell, Cashier of the Bank of Tama; C. J. Stevens Clerk of the Court; G. H. Warren, Cashier of the First National Bank of Tama City, Iowa."

J. L. Bracken & Co., Grain and Stock Buyers.—This company has been in existence since the year 1869, at Tama City, buying and shipping grain and live stock. From the formation of the company they have always sustained a good reputation for honorable and fair dealing and have always paid the highest market price for all kinds of grain and live stock. In 1875 J. L. Bracken, besides doing business at Tama City, commenced operations at Toledo. Since that date he has taken a leading position in the grain and stock trade at that point, and has shipped many hundred car loads to the Eastern markets.

Mr. Bracken is thoroughly allied with the interests of his places of business and since doing business here has gained a

goodly number of friends and the confidence of the community
as a successful business man.

J. T. Fluthers, Meat Market.—This gentleman came to Tama
in 1877, and has since been a resident of this city, and engaged in one line of trade—that of a market for the sale of fresh
meat, fish etc. He also handles live poultry, hides, tallow and
everything kept in a first-class meat market. From the first he
secured a good run of custom, which has never forsaken him
and never will as long as he remains at its head. In his private
business he exercises the same general care of all details, and
therefore has been very successful. Call at his market on Mc-
Clellan Street.

J. T. Matson, Bakery.—"Old Reliable City Bakery." We
have headed this gentleman's notice as the "Old Reliable" bakery of the city from the fact that it was established by him in
1865. Although we head it bakery, simply, yet this is by no
means all in which he deals as he keeps one of the nicest stocks
of confectioneries and family groceries in the city. His store is
situated on Third Street, where Mr. Matson, and his most obliging and respected clerk W. H. Ahlbrecht, stand ready to wait
upon their customers. Owning the store, and being so well
known in the business, he has peculiar advantages, and offers inducements which are not lost sight of by the purchasing public
as his large trade testifies.

William Corns, M. D.—One of the leading, most successful and largely patronized medical practitioners in Tama City, is
the above named gentleman. He located in this town in the
year 1865, shortly after graduating at the Keokuk Medical
College, and since that date has had a growing practice. He
loves surgery, studies science *con amore* and is a progressive man.
He is a member of the Iowa State Medical Society, and was its
Vice-President two or three years. His standing among the
medical brethern of the State is excellent. He is at present examining surgeon for pensioners. Office on Third Street.

J. H. Eastin, Tailor.—In 1876, Mr. Eastin, came to Tama
City and established himself in this business and since that date

he has held a reputation for honorable and square dealing of a very high character, and his many friends and customers constantly keep him busily engaged in the manufacture of clothing and such other articles as are adapted to his business. Persons wishing anything in his line will do well to call on him at his shop on Third Street, over J. B. Tims' grocery store, where he is always found ready to wait upon his customers.

C. W. Snyder, Furniture.—The above named gentleman is one of our best known and respected citizens. He established his present business in 1874, and being a practical man, with an indomitable perseverance, has succeeded in making it one of the most extensive and successful houses in this County, and one that will always hold a prominent position in the furniture trade. All kinds of furniture, from the most superb to the ordinary, are kept on hand, or manufactured to order, and sold at lower prices than the same can be purchased in Tama City's competing towns, as the proprietor is a practical workman and buys for cash only. In his sale rooms, on Third Street, there is every style and variety of furniture. Mr. Snyder has constantly on hand a large and complete stock of undertakers' goods. In his business transactions he is prompt and courteous.

Bank of Tama.—This bank has been in successful operation since 1871, and is one of the representative institutions of the city. It is a private bank, with stockholders who are responsible and reliable men. The business is conducted by able and competent men and since the time of its establishment it has been a great advantage to the place. It has a high reputation with those who know the bank and its officers. The capital stock amounts to over $100,000. Lewis Carmichael, an old settler and one who has been a promoter of so many enterprises of this vicinity for the past eighteen years, is President and his sons, E. L. and Charles are conducting the business; the former is cashier and the latter assistant cashier. These young men are both apt and competent scholars and have that business ability which insures success. Their father, besides attending to his duties in the bank is an extensive railroad contractor and stock raiser. He came to

this County in 1867, and was one of the first to own property in
Tama City. He is identified with the first public improvements
and has manifested himself in all interests of the town. The
banking house is situated on Third Street, and is one of the finest in the town. It is twenty-five by sixty feet, two stories high
and built of red brick, with a beautiful marble front. The inside
is systematically arranged and artistically finished.

Mills & Guernsey, Attorneys at Law.—One of the most
prominent and most thoroughly educated law firms of this place is
the above, whose establishment dates from November 1st, 1878.
Since this time they have met with abundant success, and
proven to numerous clients their legal ability. They have had
years of experience and each are close students fully posted in
the various decisions of the higher courts, and competent to engage in difficult contests with their opponents. Their office is on
the south side of Third Street where they have neatly fitted
up rooms and a large and well selected library.

W. D. Worrell, Grocer.—This young gentleman has been a
resident of Tama City for a number of years and is constantly
advancing in business capacity. He came here with his widowed mother from Marshalltown, Iowa, and found employment on
the water works, then being built, as teamster; but his aspirations were for a higher sphere in life and soon he was in the
employ of W. G. Cambridge, editor of the *Tama Citizen*, as a
printer. But soon his attention was directed to the mercantile
business, and he procured a situation in the large hardware establishment of E. G. Penrose. Here he remained three years,
giving his entire attention to the tinner's trade and clerkship in
the store, and commanded the highest respect of both his em-
ployer and customers. After a short vacation and prospecting
tour through Southern Nebraska and Kansas, he returned home
and entered into the produce trade, but soon bought one-half interest in the grocery store of A. B. Dubbs, and for months the
establishment was carried on under the firm name of Dubbs &
Worrell, but finally Mr. Dubbs sold his interest to Mr. Worrell,
and now he is sole proprietor of a fine stock of groceries and

queensware, with a deservedly large trade. Mark the progress of an energetic, wide-awake young man.

C. D. Terry & Co., Lumber Merchants.—In almost every department of trade and manufacture, Tama City offers inducements to home patrons and those outside her borders, and the lumber business forms no exception to this rule. The above named gentlemen established themselves in the lumber business in this city in 1869, having been principally managed by C. D. Terry, and B. F. Hill. About two years ago they became sole proprietors. Ever since its establishment it has been a popular yard, and posessed advantages that all could not compete with. They are wholesale and retail dealers in lumber of all kinds. They also handle coal, mixed paints, mouldings etc. They pay strict attention to their business interests. The yard is located on State Street, where they always can be found ready for business.

T. A. Bristol, Jeweler.—On Third Street near the post office is located the above gentleman. Mr. Bristol is a practical jeweler of many years experience, and is well posted in the business. He has met with good success during his business career in this place. He keeps a large and well selected stock consisting of the latest styles, in fact, everything kept in a first-class jewelry store. An especial feature of his establishment is the repairing department where all kinds of cleaning and repairing is done to perfection. The whole is presided over by Mr. Bristol, and all work is guaranteed by him. His prices are reasonable. Give him your patronage.

First National Bank.—It is necessary in times such as we are now passing through that the public should have pointed out those moneyed institutions which are sound and on a sure foundation. And in order to arrive at an intelligent conclusion in regard to the soundness of any such establishment, one of the first and most important things to be considered is how the managers have conducted their own affairs. If after due consideration we find these managers men of reputation and well tried characters, and who have managed their own affairs with large success, then we may reasonably conclude they are the best persons in any community to care for one's funds and watch over depositors' interests with caution and care. After this brief introduction, we would say that among the solid and responsible institutions of this kind is the First National Bank, of Tama City, It was organized in 1871, and stands to-day strong in its own resources and doing a large business. The bank is neatly and conveniently fitted up, and provided with vaults of recognized strength. The Yale time Safes are used.

The present officers are, B. A. Hall, President; G. H. Warren Cashier; F. N. Warren, Assistant Cashier; E. Ruggles, C. E. Covell, A. J. Tyler, C. E. Hayes, J. Brice, Jr., J. L. Bracken, J. Ramsdell and B. A. Hall, Directors. Mr. Hall is one of the oldest residents of the city and has been one of the active developers of the place. He has contributed liberally to almost every enterprise of the city, and has been a leading business man, deserving of the highst praise The same may be said of Mr. Warren, a banker of recognized ability.

Hall & Carmichael, Hardware.—Since April, 1879, this firm has been established in the hardware business. They carry one of the largest and finest stocks of shelf and heavy hardware in the County. They also deal extensively in farm implements. In connection with the hardware is a large and well equipped tin shop where all kinds of tinware is manufactured. The firm is composed of B. A. Hall and H. T. Carmichael, his son-in-law, a young man of fine business qualifications. The store is located on corner of Third and McClellan Streets.

Brooks & Holmes, Dry Goods.—One of the very foremost dry goods houses in Tama City, is that conducted by the above firm on Third Street. It was established in 1875, and since then has held a leading position, and to-day stand among the most extensive dry goods houses in the County. In addition to general dry goods they make a speciality of clothing, boots and shoes, hats and caps, upholstery goods and window draperies. In these articles they hold a leading position, and have become well known for their fine quality of goods, but above all for their accurate representations. All the advantages of a business education and of financial abilities are possessed by this firm. The firm consists of J. H. Brooks and F. R. Holmes; the former is one of our oldest citizens and respected by a host of friends, and the latter is one of Tama City's most valuable young men.

Soleman Bros, Livery and Feed Stable.—On the corner of Fourth and McClellen Streets is located one of the finest and most popular livery barns in the County. The barn was erected in the year 1877 by Henry Soleman, who assumed the management of it until March 1st, 1879, when J. F. Soleman, his brother, bought one-half interest in the business. Both take an active part in the business and are running a creditable livery. Mr. H. Soleman, besides being in connection with this barn, is proprietor of a large drug store and agricultural warehouse. He is a thorough business man and knows just how to turn the irons to keep them from burning.

Z. Solomon, Clothier.—This gentleman has been identified with the leading business men of Tama City since April, 1879. Since this date he has been largely engaged in the clothing business at his store room on Third Street, where he carrys a fine stock, consisting of clothing, hats and caps, trunks, valises and gentleman's furnishing goods, all of which he sells very cheap. Mr. Solomon is well known over the County as a man who is strictly honest, and of fine business qualifications, and we have no hesitation in pointing the public to him for good bargains in clothing etc.

Hydraulic Flouring Mills.—These mills are operated by a company composed of B. F. Crenshaw. F. B. and E. E. Ramsdell. The former of whom came to this city in 1869, while the Ramsdells are old settlers, having came to Tama County in 1853. Ever since these gentlemen have been in the city they have taken rank among the active workers of the place, giving much time and money toward the various valuable enterprises that have arisen, in order to make the city what it is to-day,—one of the most prosperous and best known in the country. In 1875, the Hydraulic Flouring Mill was erected by Mr. Crenshaw at a cost of about $12,000 and managed by him until December 1876, when he sold it to F. B. Ramsdell. In the fall of 1877, E. E. Ramsdell, his brother, bought one-half interest. Under the firm name of Ramsdell Bros. the mill done a large business shipping a great deal of flour besides supplying home markets. March 1st, 1879, Mr. B. F. Crenshaw, the founder of the mill, bought back one-third interest. Since that date the mill has been running under the firm name of Crenshaw & Ramsdell, and is doing one of the largest businesses in their line of any mill in Tama County and we will venture to say, so long as the mill is managed by these gentlemen their business will constantly increase instead of diminish. The mill is a large frame building 60x45, three stories high, and is equipped with superior machinery, with three run of burrs of the latest and best improvement which enables them to manufacture a splendid brand of flour. Mr. Crenshaw is also proprietor of the Helena Flouring Mill, which is also doing a large business, and manufacturing a splendid quality of flour.

The Paper Company.—J. Ramsdell, President; T. A. Hopkins, Agent; H. E. Ramsdell, Secretary. For a city so new as Tama and with a population of only about two thousand inhabitants, it is surprising to find so many manufacturing institutions, and yet there is room for more, all meeting with success as those in operation demonstrate. Among the most recently organized institutions may be mentioned, in this department of our work, the Tama City Paper Mills, located on the water power addition south of the Hydraulic Flouring Mills and under the supervision of A. Everhart, an old paper mill man of Milan, Illinois. These mills have now been in existence but a few months, yet being conducted by intelligent gentlemen and located in the "City of enterprise," with railroad facilities for distributing goods, we need not wonder at their successful career. Already they are shipping paper of all sizes and weights over a large area, and receiving assurances from buyers that while their paper is of the finest quality it gives general satisfaction. The machinery and general equipments of this establishment are all of the most ap-

proved kind which, with the shipping facilities and financial abil.
ity of the proprietors, assures their continued success. The proprietors are all old settlers in this County. J. Ramsdell, and his
son H. E. Ramsdell having come to the County in 1853, and
T. A. Hopkins came in 1855. They are liberal enterprising and
successful, and stand among the leading business men of the
city.

A. L. Howard, Butter Tub Factory.—In 1876, this business was established in this city and since then has been liberally
patronized. Mr. Howard is located upon the water power addition
where he manufactures a full assortment of all kinds of goods
pertaining to the butter tub and cooper business. Mr. Howard
is shipping his productions over a large portion of this State and
his work gives satisfaction, and his prices are in accordance
with the times. He employs quite a number of hands and is working up an extensive business.

UNION COMPANY.

This company was incorporated, August 31st, 1875, by a number of our leading capitalists business men and public spirited
citizens, many of whom are well versed and practical mechanics,
and fully alive to the wants of the western farmer. It is one of
the most responsible and promising institutions of Tama City, and
the persons connected with it are sufficient evidence that it has
facilities to offer in its line of a gratifying character. It gives
employment to from thirty to forty hands, among who we can
mention A. E. Axtel, foreman of the machine shops; J.
Ballhouse, foreman of the blacksmith department; D. W. Rising,

foreman of the wood room; Geo. Richards foundryman; and
C. D. Williams and G. W. Hapgood painters, all of whom rank
among the best in the State.   These works are of value to the
city, and add to the wealth of the place by sending out its
manufactures, receiving funds for the same which are principally distributed at home.   This advantage to the city and its citizens however is of no greater advantage than its valuable implements are to farmers, for from this manufactory issue some of the
most practical in use.   Among its notable farming implements
may be mentioned the improved steel plows.   These are made of
the best patent steel, extra hardened and in the most thorough
manner possible with special reference to scouring, ease of draft,
durability, and are fully warranted in every way, shape and form.

The Fearless Sulky Plow attachment is without doubt one of
the finest and best improvements now before the public.   Any
kind of a plow having either an iron or wooden beam can be used
with it.   It has the advantage of any other sulky and much
lighter and more simple.   They have also perfected a corn plow
to be attached to this sulky which saves the purchaser from ten
to fifteen dollars on a corn plow.   This attachment is an excellent thing.

The Prairie Corn Sheller is one of the neatest and most complete shellers now in the market; it is both simple and durable.
As this machine is manufactured at such a low price, many farmers throughout the country are using them, and in every case
they give satisfaction.

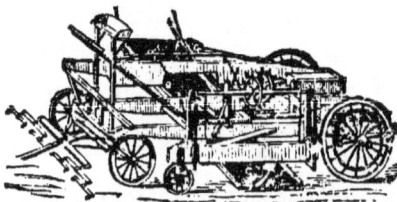

Another valuable and labor
saving machine of their manufacture is the Wauchope Grader.   This machine is almost
indispensable, and is receiving commendation wherever
used.   A correspondent to the *Western Stock and Farm
Journal* of Cedar Rapids, Iowa, under date March, 1879, says
the following of this grader:

"Now comes the tug of war, to describe one of the greatest

inventions of modern times, the Wauchope Grader. This machine is so constructed that it will plow the ground and carry the dirt by means of an elevator to the center of the road. By this means a turn-pike is built at a cost of only about twenty-five cents per rod. It is constructed on the same principal as a header for cutting grain, and it is so strongly built that it rarely gets out of order, and so arranged that two men and eight horses can run it with ease. It is not only a successful road grader, but equally as valuable as a ditcher. The testimony of of the Winnebago *Summit* is to the point as follows: "The Wauchope Road Grader, which has just been purchased by the trustees of this township built a piece of road, the length of which is sixty rods; the average width of grade sixteen feet; depth of grade eighteen inches. The road is neatly turnpiked and has a ditch on each side nine feet in width. The time occupied in the work was about four and one-half hours. Eight horses and two men did the work. The machine is warranted to build eighty rods of road a day, and we are satisfied that it will do it, and well too'. Under the old system, road building has proven both expensive and unsatisfactory. With one of these graders we should have good roads with a good deal less expense than we formerly paid for having, what in most cases were mere apologies for public highways. We are satisfied that the investment in a Wauchope Grader by our township is a good one. It will handle more earth than a dozen teams with scrapers, and handle it in better shape. It will work anywhere that a team can go. The grader is so built as to be adjusted to loading wagons where earth has to be hauled a distance, and it will keep fifteen to twenty wagons busy at a short range, to haul away the dirt which it can dig. It needs only to be seen to be appreciated, and we think it a good investment for every township."

We could quote hundreds of such testimonials as the above from various papers in the State where the Wauchope Grader has been used, but as its reputation is established it is not necessary. Since the organization of the company in the spring of 1877, hundreds of these machines have been sold in various parts of the State, and the demand is constantly increasing. The rapid introduction of this machine in Iowa is something surprising. In 1877, only about fifty were sold to townships. This year (1879) nearly the whole force of the Union Plow Company—about thirty men, with the best of machinery—have been unable to fill the orders.

Mr. G. E. Higley, the Superintendent, who has been connected with the company since January, 1877, came here from Springfield, Mass., where he had been for a number of years superintending one of the largest woodware establishments in the city. He thoroughly understands his business and is a gentleman who has made many warm friends since coming to Tama City. The same can be said of Messrs. Warren and Houghton. The manufacture and warehouse of this company are located on the water power addition and extensive and well equipped for the manufacturing of these and other machines, besides doing repairing of all kinds, and we advise those not acquainted with their manufactures to investigate or send for catalogue, price list etc. The officers are G. H. Warren, President; A. L. Houghton, Secretary and Treasurer; G. E. Higley, Superintendent. Each of these names are sufficient in themselves to inspire confidence in the responsibility of the institution.

Benjaman Thompson, M. D.—One of the most successful and leading physicians and surgeons in central Iowa, is Benjaman Thompson of Tama City. He graduated at the Eclectic Medical College of Philadelphia, Pennsylvania, in the year 1870, and shortly afterwards came to Tama City where he has since resided, and has successfully built up a large and extensive practice. Mr. Thompson is a man of sterling worth and takes an active part in the up-building of the town and community in which he lives. He is a man of ability and has a thorough knowledge of medicine and surgery. His pleasant ways and manners and sympathetic speech gains the respect of his patients. His office is in R. M. Coffin's drug store.

Mahana & Co., Wind Mill Manufacturers.—The above company established themselves at Tama City in May, 1879, and

since that time have become known as men of sterling worth.
The demand for the valuable and indispensable machines which
they manufacture is constantly increasing. Although they are
of recent invention, they have been thoroughly tested and tried
and have stood the test in every case. For a number of years
Mr. Mahana, the patentee, assisted by others, manufactured the
machines in La Moille, Bureau County, Illinois, but their ambition was to introduce them in Iowa, and after manufacturing
at Lyons this State, a considerable length of time, came to Tama
City, where we find them thoroughly in the work and manufacturing these valuable articles for the farmers of this County.
The neatest, simplest, most substantial and consequently
the cheapest machine that has come under our observation, is the
Improved Rival and Eureka Wind Mills, invented and manufactured by Mahana & Co. There is less machinery about them
than any mills in use. They have a revolving post and the
wheel is securely attached to this post, both revolving together,
while the tail is hung by hinges on the opposite side of the
post, and the self-regulating operator is secured by a T lever attached to the tail and connecting with the post. Any person can
see how perfectly simple this is. Here are secured certain results: easy running with light winds; will take care of itself in a
gale; keeps up uniform stroke in all winds; will stop when trough
is full, but will resume pumping when more water is needed.
This latter fact is an interesting one, and want of space forbids
our going into details. The manufacturers warrant to do as good
work with this mill as can be done by any higher priced machine.
The cost of the Rival is only a trifle and we advise our readers to see this admirable piece of machinery, and see it operate
before buying. The company also manufactures barbed wire.

We must not pass this sketch by without mentioning the medical ability of Mr. J. R. Mahana as a doctor. He is a graduate
of Hannemann Medical College, of Chicago, and has been a practicing physician for the past eight years. Mr. Mahana will continue practicing medicine at Tama City, and will doubtless become one of its leading and prominent physicians. He is a man
of good medical knowledge and ability.

Business Directory.

E. G. Penrose, hardware.
Brooks & Holmes, dry goods.
Thomas Murray, dry goods.
C. Homan, Flouring Mill.
E. H. Price, wagon shop.
E. A. Graves, harness shop,
W. F. Sterling, boot & shoe store.
J. F. Hegardt, meat market.
C. C. Harris, & Bro., painters.
C. L. McClung, painter.
Thomas Brice, grocer.
J. Brice Jr., grocer.
B. Thompson, doctor.
J. Nicholson, dentist.
S. W. Grove, DEMOCRAT.
H. Soleman, agricultural,
Cleveland Bros., & Gilbert, furniture.
E. R. Coyle, restaurant.
G. B. Alden, Photographer.
Ebersole & Willett, lawyer.
G. D. Sherman, Justice.
W. E. Newcomb, broom factory.
Puth Bros, clothiers and tailors.
J. H. Easton, tailor.
L. H. Brannan, Pacific Hotel.
M. Bostwick, Bostwick House.
J. M. Burge, cigar manufacturer.
Bank of Tama, E. L. Carmichael Cab'r.
C. H. Kentner, grain and stock buyer.
Mrs. S. P. Barrett, Millinery.
W. H. Cummings, blacksmith.
R. M. Coffin, druggist.
Wonser Bros., books, stationery.
J. Morrison, oysters and billiards.
G. Voss, saloon.
P. Peterson, barber.
Soleman Bros., livery and sale stable.
C. H. Kentner, insurance.
F. N. Warren, insurance.
Paper Mill Company.
A. L. Howard, butter tub factory.
Manufacturers & Builders Association.
Rhoads & Homan, builders,
H. Page, drayman.

Carmichael & Hall, hardware.
J. D. Laudi, dry goods.
M. C. Murdough, dry goods.
Crenshaw & Ramsdells, Flouring Mill.
M. C. Wilson, wagon shop.
W. Richards, boot & shoe store.
J. C. Mathews, boot & shoe, shop.
J. T. Flathers, meat market.
Williams & Hapgood, painters.
W. D. Worrell, grocer.
Tims & Jackson, grocers.
T. H. Bruhn, grocer.
Wm. Corns, doctor.
F. J. M. Wonser, HERALD.
W. H. Hawk, agricultural.
C. W. Snyder, furniture.
J. T. Matson, baker.
F. A. Bristol, jeweler.
W. H, Tiffany, lawyer.
Mills & Guernsey, lawyers.
A. W. Guernsey, Justice.
J. P. Hixon, broom factory.
Z. Solomon, clothier.
A. Mathern, & Co., brewers.
E. Harmon, Harmon House.
Delmonico House, Mrs. Felstead.
First National Bank, Geo. Warren, Cah'r
H. Day, grain and stock buyer.
Mrs. M. Ingham, Millinery.
Thomas Whitaker, produce dealer.
D. Clement, blacksmith.
H. Soleman, druggist.
B. F. Crenshaw, flour and feed.
F. Wilrodt, saloon.
Rheimer, saloon.
R. M. Coffin, express agent.
M. C. Murdough, livery.
Mills & Guernsey, insurance.
Union Plow Company.
Cleaveland Bros. & Gilbert, blind, door and sash factory.
Pearl Barley Mills.
A. Wiseman, drayman,
Thurston & Garish, printers.

CHAPTER XXIV.

This town is situated in the northern part of Perry township, on the south half of section ten, and surrounded by a country which in fertility of soil is not surpassed in the State of Iowa. The whole country for many miles around is dotted over with some of the finest and best improved farms in the County. The place was laid out on the Pacific branch of the Burlington Cedar Rapids & Northern Railroad, in the year 1873, at which time the extension reached this point, and being for a considerable length of time the terminus of the road the place was soon established, on land owned by Giles Taylor, and J. L. Bull.

On the 27th day of July, 1873, the iron horse first made its appearance in the place. To-day it has a population of nearly two thousand inhabitants. The same year J. R. Smith of Tama City, came to the place and opened a lumber yard, and built the first building on the town plat. Shortly after A. M. Batchelder and J. G. Strong erected a store building and opened a stock of drugs; from that date the work of building the new town was vigorously pursued. The music of the saw and hammer was heard on every hand. During that season a large number of buildings were erected and the population increased so rapidly that hotel accommodations in many cases could not be secured and people were compelled to resort to barns, store rooms etc., for lodging.

The town is laid out with streets running east and west, north and south, and stands upon the south bank of Wolf Creek, in a natural growth of timber. In the south eastern portion of the city is found one of the nicest parks in the State, which is used by the citizens for gatherings of all kinds, and a summer resort. This park is surrounded by a neat board fence, with a heavy growth of elm, oak and maple trees, making it beautiful and attractive. In 1875 the place grew so rapidly that it became necessary to incorporate it as a city. Accordingly, meetings and an election were held for the purpose of choosing officers, which were as follows: Mayor, Giles Taylor; Recorder, W. H. Bowen; Trustees, J. Morrison, T. H. Greelis, A. Mitchell, J. R. Smith, A. M. Batchelder, and L. Ladd. A few days afterwards the Board met and adopted such ordinances as were thought for the best interest of the place.

With reference to public schools the citizens have always taken a special pride and not without cause. From the report of the Superintendent of Schools of that place we gather the information that they are in a very flourishing condition, the general average in deportment, attendance and study being better than in any of the schools with which we are acquainted. The graded system was adopted on the completion of the new building in 1877, and has worked to the satisfaction of every one. The following named gentlemen compose the present Board of School Directors: E. D. Langley, W. W. Wilson, C. G. Johnson, G. W. McClary, C. A. Clow,———.

There are four religious denominations having organizations in this place, viz., United Presbyterian Church, on Walnut and Fourth Streets; Congregationalists, Walnut Street; Methodist Episcopal Church, Walnut and Main Streets, and the Advents. All have good comfortable church edifices.

A better class of dwelling houses are shown in this town than in many of its size in the State, while among her business houses are some fine ones, among which we can mention the banking house of Brooks & Moore, the Brooks House, Seaver & McClary's block in the business portion of the town and the Public School building. Taking all in all Traer in all branches of business is probably ahead of any town in the County. To the first settlers of the place belong the most praise for what we see to-day.

There are numerous business firms in the place worthy of special notice, among whom we mention the following:

Smith & Edwards, Dry Goods, Clothing and Groceries.— This firm is composed of two as energetic and live business men as can be found in central Iowa, S. P. Smith, formerly of Butler County, Iowa and L. H. Edwards, of Waterloo, who established business at Traer, in the year 1875. Since that time they have been doing one of the largest dry goods businesses in the city, and have made many warm friends and gained the respect and confidence of every one in the community. Their store is located on the corner of Walnut and Second Streets, where they carry a full and complete line of dry goods, groceries, clothing, boots and shoes, all of which they are selling very cheap. All the advantages of business qualifications and financial ability are possesed by this firm. Give them a call.

McCornack Bros., Lumber, Coal and Farm Implements.— The above named gentlemen have been residents of Tama County since the year 1865, locating in Perry township, where they remained upon their farms until Traer was founded, when they established themselves in the above business, and from that date have carried a full stock of the best farm machinery, together with a large stock of lumber and coal which they are selling very cheap, and their trade is greatly increasing. Their office and yards are located upon the west side of Walnut Street, between Second and Third, where they are always found ready to wait upon you. These gentlemen, since becoming residents of the County, by honest and square dealing, have gained the confidence of the public and hold a large trade.

James Fowler, Attorney at Law.—In 1856 this gentleman came to Tama County and settled at Toledo. For a number of

years, or until Traer was established, he was engaged in various
kinds of business, part of the time farming and part of the time
he was engaged in the mercantile business at Toledo. In 1873,
when Traer sprang into existence he moved to that point and engaged in the law business, since which time he has had a large
practice and met with the average success. Mr. Fowler has a
nice office over Brooks & Moore's bank, where he has a fine large
library and nicely arranged rooms with all the conveniences of
a first-class law office.

Porterfield Bros., Dry Goods.—This firm is composed of
S. M. and D. A. and W. S. Porterfield, who came to this point
from Vinton, Iowa, in 1873 and established business. Since which
time they have, by honest and fair dealing, built up a large trade
in all kinds of staple and fancy dry goods, clothing, hats, caps,
boots and shoes, valises, etc. To-day this firm stands among
the most extensive dry goods houses of this section. In addition
to their business at this point they carry on a large business at
Reinbeck, Grundy County, which was established in 1877.
Each member of this firm is esteemed among the best of Trear's
citizens, and as business men they are perfection.

W. D. Scott, M. D., Surgery a Specialty.—Among the most
successful practitioners of Traer, we may mention the name of
W. D. Scott, who has been a practicing physician of the place
since November, 1877, and who, since that date, has met with
more than ordinary success. Mr. Scott is a graduate of Hahne-
man Medical College of St Louis, and since graduating has been
in active practice both before and since settling in this County.
He loves surgery, studies science, and is a prospective man. Mr.
Scott ranks among the best educated physicians and surgeons of
the country and his practice is constantly increasing. Office in
Ortchild's building.

Moses Simon, Clothier.—A business career of five years will
either bring a man to the front or send him far to the rear. In
business there can be no middle ground for a man to occupy, he
must either go forward and keep ahead of the times or be dis-
tanced in the race by his more enterprising neighbors.

Day by day we see dropping out of sight those who were once thought to be enterprising business men, but who neglectful of the opportunities presented to them, failed to secure that success which seemed to be within easy reach. The gentleman whose name heads this item has been a resident of this city and has been in active business, and has become identified with its growth and prosperity. Although a good business man, and one that looks closely to his own interests, he yet does not allow his mind to become wholly absorbed in these matters, but in other things in which the people are interested he takes an active part, and in this way he has brought himself into notice and secured the affection and good will of thousands throughout Tama and surrounding Counties. But it is as a business man we have to deal with him in this article; as remarked it has been five years since he first began business in this city. His first location being at the corner of Main and Second Streets. Here he remained for some three years or until December 23d, 1878, when his stock was consumed by fire. Mr. Simon's loss at this time was very large as nothing whatever was saved with the exception of one or two show cases and a few other articles. But instead of becoming discouraged, as doubtless many would have done, he renewed his energies and in six days after burning out he had a new stock of goods on hand and ready again to supply his many customers. His store room at present is located on Second Street near Brooks & Moore's bank. Here he occupies a very large and neat room in which he has displayed the nicest stock of gentlemens furnishing goods that can be found in central Iowa. In this department he designs to carry a line of the best goods and his reputation for keeping superior goods at extremely low prices are made known far and wide, and his trade is constantly increasing. Mr. Simon, besides carrying on the clothing business at Tracr and Dysart, where he has a branch store and doing a large business, is agent for the Hamburg American Packet Co, North German Lloyd, the Inman and White Star Line of Steamships.

C. C. Collins, Furniture.—In 1855, this gentleman came to the County in company with his parents from WashingtonCounty,

Indiana, and settled in the southern part of Perry township in a small grove which was afterwards named in honor of his father L. B. Collins, and is still known as Collins' Grove. Here the subject of this brief sketch remained helping to carry on the farm until 1862, when he enlisted in Company F 28th Iowa, and went to war. After returning he worked at hire for a number of years or until July, 1869, when he engaged in business for himself, at Buckingham carrying a general stock of merchandise etc. In 1873, when Traer sprang into existence Mr. Collins moved to that point and engaged largely in dry goods building up an extensive trade; continued until September 1st, 1878, when he bought a fine stock of furniture, in this business he still continues carrying one of the largest stocks in the city. Mr. Collins' furniture rooms are located on Second Street, where he handles and manufactures all kinds of furniture, which he sells at lower prices than the same can be purchased in Traer's competing towns, as the proprietor owns his manufactory and buys for cash. Those needing anything in his line should not fail to call and examine his stock and prices.

Bowen & Higby, Land, Loan, Insurance and Collection Agents.—The above business was established in the year 1874, by W. H. Bowen, who came to this place from Cedar Rapids, and was conducted by him with good success until January, 1878, when M. R. Higby became interested, after which the firm was known as Bowen & Higby. Since the latter date it has been conducted in a profitable manner and to-day stands among the leading agencies of this kind in the Northwest. They do a large business in land, insurance and collections, while they make loans a specialty, infact the latter business has increased so in the last few years that nearly their whole time and attention is devoted to it in order that they may be fully prepared to give all desired information and advantages to patrons. Their office is located on Second Street, in Orchilds' building. Call and see them.

Dennis & Averill, Agricultural Implements.—Among the very foremost agricultural implement firms of this County stands that of Dennis & Averill, which was first established in the year 1866 at Tama City, having been composed of the present members since 1872. The firm is composed of J. B. Dennis and J. C. Averill, the former of whom has been a resident of Tama County, since 1866, coming to Tama City from Napoleon, Ohio, and the latter came to the County in 1871, from Highgate Springs, Vermont. In 1873, besides carrying on a large business at Tama City, a branch house was established at Traer under the management of J. C. Averill. Until 1877, these gentleman conducted business at both places, selling thousands of dollars worth of goods annually; in 1874, the firm done over one hundred and twenty-five thousand dollars worth of business which speaks well for it. In the spring of 1877, the business at Traer had so increased that it required the services of both members of the firm and J. B. Dennis sold the interest at Tama City and moved to Traer. Since the latter date the firm have carried a first-class stock of farm implements of all kinds, field seeds, etc. They have given the best inducement in prices and terms. There store is located at the corner of Second and Main Streets.

Brooks & Moore, Bankers and Collectors.—The banking firm of the above named gentleman has been in existence since 1873, and is one of the representative institutions of the city. Ever since its organization the business has been conducted by R. H. Moore, who has been identified with the leading spirits of the city since that date, and while he may not have fallen in with the views of all, yet has been liberal in promoting those enterprises which he believed intended to enhance the interests of Traer. His enterprise soon exhibited itself after his advent in aiding and liberally donating to all good enterprises. The erection of the present banking house, which is located on the corner of Walnut and Second Streets is the finest in the city, and compares with any in Iowa. The firm is composed of J. H. Brooks and R. H. Moore; the former of whom has been a resident of the County since 1856, coming here from Kane County, Illinois, and settling in Otter Creek township, where he resided upon his farm until the spring of 1866, when he moved to Tama City. Mr. Brooks is one of Tama's most highly esteemed citizens and besides railroad contracting he is engaged in farming, merchandising and banking, mainly by proxy, and strange to say making a success of every branch. The latter, R. H. Moore, has been a resident of the County since 1867, coming here from Mercer County, Pennsylvania. Mr. Moore for a number of years after coming to the County made his home at Tama City and vicinity, teaching school during the winter seasons, while in the summer he was engaged at farming, or whatever honorable employment he could obtain until the year 1871, when he received a situation in the banking house of Carmichael, Brooks & Co., where he remained until business was established at Traer, when he was sent there in charge of that bank. To-day Mr. Moore besides owning one half interest in the business is largely interested in a bank at Reinbeck, Grundy County, where they are doing a large banking business under the charge of his brother G. T. Moore. But to return to the bank which under the supervision of R. H. Moore is one of the most successful institutions in the place, whose prosperity and high standing at home and abroad gives tone and character to the city, ever stands ready to accommodate its numerous customers. The banking house was erected in 1878, is especially constructed with a view to convenience and safety, and it is conceded that no bank in the County is more secure or elegantly and conveniently fitted up. Its furniture is heavy carved hard wood, while its vaults are built up from the solid stone and provided with "time locks" thus making them doubly secure.

E. A. Bissell, Dentist.—The dental rooms of this gentleman are located over the post office, where he has nicely arranged rooms and is prepared to do all work in his line. Mr. Bissell is a graduate of the Boston Dental College, and has been in practice since 1875. From that time until 1877 he practiced in Independence, Iowa, where he had a large practice and stood well in his profession. During his four years career in Traer he has secured a large practice from the leading citizens, which go to prove the high position he has attained. Mr. Bissell does good work and guarrantees satisfaction to all.

Newcomb & Sons, Harness Manufacturers.—This firm is composed of M. A. Newcomb and his son A. G., both have been residents of this County for a great many years. For a number of years after coming to the County they resided at Tama City where they were engaged in business. In 1874 they established business at Traer, since which date they have held a leading position in the harness business, and their trade extends for many miles into the country. Besides doing repairing of all kinds they manufacture and deal in all kinds of harness, saddles, bridles, whips, collars, brushes, blankets, trunks, valises, etc. Their stock is first-class and it will pay you to call and examine prices and goods.

Brooks House, W. W. Evans, Proprietor.—Many towns of the size and attractions of Traer lack in hotel accommodations for the traveling public, which, to our mind, is one of the greatest drawbacks to the prosperity of any city. As in many other respects, Traer is alive to this important fact, and through the commendable enterprise of a number of its leading citizens, who now lay claim to having hotel accommodations to meet all necessary demands for some time to come. In 1875 the Brooks House was erected on the corner of Second and Walnut Streets, and named in honor of J. H. Brooks, of Tama City. The House is built of red brick, two stories high, with a basement. The house has all the modern improvements and conveniences. W. W. Evans, the proprietor, has been a resident of the County since 1859, coming here from Rock Island, Illinois, and settling in Grant township, remaining until 1873 when he moved to Traer and engaged in the hardware business. In 1878, he took charge of the Brooks House, and now Mr. Evans may lay claim to keeping the largest, cleanest and best hotel in the city.

George Sloss & Son, Flouring Mill.—These gentlemen are proprietors of one of the oldest flouring mills in the County, being established about the year 1856, by W. W. Leekin. In 1875 Mr. Sloss and his son became sole proprietors of the mill and have since refitted and remoddled it at a great expense, and now they have a fine one and turn out an excellent quality of flour

for which they have a large demand. The mill is located on
Wolf Creek, and is so arranged that it can be run either by water or steam making it very convenient. Mr. Sloss has long been
a resident of this County and has numerous warm friends; since
being a resident of Traer he is classed among its most valuable
citizens.

D. D. Cornick, Livery.—In 1876 this gentleman came to
Traer, from Buchannan County and established business and
has since had an encouraging run of custom. He has some as
fine rigs as there are in the County. His livery and feed stable
is located on Walnut Street north of the Brooks House, where
he is prepared to furnish his many customers with as fine rigs
as could be wished. He is a credit to the town and esteemed a
valuable citizen.

C. F. Buhmann, Cigar Manufacturer.—The cigar manufacturing establishment of the above named gentleman was established in 1874. Mr. Buhmann came here from Wynona, Minen-
sota. Since establishing business at Traer he has succeeded in
building up a large trade both in wholesale and retail, and in
every case his cigars has given entire satisfaction. He manufactures splendid brands of cigars, among which are the celebrated Belle of Traer, My Own Brand and the Tama Chief, for all
of these there is a large demand. His store is located on Second
Street where he carries a full line of all kinds of tobaccos etc. in
connection with his manufactory.

Batchelder, & Free, Druggists.—This firm is composed of
A. M. Batchelder and A. J. Free, the former has been a resident
of the County since 1864, first residing in Tama City, and the
latter has been a resident since 1853, coming here from Columbus, Ohio, and settled near Toledo in company with his father's
family. In 1873, when Traer sprang into existence Mr. Batchelder established business at that point, in company with J. G.
Strong. After a few years Mr. Strong sold out and G. T. Jones
bought an interest. The firm of Batchelder & Jones continued
until November, 1878, when Mr. Free bought Mr. Jones' interest and the firm name changed to Free & Batchelder. During

the past six years it has held a leading position and commanded an extensive trade, but never in its history has it been as popular as at the present time. They carry a full and well selected stock of everything in the drug line, paints, oils, etc. With its varied stock and well arranged apartments the store of Free & Batchelder is one of the best in the County and does honor to its energetic proprietors. Besides carrying on the drug store they are interested in the pop business; in this article they are having an extensive wholesale and retail trade. Their store is located on Second Street and their pop factory is on Main Street near the depot.

Galley & Newcomer, Dry Goods.—In 1874 business was established at this point by the above named gentlemen. The firm is composed of H. Galley and S. Newcomer, the former of whom is one of Tama County's oldest settlers and a leading dry goods merchant of Toledo. The latter is also an old settler of of the County formerly of Toledo, but now supervising the business of the above firm at Traer. Since this store has been established it has held a leading position in the dry goods trade of that place. They handle all kinds of dry goods but make a specialty of custom made boots and shoes. They have the exclusive agency in that place for the celebrated C. N. Fargo & Co. and the Miller & Co. boots and shoes, of which they claim their equal is not in Traer. Call on them.

J. H. Segner, Livery Feed and Sale Stable.—In 1876, this gentleman etablished himself in this business at Traer and since has been doing a large and paying business in the place. He turns out some fine rigs at reasonable prices. Mr. Segner for the first two years after locating at this place, besides running the livery barn was also proprietor of the Brooks House where he became well acquainted and made many friends all of whom speak of him as an honorable and valuable citizen. His livery barn is located but a few doors west of the Brooks House, where persons wishing accommodations in his line will get the best.

Seaver & McClary, Bankers and Dry Goods.—At the corner of Second and Main Streets is located the large dry goods and banking house of the above named gentlemen, who established business in the fall of 1874. Since that date they have gained a high reputation. The fine display of dry goods, notions, carpets clothing, boots and shoes, hats, caps, etc. is immense. From the first they adopted the cash system, both in buying and selling. By this means they secure goods at bottom prices and sell the same as cheap as Chicago retail houses. Their store is the finest and most attractive in the town, and commands a trade among all classes. In 1875, besides carrying on the dry goods business, the Bank of Traer was established by them. During the time it has been in existence it has done a regular banking and collection business, and has been of great advantage to the city. This department is under the supervision of Mr. Seaver, while Mr. McClary takes charge of the dry goods. Both these men came here from Jefferson County, Kansas, and since being residents of Traer have became well acquainted, highly esteemed and are good representatives of their respective positions and hold a high reputation as business men and citizens.

J. T. Weld, Hardware and Agricultural.—But a short time after Traer was founded the above named gentleman established business at that point. Since that time he has carried a full line of shelf and heavy hardware, stoves, tinware and agricultural implements. His store is located on Second Street, near Brooks and Moore's bank, where he has one of the largest and most complete stocks in the city. Mr. Weld has been a resident of Traer since 1863, coming here from Pecatonica, Illinois, where he had been in business. Since a resident of Traer Mr. Weld has become one of that city's leading hardware merchants and has established a name and trade of which he may be justly proud. He has always pushed his business in an enterprising manner and now is rewarded by a lucrative trade extending over a wide area. He has many friends and is classed among the valuable citizens of the place.

G. & N. H. Canfield, Coal and Lumber.—These gentlemen are proprietors of the oldest lumber yard in Traer, it being established by J. R. Smith in the year 1873. In the year 1877 they become sole proprietors and since have been doing an extensive business in all kinds of lumber and coal. The former member of the firm has been a resident of Traer since 1877, coming here from New Jersey, and the latter came here from Burlington, Iowa, where he had been extensively engaged in the coal trade during the year 1876. Besides having a large trade in lumber and coal they are interested in the grocery business in that place.

Greelis & Rice, Coal, Wood and Building Material.— In 1874 this business was established by T. H. Greelis who managed it with good success until September, 1877, when O. J. Rice became interested with him, since which date they have been comanding a large run of custom in coal, wood, lime, stone stucco, cement, sand, plastering hair and brick, all of which they have in stock at their office and yard on Main Street. The firm is composed of T. H. Greelis and O. J. Rice, the former has been a resident of Traer since 1874, coming here from Vinton, Iowa, formerly of Troy, New York, where he had been engaged in business. Since becoming a resident of Traer Mr. Greelis, besides being engaged in the above business, has been engaged in buying and selling town property and now owns the entire property of J. W. Traer, consisting of seventy-four lots, known as the railroad property. The latter Mr. Rice has been a resident of the County since 1856, coming here from Medina County, Ohio, and settling in Crystal township, where he remained upon his farm until 1876, when he moved to Traer and engaged in the real estate and loan business, which he followed until engaged in business with Mr. Greelis. They are both genial and obliging gentlemen and deserve success.

E. D. Rice, Hardware.—Among the oldest and most successfull men of Traer may be mentioned the above, who has been in business since 1874. The business was established by E. D. Rice and F. A. Goodenough, who managed it until February, 1879, when Mr. Goodenough sold his interest to Mr. Rice who became sole proprietor. At present Mr. Rice is carrying one of the heaviest stocks of hardware, consisting of general shelf and heavy hardware, carriage and wagon stocks, iron, nails, steel, tinware, fence wire etc., in the town. He is one of Tama County's oldest settlers, coming here in the year 1857, from Medina County, Ohio, and settling in Howard township, where he remained upon his farm until moving to Traer. While a resident of Howard township he took an active part in every good enterprise whereby the township and community would be benefited. He was a prominent mover in the Grange; was chairman of the County Grange two years, devoting a great deal of time and money for the special benefit of his brother farmers. Since residing in Traer, Mr. Rice has proven himself a liberal, enterprising and consequently successful business man and stands among the most highly respected citizens.

M. R. Wylie, Breeder of Fine Stock, Traer, Iowa.—In the stables of M. R. Wylie, at this place, may be seen as fine horses as anybody would wish to see. We are glad to see the interest that Mr. Wylie is taking in breeding the best class of horses, in this County. The following noted horses will be found in his stable at Traer: Young Invincible—This fine stallion was imported from England to Pennsylvania in the year 1876, by G. B. Hayes of that State. He is seventeen and one-half hands high, with heavy bone and muscle, and weighs two thousand pounds. He was got by Farmer's Profit, son of Young Waxwork, by Old Waxwork; dam by Great Britain, grand dam by Old Warwick, great grand dam by Old Invincible. English Champion—This horse is a dapple black, seventeen hands high and weighs one thousand and five hundred pounds. He has superior action and has proven himself to be of good blood. He was got by Cheshire Champion, who was imported to Pennsylvania, by W. Beal of that State. Dam by the imported coach horse, Bay President, great dam imported Canadian mare. Fred Grant—Is a bright bay with black dapples. He is a natural trotter and if properly trained would reach a creditable record. He was got by General Grant, son of Wapsie, by Green's Bashaw; dam by the Barklow mare, daughter of Holderman's mare, by Weatherby's Blackhawk, Profit, son of Vermont Blackhawk. Grand dam, by Matthew White's mare, Kosciusko, and bred by E. Manful, of West Liberty. Any information desired in reference to any of these horses will be cheerfully given by their owner. Call at the stable on Main Street or address, M. R. Wylie, Traer, Iowa.

Business Directory.

J. H. Smith, dry goods.
Porterfield Bros, dry goods.
Seaver & McClary, dry goods.
Mrs. H. C. Pierce, millinery,
Mrs. A. Petterson, millinery,
S. Shively, merchant tailor
Steffens&Luedemann,merchant tailors,
Pest & Canfield, grocers.
J. Atchison & Son, grocers.
W. Wade, grocer.
L. D. Knapp, grocer.
G. W. Ladd, barber.
H. Schrader, boots and shoes.
D. Bowers, boots and shoes.
I. Baldwin, restaurant.
C. C. Collins, furniture.
W. McDowall, meat market.
F. A. Adsell, meat market,
E. T. Langley, lawyer,
J. Fowler, lawyer.
Newcomb & Son, harness shop.
O. T. Brainard, justice.
E. M. Wooley, druggist,
O. D. Bonney, druggist.
J. P. Morrison, doctor.
S. Waterbury, doctor.
C. M. Ashton, doctor.
Canfield Bros, lumber, coal.
McCormack Bros, lumber, coal,
H. D. Merrimann, blacksmith.
C. H. Cram, blacksmith.
W. E. Gerry, painter.
Brooks House, W. W. Evans prop'r.
Best House, B. Best.
Schrader House, ——— ———.
Brooks & Moore's Bank, R. H. Moore
    Cashier.
O. T. Sanborn, livery,
D. D. Cornick, livery.
McCormack Bros, agricultural.
E. D. Rice, hardware.

Smith & Edwards, dry goods
Galley & Newcomer, dry goods.
M. Simon, clothier.
Mrs. L. S. Cope, millinery.
Mrs. S. Gage,
J. Stein, merchant tailor.
T. Gallogby, grocer,
C. F. Wetzel, grocer.
Grossell & Hadsell, grocers.
W. B. Gillespie, grocer.
J. Morrison, grocer.
C. M. Lathrop, barber.
H. Baxter, boots a d shoes.
G. Shay, restaurant.
J. Munson, restaurant.
J. Kingery, furniture.
J. Pritchard, meat market.
G. L. Wilber, lawyer.
D. Connell, lawyer.
N. C. Newcomb, harness shop.
J. P. Morrison, harness shop.
W. T. V. Ladd, justice,
Free & Batchelder, druggist,
W. A. Daniel, doctor.
J. L. Ladd, doctor.
W. D. Scott, doctor.
Free & Batchelder, pop manufacturers.
Johnson Bros, lumber, coal.
W. Wolf, blacksmith.
S. Hyde, blacksmith.
H. A. Hartshorn, blacksmith.
F. S. Fairchild, painter.
Clark House, C. Clark.
Pennsylvania House, ———.
Bank of Traer, C. Seaver, Cash'r.
L. H. Butler, wagon maker.
C. H. Cram, wagon maker.
J. H. Segner, livery.
Dennis & Averill, agricultural.
J. T. Weld, agricultural.
J. T. Weld, hardware.

H. M. Wooley, photographer.
L. B. Alderman, dentist.
James Morrison & Co., CLIPPER.
Bowen & Higby, land agent.
Withers & Bates, jewelry.
Sloss & Son, flouring mills.
W. W. Wilson, grain buyer.
C. A. Clow, grain buyer.
A. M. Glaze, carpenter.
W. Kinney, carpenter.

E. H. Bissell, dentist.
E. Taylor, STAR.
G. A. Rugg, book store.
C. F. Buhmann, cigar manufacturer.
S. C. Wager, boots and shoes.
M. C. Murdough, flour and feed store.
H. C. Pierce & Co. grain buyer.
D. Bedford, ice dealer.
M. D. Schaffer, carpenter.

CHAPTER XXV.

This is an enterprising town of about six hundred inhabitants situated on the Chicago & Northwestern Railroad about seven miles west of Tama City. It is beautifully located and is one of the most thrifty and enterprising towns in the County. It is located on section twenty-one and twenty-eight and covers about one hundred and twenty acres of land. Miron Blodgett, and Phineas Helm, were the original owners of this land, and for a number of years before this town was established used it for farming purposes.

The first business established at this point was by Dr. John Doe, in the fall of 1863, who opened a stock of dry goods in a small building which was moved from Indiantown. E. Ruggles who had been engaged in business at the latter place, prior to the road reaching Montour, was the next to erect a store and engage in business at the new town. From this date, 1863, the place grew very rapidly and to-day it is well represented in all branches of business as our business directory will show. The first dwelling house was erected by B. McCullen, and the first hotel was the Orford House, moved here from Indiantown. The railroad depot was built by the people, and as soon as this was done it gave an impetus to the place and from that time to the present date the town has continued to grow. It was called

Orford at the request of some of the citizens after the well known Orford of Vermont, but since changed to Montour, the present name. The scenery in and around town is truly beautiful. The bluffs here are its true mine of wealth; not only do they add charms to the place, but they are composed of a formation which at no distant day will cause the town of Montour to become a place of no small note. One-fourth mile west of the town are the kilns of the Orford Lime Company, where are deposits of oolitic limestone of large quantities, from which they are manufacturing lime and doing a good shipping business. This, from its appearance, belongs to the sub-carboniferous era, for the whole formation seems to consist of deposits of fish bones, shell, spines, etc. The finest however, has the appearance of the spawn of millions of fish being thrown together and cemented in one solid mass; and upon examination it is almost impossible to find a specimen in which traces of organic life cannot be seen. It is from appearance a fine carbonate of lime, minus sand or quartz, but seems held together by a crystalized calcareous spar. It varies in color, sometimes being of grayish white with sections of light blue, and sometimes of a dark cream running through it. It is quite soft when first quarried but grows hard upon exposure. The deposit here is about twelve to fifteen feet in thickness, and the lime manufactured from this cannot be surpassed, it having now an almost universal reputation. This business adds greatly to the interest of the town.

On the sixth day of December, A. D. 1870, a vote was taken for or against organizing as a town under the general laws of the State, resulting in its almost unanimous adoption, only two votes being polled against it, and the following named gentleman were elected to the various offices: Mayor, J. W. Niman; Trustees, H. Winchell, J. H. Stevens, S. Ellis, J. White; Recorder, T. R. Oldham. The present officers are as follows: Mayor, H. J. Stevens; Recorder, W. C. Burgess; Trustees, T. P. Smith, H. C. Burgess, R. E. Tewksbury, H. C. Waggenor, A. B. Gage, and R. M. Tenney.

With reference to the public schools of the place the citizens take an especial pride, and their schools rank among the best in the County. In the southern part of town between Main and Division Streets is located a fine brick school building the main part of which is 30x54, with two large wings 14x26. This building was erected in the year 1877 at a cost of about $9,000, is quite showy, and neat, yet well proportioned. The foundation is of limestone, while the main walls are of red brick. It is in height two stories and contains three large and nicely arranged school rooms, with two recitation rooms, each being provided with the best modern school furniture and every appliance that would aid one in acquiring knowledge. Everything in connection with the building is in good taste and reflects great credit upon the city,

The public schools for the past two or three years have been conducted by W. H. Black, who has succeeded in a perfect organization of every department of the schools, and has filled his position to the satisfaction of the people. The following are the present school board: T. P. Smith, J. H. Stevens, A. N. Poyneer, H. D. Williams, H. G. Wallace, R. E. Tewksbury.

There are a number of live merchants in the town, among whom we may mention the following named firms.

Butler & Cronk, Grain and Live Stock Dealers.—This is one of the strongest and most reliable firms doing business in Montour and is composed of Philip Butler and J. G. Cronk, both of whom are old settlers in Tama County, the former came to Indian Village township, from Linn County, in company with his father's family in the year 1853, and located upon a farm. Since residing here, Mr. Butler has been extensively engaged in farming and now owns over 1,400 acres of land the most of which is under cultivation. Besides attending to the duties of his farm he is a member of the above firm at Montour where they are doing a large business. Politically Mr. Butler is a Democrat, the principles of that party being near and dear to his heart. Though the township in which he resides is strongly Republican, at the last general election he was elected justice of the peace by a large majority. The latter, Mr. Cronk, came to the County from Morrow County, Ohio, and settled in Highland township in 1857, residing upon his farm which consists of over 600 acres, until 1877 when he removed to Montour. He also carries on his farm in connection with the above business. These gentleman are both honorable and highly respected citizens and since doing business, at this point have made many friends.

Millard & Rockwell, Blacksmiths. Smith & Kelley, Wagon Makers.—Under one roof these two firms are doing business on Main Street, south of the railroad track, and since establishing this business they have been doing a large business in all kinds of blacksmithing, wagon and carriage manufacturing and repairing. They have built a reputation for honest work and square dealing. In connection with the shops is a machine and repair shop, operated by W. A. Downs, a young but accomplished, man just starting in a business life who is building up an extensive trade. These gentlemen are all good citizens, have made many friends and classed among the valuable citizens of the town.

E. Ruggles, Dry Goods.—The oldest and most thoroughly established business at this point is that of the above named gentleman. Mr. Ruggles came to this County in 1854 from Ogle County, Illinois, and established business at Indiantown, where he remained until removing to Montour in 1864. Since that date he has been carrying a full line of dry goods, clothing, boots, shoes, hats, caps, groceries, crockery etc., and commands a trade that extends for many miles around. His store is located on the corner of Elm and Main Streets. Since doing business here Mr. Ruggles has gained a reputation for enterprise and fair dealing, and has become popular as a dry goods merchant of that thriving and stirring place.

J. L. Waggenor, Hardware.—For all kinds of shelf and heavy hardware, stoves, tinware, wagon stock, etc. persons residing in and around the vicinity of Montour will do well to call on this gentleman, on Main Street and examine his stock and prices. Mr. Waggenor first came to the County from Marshall County and established business at Tama City remaining in the latter place until 1867, when he removed to Montour. Here we now find him doing a large business. He is a man that can be relied upon, is prompt and gives his entire attention to his business, but never neglects the best interests of the community in which he lives.

Weimer & Co., Restaurant.—Among the late branches of business established in this town is the restaurant and ice cream stand of the above named firm, located on Elm Street, in the post office building. Here they have nicely fitted up rooms with all the conveniences of a first-class restaurant. They have in stock a full line of candies, smoking and chewing tobaccos, nuts, pies, cakes, etc. The firm is composed of L. Bingham and W. Weimer, the former has been a resident of the County since 1870, and besides being interested in the above business is post master, which office he has held since 1877. The latter is a young man of fine business qualifications, and no doubt will make a success of whatever he undertakes.

H. C. Hutson, Druggist.—This gentleman is classed among the oldest and most highly respected citizens of Montour, being a resident of that place since 1865, coming here from Maryland. Until 1872 Mr. Hutson practiced medicine at this place retaining a large practice, when he engaged in the drug business. Since entering into this occupation he has been carrying a full and complete stock of drugs, books, stationery, wall paper, window curtains, etc., in his store room on Elm Street. Call and see him and you will find a liberal, enterprising, jovial good fellow.

Smith Bros.—This firm is composed of T. P. and Jeremiah Smith, the former has been a resident of the place since 1867, and the latter since 1868, both came here from Massachusetts. Since becoming residents of Montour they have been engaged in active business and classed among the leading spirits of the place. At their office and yard, on Main Street, they are handling agricultural implements, lumber, plastering hair, coal, salt, cement, etc.; in each article they are having a large run of custom. Besides carrying on the above business they are largely interested in, and assume the management of the Orford Lime

Company's business. They are manufacturing a splendid article of lime at the kilns, one-fourth mile west of the town, which meets with rapid and ready sale.

L. Matthews, Dry Goods.—One among the oldest and reliable dry goods houses of central Iowa, stands that of the above named gentleman, established in the year 1866. Mr. Matthews came to this point from Minnesota, formerly of Greene County, New York and since that date has taken the lead in the dry goods business at Montour. His store is without doubt the finest and largest in the town being one hundred and nine feet deep. He commands a large trade among all classes of citizens. It is his aim to keep a full line of staple dry goods, dress goods, clothing, boots, shoes, groceries, hardware, etc. He buys for cash and secures goods at bottom prices and therefore sells goods very cheap. Mr. Matthews is among the solid and substantial business men, and one who has liberally contributed to the up-building of the town.

C. J. Stevens & Co., Bankers.—The banking business at this point has been carried on since 1873, first by O. B. Dutton & Son, then by Stevens, Harrison & Warren, and at present by C. J. Stevens & Co., who have had charge of the business since November, 1875. The firm is composed of C. J. Stevens and H. J. Stevens: the former has been a resident of the County since 1855, coming here from New York, and settling in Indian Village township. He is a farmer by occupation, but is at present our popular County Clerk, filling this office since 1874. The latter has been a resident of the County since 1875, coming here from the same State. Since residing at Montour, Mr. H. J. Stevens has had charge of the business at that point and has succeeded in building up a large banking custom and is at present Mayor of the town. They are both honorable and reputable citizens and are ranked among the leading and most respected citizens of the County.

E. M. Poyneer, Grocer.—In 1859 this gentleman settled in this County, Indian Village township, upon a farm. Here he remained until the year 1874, when he removed to Montour, and engaged in the banking business continuing for a number of years.

In 1878 he established himself in the grocery business and at his store, on Elm Street, he is carrying a fine stock of groceries which he is selling at bottom prices. Mr. Poyneer is a gentleman of acknowleged business ability, and always works for the best interests of the town and community in which he lives.

H. G. Wallace, Stock and Grain Dealer.—This gentleman is the oldest stock and grain dealer in the place, coming here from Lee County, Ills., in the year 1865, and built the first elevator inside the corporation. Since residing here Mr. Wallace has been engaged in the above business, and has built a reputation for honorable and square dealing and is known over the greater portion of Tama County as such. He is a credit to the stock and grain business, an enterprising business man, and has a large circle of patrons and friends.

D. R. Way, Dry Goods.—In the store of D. R. Way, located on the corner of Main and Elm Streets may be found one of the nicest and most complete stock of general dry goods, groceries, clothing, boots, shoes, queensware, etc. in the town, and at prices hard to beat. Mr. Way has been a business resident of Montour since 1866, coming here from Montezuma, Poweshiek County, and since that time has been active in the dry goods business. He does business in his own store room which saves paying rent; this advantage is given his patrons. Give him a call.

B. W. Fellows, Farm Machinery.—Persons wishing anything in the way of farm machinery, repairs, mowers, plows, rakes, pumps, harvesters, cultivators, planters, etc., will do well to call and see Mr. Fellows. He is selling goods very cheap at his store rooms on Elm Street. As he is an old settler in this County, coming here from New York and settling in Indian Village township in the year 1855, he is well acquainted, has many friends and a good run of custom, and since establishing the above business he has constantly been increasing it. Give him a call.

Business Directory.

E. Ruggles, dry goods.	D. R. Way, dry goods,
L. Matthews, dry goods.	J. C. Millard, dry goods.

H. C. Hutson, druggist.
Mrs. A. Doty, millinery.
J. L. Waggenor, hardware.
J. T. Mckee, restaurant.
Horn Bros, grocers.
E. M. Poyneer, grocer.
R. Montgomery, blacksmith.
Millard & Rockwell, blacksmiths.
A. A. Voiles & Kellogg, wagon makers,
Butler & Cronk, grain and stock.
B. W. Fellows, agricultural.
P. F. Long, meat market.
J. B. Roberts, painter.
Charles Gray, flour and feed.
Smith Bros., lumber.

J. H. Stevens, druggist,
C. H. Roberts, attorney.
A. B. Gage, Gage House.
Weimer & Co., restaurant.
J. L. Waggenor, & Co, grocers.
L. Bingham, post master.
L, F. Kellogg, blacksmith.
H. H. Alexander, wagon maker.
W. Calkins, furniture.
H. G. Wallace, grain and stock.
Exchange Bank, H. J. Stevens,   Cashier.
D. E. Dickinson, shoe shop.
J. Gass, harness shop.
E. Finch, livery and feed stable.

CHAPTER XXVI.

This beautiful little town is located in the eastern part of Clark township on section thirteen, and was named in honor of Hon. Joseph Dysart, ex State Senator, from Tama and Benton Counties and ex-Lieutenant Governor of this State. It is surrounded by as fine a tract of prairie land as can be found in central Iowa. In the fall of 1872 the town was established on land belonging to J. W. Crisman, and is located on the Pacific Branch of the Burlington, Cedar Rapids & Northern Railroad. The first train made its appearance in the town on the 27th day of December, 1873, and as it was the terminus of the road until August of the following year the town grew rapidly and when the road moved on her progress did not stop, and to-day there is a population of six hundred souls rejoicing over what her future promises to be. The first dwelling house was erected by Mr. Levi Johnston of Belle Plaine. Mr. William Davidson was the first to erect a store room and commence business. He opened, on January 1st, 1873, a fine general stock. About the same time Brown, Doty & Co , built a warehouse and commenced buying and shipping grain. Then followed S. Hanlin & Son, C. Johnson and others who established business. Now the town is well represented in all branches of business and has become a place of considearble importance. The town is situated on high rolling ground and surrounded by a fine and richly producing country.   This land, once a broad unbroken prairie, is now converted into bountiful farms some as fine as there are in central Iowa.

No efforts have yet been made to establish manufacturing, and therefore, the merchants are dependent upon the trade of the surrounding country.

In educational pursuits Dysart has kept pace with her neighboring towns.   In the southern portion of the town we find a beautiful frame building which is used for school purposes.   It is large, two stories high with a dome rising from the east wing from which can be obtained a view of the town and surrounding country.   The building is entered from the north and south sides into a large hall.   From this hall a stairway leads to the second floor.   The building contains, besides the halls, four large and commodious school rooms, each well furnished with the best furniture.

There are two religious denominations in the place, Methodist and Presbyterian.   Each of these have fine church buildings of which we have spoken in another chapter.

The business portion of the town is substantially built, some large and commodious buildings reflect credit upon the enterprising men of her business circle.   Among the businesss men of the place we make special mention of the following:

A. Brannaman & Co., Bankers.—This business was established in the year 1877, by the above firm.   They done business in a rented room until the summer of 1878, when they erected the present building on Main Street.   It is a fine brick structure twenty feet wide and thirty-two feet long, and is nicely arranged, with all the conveniences of modern times.   The company is in a prosperous condition and composed of A. Brannaman, C. E. Morris and E. A. Morris, with A. Brannaman as cashier and M. M. Morris, assistant cashier.   Under the management of these able gentlemen the bank is doing a large business and giving entire satisfaction.   The members of this firm are among the leading citizens and are always ready to assist in advancing the best interests of their town.

R. M. Horton, Attorney at Law.—This gentleman has been a resident of Dysart since 1876, coming here from Lewiston Ill. Since being a resident of the place he has been extensively engaged in the practice of law and the collection business. Mr. Horton is a gentleman who is well read in law and has had over sixteen years practice. He thoroughly understands his business, and is an able man to consult Since residing in this place has made many warm friends and is classed among the highly respected citizens of the town.

W. O. Beam, M. D.—For a number of years this gentleman has been a resident of Tama County, locating first at Waltham, where he remained practicing medicine until July, 1878, when he moved to Dysart, and since has had a growing practice. Mr. Beam is a graduate of the Medical Department of the Iowa State University. He is a gentleman of acknowledged ability and well educated in the medical profession. He enjoys the confidence of the community in which he resides. His office is located over Wm. Davidson's dry goods store.

C. W. Cooper, Blacksmith and Wagon Maker.—One of the best and successful business men in Tama County is C. W. Cooper. He manufactures wagons, buggies and sleighs besides carrying on blacksmithing. His shops are located on the corner of Wilson and Tilford Streets in Dysart. This gentleman is a native of Canada, being born there in the year 1845. He learned his trade from his father, who was a successful blacksmith and mechanic. After Mr. Cooper reached his twenty-first year he left home and went to Pennsylvania where remained until the year 1869, when he came to this State and settled in Cedar Rapids. In 1871, he moved to Vinton and again followed the old line of trade. He remained here until 1875 when he moved to Dysart. Since this he has had a large run of custom in all his branches of business and takes great pleasure in saying to his many patrons and the farmers in general that he has recently erected a wagon and paint shop and is fully prepared to do all kinds of work in this line, besides doing all kinds of blacksmithing. Mr. Cooper has in his employ a set of hands that are second to none in Tama or Benton Counties. He is setting horse shoes for ten cents; new shoes twenty-five cents; plows layed, two dollars and fifty cents; plows sharpened for twenty-five cents and tires set for one dollar per set. His shops are located west of Main Street on the corner of Wilson and Tilford Streets, where he has two large and nicely arranged shops, one is used as the blacksmith shop and the other as a wagon and paint shop. The latter is a large two story building, the first floor is used as the wagon shop and the upper for a paint shop. In each of these departments Mr. Cooper is fully prepared to do first class work, on very short notice. He is manufacturing wagons which he sells for sixty dollars, and warrants them for two years. He is manufacturing buggies and sleighs at equally as low price. Mr. Cooper enjoys the confidence of the community in which he resides and we can truly say that it would be difficult to become acquainted with a more genial and social gentleman than C. W. Cooper. When ever you want anything in his line don't forget Mr. Cooper.

N. C. Rice, Attorney at Law.—One of Dysart's most successful lawyers is N. C. Rice, who has been a resident of Tama County since the year 1855. For a number of years after coming to this County, Mr. Rice resided in Perry township upon his farm. Besides carrying on the farm he read law and was admitted to the bar, and since has had an encouraging practice. Mr. Rice has proven his ability as a lawyer and counselor, and has gained the respect of all.

Wm. Davidson, Dry Goods and Groceries.—This gentleman is proprietor of the leading dry goods and grocery house of the place, which was established in the year 1873. Mr. Davidson has been a resident of Tama County since 1870, coming here from Canada, and locating at Buckingham. In 1871, he established business at Mooreville, a small village and post office in the northeastern part of Geneseo township, remaining until moving to Dysart. Since the latter date he has carried a full line of dry goods, boots, shoes, hats, caps, staple and fancy groceries, etc., and has taken the lead in trade. Call and see him and he will sell you goods cheap, as his long business experience enables him to buy goods at bottom figures; this together with his good judgment in selecting enables him to offer his patrons superior inducements.

J. H. Pinkerton, Druggist.—This gentleman has ranked among the first-class and fluential business men of Dysart since 1874. Since this date he has been engaged in the drug business. Mr. Pinkerton is now carrying a full line of drugs, together with paints, oils, stationery, wall paper, toilet goods and all kinds of school books. His store is located on Main Street, where he ever stands ready to wait upon his numerous customers. Call on him and you will find him a gentleman who will do well by you.

W. H. Sherwin & Son, Hardware and Furniture.—In 1877, these gentlemen established business at this point, buying the hardware stock of S. B. Yeoman. Since this time they have carried a full line of goods consisting of hardware, tinware, stoves, iron, etc., which they are selling very cheap. They are also proprietors of a furniture store which is located three doors south of the hardware, where they carry a full line of furniture consisting of everything kept in a first-class stock. This department is under the management of H. P. Sherwin, while the hardware is managed by his father, W. H. Sherwin. Both these gentlemen are liberal, enterprising and consequently successful business men and rank among the foremost citizens of the place.

J. E. Hollabaugh, Grocer.—For all kinds of staple and fancy groceries, crockery, glassware, fish, salt and dried fruits call at the store of the above named gentleman and he or his obliging clerks will show you a first-class article. Mr. Hollabaugh has been engaged in business at this point since 1876, coming here from Vinton. Since that date he has succeeded in building up a large and increasing trade. His store is located on Main Street. Persons wishing anything in the grocery line will do well to call and see him.

C. Ellis & Son, Lumber Dealers.—On Wilson Street is located the oldest lumber yard in the town, being established in the year 1874. In September, 1878, the business passed into the hands of the above named gentlemen.   They are at present conducting the business at this point through their agent H. H. Allison, a gentleman of fine business qualifications, who by attentive work and honest dealing is working up a fine business.   They handle all kinds of lumber, lath, shingles, sash, doors, blinds, building paper etc., together with coal, all of which they are selling at very low prices.

H. W. Howard, Wagon and Repair Shop.—Since 1866, this gentleman has been a resident of this County, coming here from Jackson County, Iowa, and settled at Tama City.   Mr. Howard by trade is a carpenter, and for a number of years before settling at this point followed that business.   In 1877 he moved here and engaged in the above business.   Since that date he has been having a good run of custom in wagon and machine repairing.   His shops are located on Wilson Street, where you will always find him ready for business.

Business Directory.

A. Brannaman & Co., bankers.
C. P. Fedderson, dry goods.
G. W. McDonald, dry goods
S. Horton, grocer.
S. P. Black, doctor.
J. H. Pinkerton, druggist.
J. P. Schloe, meat market.
L. D. Hallett & Co, harness.
Simon & Werthim, clothier.
A. M. Woodward, jeweler
Wm Harrison, hardware.
Mrs M. H. Lavy, millinery,
Mrs M. L. Smith, millinery.
Central House,
G. Wood, boot and shoe maker.
C. Ellis & Son, lumber.
R. Hyatt, flour and feed.
Paysley Bros. liveries.
H. W. Howard, wagon maker.
E. Edmonds, wagon maker.
A. Arbuthnot, grain buyer.
H. L. Brannaman, grain buyer.
Innis & Hanks, stock.
R. M. Horton, lawyer.
T. N. Ives, REPORTER.

W. Davidson, dry goods.
Miller & Betebenner, dry goods.
J. E. Hallabough, grocer.
W. O. Beam, doctor.
Manrid & Haney, druggists.
C. A. Gambrill, bakery.
C. Duncan, harness.
J. Keellman, taylor.
U. S. Miller, jeweler.
Sherwin & Son. Hardware.
Sherwin & Son. furniture.
Mrs A. M. Crady, millinery.
Dysart House.
City Hotel.
A. Mussmann, boot and shoe maker.
C. E. Morris & Co, coal.
Furrow & Stewart, livery.
W. Bradbrook, blacksmith.
C. W. Cooper, wagon maker.
C. Kenaston, wagon maker.
D. A. Innis, grain buyer.
Hill Bros, stock.
N. C. Rice, lawyer.
D. E. Hallet, agricultural dealer.

CHAPTER XXVII

CHELSEA.

This town was laid out in 1863, by C. S. Breese, and J. Hunter, on sections seventeen and eighteen. It is a bustling little town situated on the Chicago & Northwestern Railroad, about ten miles east of Tama City, and has a population of about five hundred. It is mostly surrounded by prairie which extends north and west for quite a distance and south about one mile to the Iowa River. The first store building erected in the place was by J. R. Graham, and the first stock of merchandise of any kind was a grocery and dry good stock, opened by him. Shortly after, his brother W. H. Graham opened a dry good store, followed by M. Smith and others, who came in and engaged in business.

At an election held January 28th, 1878, a vote was taken for or against the incorporation of the town, and on March 3d, of the same year, the following officers were elected: Mayor, H. E. Covell; Recorder, J. W. Shaler; Trustees, F. Roach, H. Cory, J. H. Mercer, J. Sittler, and J. S. Ormiston; Assessor, F. Roach. At present the officers are as follows: Mayor, H. E. Covell; Recorder J. W. Shaler; Trustees, M. Smith, J. S. Ormiston, J. Sittler, J. H. Mercer, J. Hannify, and J. Musle.

During the first few years of its existence the town grew very rapidly, notwithstanding the cry of hard times was heard upon every hand, and to-day it is steadily increasing in population

though slow. The town is a large grain market, there being
thousands of bushels of oats, wheat and corn shipped from this
point annually besides hundreds of car loads of hogs and cattle,
there are at present one grocery store, four dry good stores, one
drug store, two hardwares, two shoe shops, one harness shop, one
exchange store, three blacksmith shops, one wagon shop, one
lumber yard, one millinery, one poultry firm, two saw mills, besides two doctors and two grain buyers, in the place, all of whom
are doing a fair business.

The mercantile trade of Chelsea is better than usually enjoyed
by towns of its size, and her business men, as a class, are live,
enterprising men, and work for the prosperity of the town.
Among the number we take pleasure in referring to the following
named firms:

M. Smith & Son.—This is one of the oldest firms in the town
as well as the largest one in trade. The business was first established in West Irving, by Mr. Smith, in the year 1856. Here
he done business until 1866, when he moved to Chelsea where
he still remains. Since moving to this point he has taken his
son P. R. Smith, a young man of splendid business qualifications,
in with him, and they are having a large trade. Mr. Smith is
also post master which position he has held for ten years, giving
satisfaction to all. They carry a full line of dry goods, groceries,
hardware, boots and shoes, hats, caps, etc, which they take pleasure in showing, and are never undersold. Call and see them;
they are both liberal and enterprising gentleman and will do well
by you.

J. W. Shaler.—This gentleman has been a resident of Chelsea
since March 1872, and until July, 1877, was in the employ of the
Chicago & Northwestern Railroad company as station agent.
After quitting the employ of the company he established himself
in the grain business. To-day Mr. Shaler, besides buying grain,
is successfully carrying on the lumber, coal, and pump business;
in each branch he holds a large trade, extending for many
miles around the village. Mr. Shaler is a liberal, enterprising,
and consequently a successful business man, and stands among the

leading business men of the city, and is at present efficiently serving the city as Recorder, and filling the offices of township clerk and justice of the peace, besides serving the Chicago & Northwestern railroad company as express agent, which appointment dates from April 26th, 1879.

Wilson & Ormiston, Physicians and Surgeons.—This very prominent and successful medical firm is composed of G. W. Wilson, and J. S. Ormiston, both of whom are young men of high standing and good character, and graduates of the Medical Department of the Iowa State University, the former of whom graduated in the year 1876, and the latter in 1877. Shortly after graduating these gentleman located at Chelsea, since which date they have been having a good practice, among all classes of citizens, and now they are recognized as one of the reputable, permanent and leading medical firms of the County. Their office is located in White & Co's, drug store, where they may always be found and ever ready to attend to your wants.

A. Z. Rawson.—This gentleman came to Tama County, from Stebbin County, Indiana, and settled at Chelsea in the year 1865. For a number of years after locating at this point he followed the carpenter business. In the year 1870, Mr. Rawson opened a wagon shop, and has since been doing a good business. His shop is located on Seneca Street, where he is prepared to do all kinds of wagon and carriage repairing besides machine repairing, on short notice, small pay, and in good style. Call and see him.

Mr. Henry Cory.—In 1864, Mr. Cory came to this County from Belmont County, Ohio, and settled in Columbia township, here he remained until 1871, when he moved to Richland township, remaining until settling in Chelsea in the year 1876. Since locating at this point Mr. Cory has been quite extensively engaged in the grocery and provision business, and holds a large trade, for many miles around the city, and is rewarded with a large and growing business. Store on Station Street.

Business Directory.

H. Cory, grocer.   Smith & Son, dry goods.

M. Weaver, dry goods.
F. Simon, dry goods.
L. Cumte, Hardware.
J. Holepeck, shoe shop.
W, H. Graham. exchange store.
T. Morris, blacksmith.
A. Z. Rawson, wagon maker.
A. E. Covel, cattle buyer.
Dudley & Smith, saw mill.
Spence & Son, saw mill.
J. S. Ormiston, doctor.

J. H. Mercer, dry goods.
White & Co. druggist.
J. Sittler, shoe shop.
J. Mussell, harness.
A. Ennis, blacksmith,
J. Iseman, blacksmith.
J. W. Shaler, lumber.
Wolraven & Southard, poultry and fur
    dealers.
G W. Wilson, doctor.
Mrs. Coe, & Wilkinson, millinery.

CHAPTER. XXVIII

The land on which Indiantown now stands was entered at a very early day, and for a number of years before Montour was founded there was considerable business done at this point. It is located on the Iowa river about one mile north of Montour. It derived its name from the fact that at an early day there was a great many Indians living in that vicinity, but is now known to a great many by the name of Butlerville. At present there is one dry goods store, post office, one grocery store, one blacksmith shop and one flouring mill, which comprise the business facilities of the place. Besides these there are a number of dwellings and a school house.

C. Gray, Flouring Mill.—This gentlman is proprietor of one of the oldest flouring mills in the County, which was established in the year 1855, by Fish & Helm. Since that date it has been in running operation and retained a reputation as a first-class mill. Mr. Gray become its proprietor in 1856 and since that date, from time to time as the mill needed, he has added new machinery and repaired the building, and now it stands nearly as good as new. It has three run of stone and all the latest improvements. It is located upon the Iowa river about one-half mile north, east of Indiantown. Mr. Gray is well known throughout the County and is respected as one of its best citizens. In connection with the mill he has an exchange store at Montour for the accommodation of his custom at that place.

J. J. Lavelley, Piano Tuner and Repairer.—This gentleman is located at Indiantown where he is permanently established. He has had years of experience in this business and thoroughly understands it. He is also general salesman for the Sweep Stake Washing Machine. He is having a good trade in this machine, and it gives general satisfaction.

LEGRAND STATION.

We can only speak of LeGrand Station without going outside of our territory as the main town is situated in Marshall County and depot just over the boundary line in this County. At the station is only the depot, two or three dwelling houses, an elevator and a lumber yard. The station is located on the Chicago & Northwestern Railroad, about one-half mile east of the main town. Notwithstanding the size of the place we speak with pleasure of the business of Heald & Nevill.

These gentlemen have been engaged in business at this point for a number of years, handling coal, lumber, sash, blinds, doors, besides buying grain. The firm is composed of Sidwell Heald and B. G. Nevill, both are men of splendid business qualifications and high standing in society. Since they have been doing business at this point they have succeeded in building up a large run of custom and yet it steadily increases. Their agreeable ways and honorable dealings make it pleasant to do business with them.

MONTICELLO.

Monticello is located in the southern part of Howard township on land entered by George Zehrung and Christian Bruner, and lays in the midst of a beautiful farming community, four miles northwest of Toledo. For a number of years after it was established those who were doing business there enjoyed a season of prosperity and every thing looked favorable for the up-building of a considerable town, but after Toledo become the County seat, things changed, and it was but a few years until most of the town moved to Toledo. The first store built in the place was by Peter Brush, who filled it with a general stock of merchandise. At present there is no business done at Monticello save one blacksmith shop and a practicing physician of whom we make mention.

J. Ballard, Physician and Surgeon.—This gentleman is among the leading practitioners of Tama County, and is located in Monticello where he has an extensive practice. He is regarded as one of the best read and education physicians in this County. Mr. Ballard has attended two courses of lectures at Ann Arbor, Michigan; one at Chicago and one at Iowa City. After finishing these he located in Toledo, but in the fall of 1878 moved to Monticello. Since locating here he has had a creditable practice and holds a prominent position in his chosen profession.

Bruner & Reedy, Flouring Mills.—In speaking of these gentlemen and their mills we can say that they are proprietors of the oldest mills in the County. They were established by Christian Bruner, father of one of the present proprietors, in the year 1854. The proprietors are both young men of excellent business qualifications; they are enterprising and successful in their chosen occupation. Their mills are located about one-half mile west of Monticello and are known as The Monticello Mills. The building is a large frame one, four stories high, and equipped with superior machinery. Besides doing the milling business these gentlemen are dealing quite extensively in live stock.

WALTHAM.

This village is located in York township on section three, and is surrounded by a fine country. The place was surveyed by H. Jacobs, in the year 1868, and for a number of years there was considerable business done at this point. The first store was opened by George Mason, and consisted of a general stock of dry goods, groceries, hardware etc. At present there are two grocery and dry goods stories, two blacksmith shop, post office, one harness shop, one shoe shop, and one physician.

IRVING.

This beautiful litte hamlet is located in the extreme northeastern corner of Salt Creek township, and lays half in Benton and half in Tama Counties. The land on which it is located was entered by L. Marsh, in the year 1853. For a number of years before the town was laid out, Mr. Marsh erected a store building and commenced business at this point carrying a complete stock consisting of everything kept in a pioneer store until the year 1856 when the services of N. C. Wieting were secured and the town was surveyed. From this date up to 1862, there was considerable business done at the place, and everything bid fair for a large and enterprising town, but after the railroad reached Belle Plaine, the business mostly moved to that place and now there is nothing left but one dry goods store, one grocery store, post office, one blacksmith shop, one flouring mill and one shoe shop.

HAVEN.

This town is located in Richland township, and, was laid out by T. H. Marshall and I. M. Strong, who entered the land about the year 1854. It is located in a beautiful surrounding country, which is thickly settled and well improved, and doubtless affords trade sufficient to sustain quite a village. The following comprises the business facilities of the place: two blacksmith shops two stores, one shoe shop and one practicing physician.

HELENA.

This place is located in Richland township and was surveyed by J. Marshall, under direction of J. W. Clem and N. B. Hiatt, who entered the land in 1854. Shortly after this a store building was erected by Lewis Vogel, who opened a stock of general merchandise. Mr. Vogel followed the mercantile business until his death, then his wife took charge of the stock and is still continuing the business. Besides this there is a shoe shop carried on by Lewis Schwerdtfeger.

MOOREVILLE.

This town consists of a post office, one dry goods and grocery store, two blacksmith shops, one flouring mill and one practicing physician, and a few dwellings. It is located on the County line, on section 24, Geneseo township. It is in the midst of a beautiful farming country. The first store at this place was erected by William Davidson, in the year 1869.

BADGER HILL.

This is a small village established about the year 1874, in the northern part of of Spring Creek township, and contains one store by P. G. and M. L. Hess, one wagon shop, by J. P. Gage, one flouring mill, by D. G. Wescott, and one blacksmith shop, by H. Galloway, besides one church belonging to the United Brethren denomination.

P. G. & M. L. Hess, Dry Goods.—In the year 1874, these gentlemen came to this County from Morrow County, Ohio, and shortly after established business at this point, since which date they have been doing a large business in dry goods, groceries, tobaccos, cigars, paints, oil, window glass, hats, caps, boots and shoes, ready made clothing, hardware, patent medicines, drugs etc., besides acting as agent for the American Sewing Machine. As these gentlemen are located in a fine country, and claim that they can and will sell goods much cheaper than merchants can in incorporated towns, where they are obliged to pay high rents, high city taxes, high insurance, and put on city style. All kinds of produce taken in exchange for goods.

Wescott & Myers, Flouring Mill.—This firm is composed of D. G. Wescott, and J. H. Myers, two as honorable gentlemen and good citizens as ever settled in Spring Creek township, who established the Badger Hill Flouring Mill, at Badger Hill, in the year 1871. This mill is located on Wolf Creek, and is run by water power. Since the mill was established it has had an excellent run of custom and done a large business. They manufacture a first-class brand of flour, and consequently it gives entire satisfaction, besides they are doing a large exchange business which enables those living at a distance to visit their mill and return the same day. Try the Badger Hill flour, and you will like it.

Hugh Galloway, Blacksmith.—Badger Hill, though but a small place, will rank among our larger towns for first-class work and every thing pertaining to the blacksmithing business. Mr. Galloway established business at this point two or three years ago and since that time has been doing an excellent business, in the way of horse shoeing, repairing of all kinds. His shop is located north of Hess Bros., dry goods store where you will always find him ready to wait upon you and do your work in good style, at reasonable prices. Give him a call.

UNION GROVE.

This is the name of a post office, in the southern part of Spring Creek township. It also has one store and one blacksmith shop.

Joseph Schichtl, Dry Goods.—This gentleman has been located at this point (Union Grove,) for a number of years and ever since coming here has been engaged in this line of trade. He handles all kinds of dry goods boots, and shoes, grocery, hardware, tobaccos, cigars, queensware wood and willow ware, and every thing kept in a first-class country store. He takes all kind of produce in exchange for goods for which he pays the highest price. He sells goods very low and handles the best quality is why he has been so successful and holds such a large trade. Mr. Schichtl, is also post master, and justee of the peace. Since locating in the township has made many friends, in all his business transactions he is honorable, liberal, and strictly honest and consequently is ranked among the leading men of the township.

Schichtl & Graham, Blacksmiths.—For all kinds of blacksmithing, and machine repairing; call upon the above named gentlemen, at their shop at Union Grove, and we will warrant you a first-class job, on short notice and reasonable price. These gentlemen have been engaged in business at this point for a number of years during the time they have had a large run of custom and as they guarantee all of their work, their business is lasting and constantly increasing. These gentleman are also liberal, enterprising and successful business men, and have made many warm friends, in the vicinity where they are acquainted.

CHAPTER XXIX

MISCELLANEOUS.

Frank Fruhm & Bro., Blacksmith and Wagon Shops.— This shop was established by three gentlemen in the year 1868, in the south-west corner of Crystal township, since which time they have been doing a large business in manufacturing lumber wagons, spring wagons, etc., which they are selling very cheap, besides having a large run of blacksmithing in which line they do all kinds of horse-shoeing, wagon repairing and machine repairing, which is done in a workmanlike manner and at reasonable prices. Call and see them, and they will do you a good job.

Joshua Leonard, Breeder of Fine Stock.—Mr. Leonard has been a resident of Geneseo township since 1860, coming here from Michigan. Of late years, besides carrying on the farm, he has been paying considerable attention to fine stock raising, and when we called upon him he showed us some very fine stock indeed, which we will venture to say will rank with any in the County or State. His stock are all first-class and but a few years more and Mr. Leonard, with his blooded cattle, hogs etc., will make a fine display at our County Fairs, and carry away the ribbons.

John Wild, Brick Maker.—In 1865, this gentleman settled in Toledo, and has been a resident of the township ever since; is well known over the entire southern portion of the County, by the good quality of brick he makes, and as Mr. Wild has been at this business since settling in the County his reputation is thoroughly established. Mr. Wild since locating his brick yard upon his farm one mile and a quarter west of Toledo has made a splendid quality of brick and has a large trade. In 1878 alone, he sold over 600,000, furnishing the brick for the new school house, Toledo Savings Bank and numerous other fine buildings at Toledo which speaks well for his brick and prices.

William W. Munson, Blooded Stock Dealer.—This gentleman has been a resident of Tama County for a number of years and is a citizen of Howard township. For the past few years he has turned his attention to the breeding of fine durham cattle and poland-china hogs, besides other noted grades. Among his herds we can safely say are some of the nicest animals we have seen in the County. Mr. Munson is a young man of excellent qualifications and will no doubt make a success of whatever he undertakes. His farm is located in the eastern part of the township. He is among the successful and enterprising farmers and stock raisers of the County.

W. A. McAnulty, Blacksmith.—This gentleman is an old settler in this County, having come here in the year 1857, from Berks County, Pennsylvania, and settled in Howard township, in company with his widowed mother, brothers and sisters. Farming has always been his occupation, but of late years, besides carrying on the farm, he has turned his attention to the blacksmithing business. In this trade he exhibits skill and thoroughly understands how to execute a good job. His shop is upon his farm on section thirteen, Howard township, where he manufactures the celebrated iron drag which gives entire satisfaction, and is prepared to do all kinds of blacksmithing.

S. E. Wilson, Dry Goods and Groceries.—In Fifteen Mile Grove we find the above named gentleman in a neatly and well filled dry goods and grocery store. He established business at this point in the year 1876. Since that date he has built up a large trade and carries a first-class line of dry goods, notions, groceries, tobaccos, crockery, queensware, etc. He handles all kinds of country produce which he takes in exchange for goods. Mr. Wilson is a promising young man and possesses good busi qualifications.

L. P. Dinsdale & Son, Breeders of Fine Stock.—These gentlemen have resided in Tama County for a number of years, and have gradually been turning their attention to fine stock until now their Allendale herd of short horns will rank with any in this section, as they have selected their stock from some of the best herds in the country and always with regard to individual merit of the animals. They have representatives of the following noted families: Young Mary, Lady Jane, by Whittington Rose, by Skipton; Amelia, by Plato, Adelaide, by Magnum Bonum; Rose Mary, by Flash; Galatea, by Fredrick, and others. The stock farm is located six miles west of Tracr, where is always found a large number of these superior cattle for sale.

Thomas Shunn, Brick.—This gentleman came to Tama County from Canada in the year 1863 and settled in Toledo township. In 1870 he bought a farm in Carroll township and since has been manufacturing a splendid quality of brick. Mr. Shunn claims that he makes a better article and can sell cheaper than any other yard in the County.

Andrew McCosh, Breeder of Fine Stock.—Among the fine stock men of Tama County may be mentioned the above named gentleman. Mr. McCosh has been a resident of this County for nearly twenty years. Since that time, besides carrying on his farm in the western part of Perry township, four miles west of Tracr, he gradually worked himself into an extensive fine stock business, and now has some of the finest durham cattle, cottswool sheep and Poland-China hogs in the County. Any one wishing to buy fine stock will do well to call and see Mr. McCash before buying.